Libraries

VICTORIAN RAILWAYMEN

MR. THOMAS HAMERTON, INSPECTOR OF THE SOUTH EASTERN RAILWAY (d. 1858)

VICTORIAN RAILWAYMEN

The Emergence and Growth of Railway Labour
1830—1870

Dr. P. W. KINGSFORD
Senior Research Fellow, Hatfield College, Herts.

FRANK CASS & CO. LTD.
1970

First published in 1970 by
FRANK CASS AND COMPANY LIMITED
67 Great Russell Street, London WC1B 3BT

Copyright © 1970 P. W. Kingsford

All rights reserved. No part of this publication may be reproduced in any form or by any means, electronic, mechanical, photocopying, recording or otherwise without the prior permission of Frank Cass and Company Limited in writing,

ISBN 0 7146 1331 2

Printed in Great Britain by Clarke, Doble & Brendon Ltd.
Plymouth and London

CONTENTS

	Page
Acknowledgements	ix
Introduction	xi

Part I. LABOUR ECONOMY
Ch. 1 Recruitment	1
Ch. 2 Discipline	13
Ch. 3 Wastage	35
Ch. 4 Mobility and Rationalisation	55
Ch. 5 Industrial Relations	64

PART II. SOCIAL ECONOMY
Ch. 6 Incomes and Hours of Work	88
Ch. 7 Housing	121
Ch. 8 Advancement and Promotion	128
Ch. 9 Security	148
Ch. 10 Thrift and Self Help	170

Bibliography	182
Index	189
Appendices	193

MAPS

Railway Map of England and Wales
   Railways opened to end of year 1839
Railway Map of England and Wales   *Facing*
   Railways completed and opened to end of year 1852   *Appendix*
Map of Great Britain showing the Systems of   *II*
   Railways now under the control of the
   Principal Railway Companies, 1872

ILLUSTRATIONS

Mr. Thomas Hamerton, Inspector of the South Eastern Railway (d. 1858)	*Frontispiece*
Somerset & Dorset Railway Locomotive No. 11 (nicknamed 'Bluebottle') 1861	*Facing page* 74
London, Brighton & South Coast Railway Personnel, 1881 (left to right: Van Guard, Carman, Head Porter, General Porter, Cloak Room Porter, Station Superintendent's Clerk)	75
London, Brighton & South Coast Railway Personnel, 1881 (left to right: Ticket Collector, Ticket Inspector, Station Superintendent, Station Inspector, Guard, Policeman)	90
London, Brighton & South Coast Railway Personnel, 1881 (left to right: Luggage Labeller, Lampman, Signalman, Telegraph Clerk, Station Messenger, Telegraph Messenger)	91

All illustrations reproduced by kind permission of the Museum of British Transport, Clapham, London, SW4

ACKNOWLEDGEMENTS

I am deeply indebted to Mr. H.L. Beales who supervised the Ph.D. thesis on which this book is based. It is a great pleasure to acknowledge this. His guidance and encouragement meant a very great deal. I would also like to thank Dr. P.S. Bagwell for permission to quote from his book, *The Railwaymen,* the British Transport Commission for permission to reproduce documents, and Mrs. Patricia Levin for help with the typing.

INTRODUCTION

Much has been written about the physical development of the railway system in Britain, the enormous investment of capital involved and the crucial effects on economic and industrial growth in the nineteenth century, but very little has been said about the most important social aspect of this phenomenon. I mean the emergence and rapid growth of an entirely new and very large occupation for working men, that of operating the railways. This book is not about the men who constructed the railways, the navvies and labourers. It is about the men who ran them, the enginemen, signalmen, guards, porters, clerks and station masters. Their numbers grew, as the navvies diminished, from 1825 when they worked the Stockton and Darlington Railway, until by 1870, the year before they were able to establish their own trade unions, there was a great army of a quarter of a million men doing work of a kind that had never been done before. No attempt has yet been made to analyse the nature and growth of this army, with its own peculiar discipline, in the first forty-five years of its existence.

The prerequisite for the employment of labour on such a scale was investment of great amounts of capital. Savings from investors, the merchants, the landed gentry, the professional people poured into the railway companies in a flood from the mid-eighteen-thirties. The volume of the paid-up capital of the companies, the funds they received, rose dramatically in a series of ebbs and flows and this gives one picture of investment, but it is only the one seen by the investors. The picture as seen by the railwaymen was the solid one of rails, stations, rolling stock and locomotives, the objects for employment of their labour. The amount of investment in their sense is far more significant. It is the amounts actually expended by the companies on providing all kinds of buildings, plant and equipment and on maintaining it in proper shape, excluding all expenditure, considerable as it was, on buying land and legal and parliamentary approval. This investment though not so great as the volume of paid-up capital, grew rapidly. The sum of £40,000 invested in 1825 grew to £166 millions by 1850 and more than trebled again by 1875. It grew continuously but in three great waves. Whichever way investment is regarded there is no doubt about its scale of growth. It was the kind of growth which in other less advanced or developed countries was the key influence in developing modern industry and commerce. In terms of capital expenditure the railways exceeded house building in this period and were far ahead of merchant shipbuilding. Rapid as this growth was the railwaymen increased in number even more rapidly. In the short space of twenty-five years the little groups of enginemen and policemen on the Stockton & Darlington grew by 1850 to a body of 60,000 men, scattered along the length and breadth of Britain. During the next quarter of a century they multiplied five times over. This occupation was a new and solid pillar in the social structure of nineteenth-century Britain.

The growth of this new employment, like the capital investment, did not proceed evenly; at some times it was more rapid than others. Table 1 illustrates this point.

TABLE 1
Persons Employed in Railways open in U.K.

Year	(1) Number	(2) Per cent increases over preceding figure	(3) Yearly average of column 2
1847	47.218		
1850	59,974	27	9
1855	97,952	63	13
1860	127,450	30	6
1873	274,535	115	9
1884	367.793	34	3

The expansion of employment followed the waves of investment of capital. Thus the most rapid expansion between 1850 and 1855 followed a peak of investment by railway companies in 1849, and the high rate of expansion between 1860 and 1873 was linked with a peak of investment in 1865.

Railway employment not only grew rapidly it grew more rapidly than any other employment during the early and mid-Victorian years and so became more and more significant as a section of the whole working population. In 1850 it was the thirty-third largest occupation in the United Kingdom and nearly 1 per cent of the working population, by 1860 it was already in the fifteenth place and nearly 2 per cent and by 1870 it had risen to the sixth and over 3 per cent.

Within this new and substantial pillar of the social system there developed a complex sub-system. As soon as the railways became big organisations the division of labour proceeded apace and the types of work crystallised into a large number of grades of employee. These were, for the most part, linked in terms of pay and status in an elaborate hierarchy. The main pattern was established by 1850, became more elaborate in the following decades and by 1870 there were not far short of a hundred grades of post on the railways. This was perhaps the most important characteristic of railway service and of railway servants, as the railwaymen alone among industrial workers were called. It continued as a major obstacle to the attempts to form a trade union at the end of this period. The 'grade notion' effectively preserved the distinctions between grades, which were social as well as authoritarian. 'The man in one of the higher grades was regarded as socially superior to the lower grade man', wrote a railwayman who worked in a goods yard in the north at the end of the nineteenth century. 'The goods porter was looked upon as an inferior animal by the shunter. The shunter was tolerated as a necessary evil by the goods guard, who had wild hopes that some time he would be able to look a passenger guard squarely in the eyes as a man and brother of equal rank.'[1]

This book is in two parts: part I deals with the labour economy of the railwaymen, and part II with their social economy. By labour economy I mean those aspects of labour on the railway which concern its use by the railway companies; by social economy, those aspects which concern the standard of living and the railwaymen in their social context. There is, necessarily, some overlap between the two parts. The material used has been limited mainly to England and Wales and in general the men in the railway workshops have been excluded.

In part I, chapters 1 to 5, the questions I have dealt with are recruitment, discipline, wastage, mobility and rationalisation, and industrial relations. These have seemed to me to be the key questions affecting the use of labour by the railway companies. Recruitment of servants was, of course, a continuous and major task for the railways throughout the whole period. But it was not difficult to find large numbers of men from agricultural labourers, the general labourers, the domestic servants and the discharged soldiers and sailors. This new occupation was continually increased and replenished from a number of other occupations marked by the habit of obedience and filled by men who were amenable to control by their superiors. Such control was exercised by means of strict discipline. It was a discipline

---

1. R. Kenney, *Men and Rails*, 1913, p. 149.

not only of timekeeping but of safety and, because of the dangers to the public inherent in error at work, it had the power of the law behind it. Very strict, not to say harsh at first, even quasi military, it became less severe as discipline became second nature to railwaymen. It bred, on the one hand, comradeship among men whose mistakes could be fatal to each other and, on the other hand, submission to the word of their masters. Alongside these characteristics of railway labour must be placed the fact that there was a continual movement of men out of the industry, chiefly young men in search of better pay. This amounted to a considerable wastage of the labour force, particularly when the loss of men through the large amount of occupational injury and sickness which was peculiar to railways is added to it, as shown in chapter 3. However, wastage was never a serious problem for the companies; partly because there was an ample supply of recruits and partly because at least half of the men were unskilled and even what may be called the skilled men (workshop artisans excluded) did not need much training.

Movement of a different kind was more significant. Mobility was an essential and peculiar feature of work on the line. Most men were moved from station to station, often because of promotion, sometimes as a punishment. The high degree of mobility was certainly essential to effective control of labour by the companies. Yet control of this cost, or rationalisation of labour, was rarely attempted. There were, of course, isolated examples in times of financial stringency, as shown in chapter 4, but a consistent policy of elimination of waste is hardly to be expected in conditions of rapid expansion. All these considerations have a direct connection with the nature of the industrial relations in this period before the railwaymen's amalgamated society appeared. Serious disputes were infrequent and invariably limited to one section of men or one locality, and the few attempts to form trade unions were unsuccessful.

Considered as a factor in the great and essential contribution made by the railways to the economic growth of Britain in the nineteenth century the labour employed was an asset in the sense that it was not dear, yet adequate to the nature of the work required from it, well disciplined, easily controlled, both respectable and respectful.

In part II, chapters 6 to 10, where an attempt is made to place the railwaymen in their social context, the basic questions discussed are earnings and hours of work, housing, advancement and promotion, security, and thrift and self help. Wages, the most important part of the standard of living, varied widely over a great number of grades. At one extreme the porter's wage was at a somewhat higher level than the agricultural labourer's, and at the other the engine driver's, rather more than the skilled artisan's. There was little general change over the whole period, some grades showing a slight advance or retreat. On the other hand the excessively long hours of work, which were common at first, did gradually become less, and real wages rose somewhat accordingly.

As well as wages and hours of work there were other elements in the standard of living, some more important than others. Housing was one. But although the railway cottage, the station master's house and the railway town like Swindon are evidence of what the companies did, housing was in fact provided for only a small minority of men in the service. As shown in chapter 7, housing by the companies added little to the income of railwaymen as a whole. More important was the railwayman's prospect of advancement, his chance to 'raise himself in the scale of society', in an age when the opportunities for the poor boy to better himself were continually emphasised. That prospect was certainly better than in the occupations from which he had come; for many, it was distinctly possible to rise to better paid work, for most, length of service meant advance up a scale of increments in wages. But most valuable of all, in an age of insecurity, was the security of employment, and this was high compared with most occupations. Provided he survived the hazards of the discipline system and was well behaved the railwayman could reckon to keep his job so long as he was fit to undertake it. One thing that went to ensure this situation was the inability of the management to coordinate the amount of labour employed with fluctuations in revenue; another was its desire to keep experienced men. Of course this was not the whole story. As shown in chapter 9, a man's security was often threatened by those risks of injury, sickness and death which were peculiarly high on the railways. While the companies made some provision for this — a small cash payment or pension for the loss of a limb, it was at best a meagre one.

Finally, how far were these men able to practise the contemporary virtues of thrift and self help? An examination of savings banks and friendly societies in chapter 10 shows that only some of the aristocracy, engine drivers, passenger guards, station masters, could and did save any considerable sums. One man spoke for the great majority when he said, 'I would save if I could and I will if you will only show me how it is possible to provide for a wife and children on such small wages'. Nevertheless, considered in relation to the working class standard of living, that of the railwaymen was probably above the average. His average wage was above the general average for the period. 'The working man knows he will be a working man all his life. What he wants is security, regularity of payment, freedom from anxiety and short hours.'[1] Although the railwayman lacked the last two of these he notably had the first two. The influence of these characteristics lasted into the twentieth century.

---

1. *Pall Mall Gazette.* 1 Jan. 1867.

Chapter 1

RECRUITMENT

The system and methods of recruitment were among the most important influences on the economic and social character of railway labour. The subject is discussed in this chapter under the following headings: the sources of labour or fields of recruitment and the patronage system; the standards and quality required and enforced; the difficulties, if any, in recruitment of the required quality of labour.

An analysis of labour employed, by the chief grades, as shown in Table II gives a preliminary idea of the problem and of the numerous types of occupation which had to be filled. The grades may be put into seven main groups: managerial, clerical, supervisory, skilled operating, unskilled, artificers, and miscellaneous. This is shown in Table III. Managerial includes managers, secretaries, engineers, accountants, storekeepers. Supervisory includes station masters, inspectors and foremen. Skilled includes engine drivers, guards and switchmen. Unskilled includes all others except artificers and miscellaneous. The division between skilled and unskilled has been made on the basis of the training and experience required, responsibility and wages. The figures for 1847 are incomplete and not strictly comparable with others. The low supervisory percentage in that year is accounted for by the fact that there are no figures for station masters and inspectors.

The decrease in the managerial proportion may be due to amalgamation. In spite of that development, however, the clerical and supervisory together increased considerably. The proportion between skilled and unskilled changed slightly in favour of the skilled but a considerable number of the miscellaneous must be included in the unskilled. The high percentage of miscellaneous in 1884 makes the figures for that year hardly comparable.

Table II
Persons Employed by Grades

Grade	Percentage of Total Employed					
	1847	1850	1855	1860	1873	1884
Manager / Secretary / Treasurer / Engineer / Superintendent / Storekeeper / Accountant / Cashier	1.7	1.4	1.2	1.0	.5	.2
Inspector	-	.9	.8	.8	.9	1.0
Station Master	-	2.8	2.2	2.4	2.1	1.7
Ticket Collector	-	-	.3	.4	.5	.6
Draughtsman	.2	.2	.2	.1	.1	.1
Clerk	7.3	7.4	7.9	7.9	10.8	9.2
Foreman	1.7	1.6	1.2	1.4	.9	.8
Engine Driver	3.1	3.4	3.2	3.1	3.5	3.5
Fireman	3.2	3.6	3.6	3.2	3.6	3.5
Guard	2.5	3.3	3.3	3.5	3.7	3.6
Artificers	23.0	19.4	21.7	19.7	13.4	15.2
Switchman	2.2	3.0	2.9	2.6	4.7	5.2
Gatekeeper	.9	2.7	2.5	2.1	.7	.4
Policeman	18.3	3.8	1.6	2.0	.6	.5
Porter	-	14.4	14.8	15.2	20.1	12.2
Platelayer	8.8	8.6	7.3	7.8	11.8	8.1
Labourer	26.6	23.1	22.9	23.6	17.4	19.2
Miscellaneous	.5	.4	2.4	3.2	5.9	11.0
Telegraphs	-	-	-	-	-	1.0
Steamboats etc.	-	-	-	-	-	1.6
Canals	-	-	-	-	-	.5
Hotels etc.	-	-	-	-	-	.7

Sources of Labour

The generally accepted view that the main field of recruitment for the greater part of labour was from agriculture can be broadly confirmed. 'In agricultural districts where wages were very low, fifteen shillings per week as a commencing wage for a porter enabled the company to obtain, without difficulty, as many men as they required, especially as the chances of promotion afforded to the men

Table III
Persons Employed by Groups

Group	Percentage of Total Employed					
	1847	1850	1855	1860	1873	1884
Managerial	1.7	1.4	1.2	1.0	.4	.2
Clerical	7.5	7.6	8.1	8.0	10.9	10.3
Supervisory	1.7	5.3	4.2	4.6	3.9	3.5
Skilled	7.8	9.7	9.4	9.2	11.9	12.3
Unskilled	57.8	56.2	53.0	54.3	53.6	44.7
Artificers	23.0	19.4	21.7	19.7	13.4	15.2
Miscellaneous	.5	.4	2.4	3.2	5.9	13.8

a prospect of advancement far beyond what they were likely to attain in agricultural pursuits.' This statement by a railway manager in 1879 is confirmed by an examination of applications for employment from 1840 onwards. A similar reference to the employment provided by the railways in agricultural districts was made by the 1867 Royal Commission on Railways.[1] The suggestion then was that the parishes had been indirectly relieved of much pauperism. However there seems to have been little direct help to the parishes by the employment of paupers and when in 1843 the railways were requested to follow the farmers' example by taking on unemployed men the request was passed over to the contractors with the comment that the railways could employ only 'trained men'. In 1876 evidence given before a Parliamentary committee stated that labour was previously drawn from agricultural districts where wages were lowest. This, it was said, gave the railways a special advantage over other employers since they were put to no cost of conveyance for their workers.[2] Whatever the substance of this point, local recruitment was often the rule. On the Liverpool & Manchester in 1832 out of about 600 men employed, about 540 were recruited locally. It was also the policy in 1848 on the Great Northern when, prior to opening the line, the directors ordered the porters and gatekeepers to be selected from local men.

The broad generalisation that agriculture was the main field of recruitment requires, however, some qualification. It is largely true of

---

1. Royal Commission on Railways, 1867. Report of Sir Rowland Hill.
2. Report of S.C. on Employer's Liability, 1876. Evidence of F.W. Evans.

the majority in the traffic grades, the men who required little skill at first, porters, police, brakesmen, switchmen and the permanent way men, the grades from which those with more skill developed. It does not apply to others such as enginemen, gangers, guards. Even in the general traffic grades, men who had been in gentlemen's service were always acceptable. Discharged soldiers were preferred and the minimum age of entry for police and porters was raised in their favour. In the early years the railway contractors were also to some slight extent a source of supply of unskilled men. According to Edwin Chadwick railway construction labourers were either discharged, returned to agricultural work, or became vagrant and increased the prison population.[1] But contractors' men who were injured at work were often given preference for employment when the railways opened, a policy which became general as the Midland and other lines adopted it. The early police, jacks of all trades, transferred in the same way from construction to operation. When these men were first appointed they were, although paid by the railways, supervised by the local magistrates, and their duty was to preserve order among the construction labourers. Many of them were retained by the railways, after construction had been completed 'if they conducted themselves properly' and their duties then became those of keeping the railway line free from obstruction, which in turn developed into the work of signalling.

The police were so much the prototype of many subsequent grades, such as signalmen, switchmen and ticket collectors, that they are worth special mention. Inevitably they were modelled on the recently established Metropolitan Police, with similar uniforms and beaver top hats, and with similar wages and duties. They were sometimes recruited from the metropolitan police and city police elsewhere. In 1840 wages in London were very much the same for both, viz. railway police – 17s to 19s per week, civil police – 17s to 21s per week. But there were certain advantages and opportunities for advancement on the railways, not open to the civil police.

The enginemen were in quite a different class and from the first they showed a peculiar sense of independence. In the thirties and forties the demand for them was greater than the supply; they could 'dictate their own terms in a great degree'. It was difficult to get skilful and reliable men. They were recruited, not from blacksmiths as one member of the 1839 Select Committee supposed, but mainly from labourers who showed a particular aptitude for the work, wherever they could be obtained. The length of training depended on that aptitude, but training presented no difficulty since the men were

---

1. Statistical Society, Manchester Papers, 1845/6.

not required to have much knowledge of the locomotives. They were, however, 'men of great activity and great ability to get out of a difficulty'.[1] Brunel considered it an advantage if they were illiterate and many of them were so. A few no doubt, like James Hurst of the Great Western, came directly to the company from the decaying hand loom weavers without the advantage of any schooling. The enginemen, however, were almost the only men who had had some training. Their original school was the colliery lines of Northumberland and Durham, particularly Killingworth Colliery. The men trained there drove the locomotives in the north east, and enginemen from the north east were taken to the Liverpool & Manchester by George Stephenson. A little later Daniel Gooch, locomotive superintendent of the Great Western, himself a Tynesider, recruited most of his enginemen from the north, men such as the same James Hurst who, after being labourer, fireman and engine driver on the Liverpool & Manchester, became driver on the Great Western.

The previous occupations of railwaymen seem to have become somewhat more varied after the early years. In 1858 the total establishment of twenty-eight men at Sheffield passenger station showed the following previous occupations:- twelve labourers, three soldiers, two police, two domestic servants, one spinner, one ostler, one groom and four from other railways. In 1857 applicants for employment on the London & North Western included a footman applying for the post of porter, a joiner for that of foreman, a provision merchant for a clerk's job, a painter for a porter's or policeman's. And examination of a number of applications on the London, Brighton & South Coast between 1858 and 1879 confirms that the sources of recruitment became more various. Out of fifty-five applicants, eight were soldiers, seven agricultural labourers, seven general labourers, seven domestic servants and six shop assistants.

Methods of Recruitment.

The outstanding feature is the system of patronage which was maintained throughout the greater part of this period. It was valued and carefully preserved by the directors, though limited usually only to the traffic grades and clerks. Its persistence probably had some effect on the continued prevalence of family connection in railway service into the twentieth century.

Patronage on the railways, as elsewhere, became prominent as soon as there were any considerable number of places to fill. In 1832, the Liverpool & Manchester directors issued a statement to deny it.

---

1. Report of S.C. on Railways, 1839. Evidence of Capt. Moorson and E. Bury.

Complaints had been made, not so much that the men working the new railway had become 'objects of favour and patronage', but that the directors had delegated the privilege to George Stephenson, a 'foreigner'. The directors replied that only sixty out of about six hundred had any connection with Stephenson, but they omitted to mention whether the other five hundred and forty had any connection with them. A few years later the system was fully working. Directors nominated in rotation to all vacancies for the police, porters, clerks and traffic grades generally. Prior to the opening of the York & North Midland, an 'election' of policemen, guards and porters was carried out. When the Great Northern from Peterborough to Lincoln and the East Lincolnshire Railway were opened in 1848 the appointments were fully organised. Out of one hundred and thirty-five appointments one hundred and ten were offered to the directors 'in equal proportion as to pecuniary amount, or as nearly as from the number and nature of the appointments can be done, the chairman having double the number of the other directors'. This was arranged in detail. The 'distribution of patronage' among the eighteen directors was made on the following basis:

Chairman

1 clerk @ £150 p.a. & lodging	150	0	0
2 clerks @ 25/- p.w. & lodging	130	0	0
1 guard @ 27/6 p.w. clothes	71	10	0
2 pointsmen @ 17/6 p.w., clothes & lodging	91	0	0
4 porters @ 17/6 p.w., clothes	182	0	0
1 gatekeeper 15/- p.w., clothes & lodging	39	0	0
1 gatekeeper 12/- p.w., clothes & lodging	31	4	0
12 offices amounting to	694	14	0

A Director

1 clerk @ £150 p.a.	150	0	0
1 guard @ 27/6 p.w.	71	10	0
2 porters @ 17/6 p.w.	91	0	0
1 gatekeeper @ 15/- p.w.	39	0	0
1 gatekeeper @ 12/- p.w.	31	4	0
6 offices amounting to	382	14	0

Decisions were taken on the future method of filling vacancies. Those caused by death were to be nominated by the directors in alphabetical rotation, commencing with the chairman and deputy chairman, the chairman to have two nominations, the other directors to have one each. Vacancies caused by dismissal, resignation or the creation of new posts were to be ballotted for by the directors present.

This system was still fully working in the sixties. In the staff character books on the London & South Western the name of the director who had nominated each member of the staff had to be entered. On the London & North Western vacancies for porters, police, clerks and clerical apprentices were classed in districts, and the manager applied to the directors resident there for nominations. Applicants for employment, even if recommended by a member of the nobility, were told that they must be nominated by a director 'in the usual rotation'. It was probably not until the seventies that, because of its inadequacy to deal with the greatly increased number of servants, the system began to be inoperative. The regulations on the London & North Western still provided for all vacancies in the traffic and clerical grades to be nominated by the directors and in some cases every fifth nomination was at the disposal of the chairman. Special recommendation by a director could except a man from the general rules as to minimum stature of entrants. But by the end of the decade the system had become a formality. The directors signed blank nomination forms which were completed by the officials.

Patronage was an important factor in securing the respectability, loyalty and reliability of railwaymen. But before it could be exercised applications had to be made, recommendations and testimonials produced and due regard paid to any circumstances deserving special consideration. In the following application of 1842 for the elevated position of porter, humility is perhaps the chief note.

> 'The humble petition of William Bullock a resident inhabitant of the Parish of Steventon in the County of Berks respectfully sheweth that your petitioner is anxious to obtain employment as a Porter on your line of Railway. We the undersigned inhabitants of the said Parish do recommend him as being a sober, honest, industrious person as a candidate for that office, he therefore solicits the kind approval of your honourable company hoping they will be pleased to grant him an early appointment and should he be the object of your choice will no doubt to the utmost of his abilities merit your confidence and approbation in discharging the duties committed to his care.'

The kind of application which was expected is shown by the following model for specimens of applicants' handwriting on the G.W.R. in 1837.

> 'Gentlemen: Understanding that the situation lately occupied by Mr. John Day has become vacant, I have taken the liberty of intruding myself upon your notice as a Candidate for the

same, and should you be pleased to confer upon me the appointment it shall be my constant endeavour to fulfil its duties at all times to the best of my ability.'

Recommendation by 'one housekeeper of undoubted respectability' was essential to appointment. Records of the persons who had recommended applicants were kept for future reference. The establishment list at Sheffield in 1858 shows, for nearly all the men, the names of those by whom they were recommended, although it may have been ten years since they began work with the company. Applications for employment addressed to the Marquis of Chandos, director of the L. & N.W., admittedly a special case, show recommendations by nine clergymen, two churchwardens, two solicitors, two schoolmasters, a lawyer, a farmer and a titled lady. In this particular case there were circumstances deserving special consideration since the applicants' families were avowed supporters of the Marquis's political interest. However, there does not seem to have been much political motive in patronage. The production of testimonials was generally a further prerequisite of appointment. This was strictly observed. Thus on the formation of the Great Western establishment at Bristol and Bath testimonials were referred to in each case, some applications being deferred for testimonials to be produced, and this practice was consistently followed in later years. The application forms required testimonials from the previous employer. On the Sheffield & Manchester testimonials of the 'different candidates now applying for situations on the opening of the line' had first to be examined. On the opening of a section of the Great Northern the directors, after having had the patronage allotted to them, were requested to send testimonials with the names of their nominees. Later, in 1860 on the L. & S.W., all candidates for porters' situations were required to produce 'responsible testimonials of character', and these were to be kept for reference in case of misconduct. The companies' claim that great precautions were taken in appointing men, to the extent of obtaining testimonials from three previous employers, had a great deal of truth; their complaint that they had to resist attempts by members of the public to recommend undesirables was also probably borne out.[1]

Considerable pains were therefore taken to ensure that railway servants were respectable men of reliable character. The qualities required were expressed in some of the sentences which applicants to the Great Western in 1837 were required to copy in giving samples of their handwriting:

---

1. Report of S.C. on Accidents on Railways, 1858. Evidence of J. Allport.

'Zealously strive to Excel. Industry is commendable. Perseverance deserves Success. Quietude of mind is a Treasure.'[1]
The testimonial for William Windus of Hagbourne, Berks, appointed as a policeman, said he was 'sober, honest and with a steady character' and was signed by the vicar, churchwardens and overseers of his parish. Naturally enough any connection with the liquor trade was discouraged. It was considered 'inexpedient' to employ men who had been in the service of publicans. Men were dismissed if they were found to be keeping a public house, although this, in fact, was in line with the general prohibition against engaging in trade. Respectability extended to appearance. Station masters were enjoined to ensure that servants were 'clean in their persons and clothes, shaved and with their shoes brushed'.

Quality of Labour Required

The physical standards were fairly high, for the traffic grades at least, since there was in general no shortage of supply and the railways could afford to pick and choose. In the 1840s for instance, there were quite frequently waiting lists of men approved for future employment as policemen, porters, and guards. Medical examination, in which good health, physical strength and good eyesight were required, was compulsory from the fifties if not before.[2] The maximum age at entry varied from railway to railway and from time to time between twenty-eight and forty. Minimum heights were also fixed and varied similarly but seem to have been reduced with time. The minimum for porters on the Great Western in 1842 was five feet nine inches; in 1870 on the London & North Western it was reduced to five feet seven inches and again in 1872 to five feet six inches. It is claimed that the railways were able to reject those 'that suffered from any deformity or physical blemish, of evil appearance and even with red hair'. The educational standards were surprisingly high in view of what is known about the lack of attainments of engine drivers in the early years and in view of the general standard of literacy in Britain. In 1847 it was considered adequate if the enginemen had had the rules and regulations read to them; they did not need to be able to read them themselves. But even the porters on the Great Western in 1842 had to be able to read and write and be 'generally intelligent'. In 1849 the London, Brighton & South Coast laid it down that no one should be appointed as guard, porter, policeman or switchman unless he could read and write. And by

---

1. Great Western Rly. Specimens for Applicants, 1837.
2. Report of S.C. on Accidents on Railways, 1858. Evidence of H.P. Bruyeres.

1874, if not before, all wages-paid staff on the London & North Western had to be able to read and write with 'reasonable facility' and all new entrants had to pass an examination accordingly.

Difficulties in Recruitment

There was generally no difficulty in obtaining recruits, with the exception of enginemen in the first few years. There were, for instance, 'great numbers of applications from residents in the potteries' on the opening of part of the N. Staffs line in 1848.[1] But it was also necessary to recruit men with the required qualities.

The early difficulties with enginemen have already been noted. Skilful men were difficult to get owing to the greatly increasing demand for them at that time. The men who were employed had not always attained as high a skill as they should have; firemen were promoted to driver without adequate qualifications. The suggestion was made that all enginemen should be required to give security of at least £200 for good conduct, but they were strong enough to defeat it. This 'serious evil' of incompetent drivers eventually cured itself, but in 1840 it still gave rise to discussions in the press and recommendations for improvement. Among these ideas were those of examination and periodic licensing, good wages, extra inducements for economy and punctuality, and strict punishment of errors.[2] The last two of these were certainly put into practice, while the wages were definitely good for the times. The real trouble apparently was that the enginemen were 'taken from a class where habits of sobriety, carefulness and control are much less common than in a more elevated condition of society', and this, it seems, produced a 'consciousness of inferiority'. Concern was naturally expressed too about the character of the switchmen who also held life in their hands. They should be 'of the better class of workmen and they should receive higher wages as well as give some security'. In fact, in those early years, these men were usually promoted policemen.

But the general position throughout this period was that the railways did not run short of men whom they were willing to appoint. The degree of their subsequent unsatisfactoriness is another matter and one which is illustrated by the disciplinary system (Chapter 2) and by complaints from the public, of which there were a considerable number recorded, particularly in the forties. In this position the railways could afford, for instance, to refuse to re-engage men who had left. On the London & South Western in 1860 it was not considered desirable to re-employ officials who had left the

---

1. N. Staffs Railway. Report to Board, 1848.
2. *Railway Times*, 1839, 1840.

service. By 1870 on the London & North Western persons who left the service for any reason were not re-engaged.

There was one difficulty in maintaining control over recruitment, particularly of men with skill or experience. In the early years there was considerable movement of labour between railways and later some competition between managements for it. It was in this connection that a registry of servants was suggested in parliament in order to prevent men who had been dismissed by one company from being engaged by another.[1] In the forties there was inter-railway recruitment of clerks; similarly in the fifties of porters. In 1865 the Great Western complained of two incidents. An inspector, who had been dismissed for carelessness but whose punishment had been reduced to a fine of £10, was engaged by another company without any reference, and a foreman had been enticed away by another company with an offer of increased wages. In the latter case it was contrary to an understanding with the other company. This kind of mobility continued, for by 1877, at least on the Midland, men who had left for another company were not to be re-engaged.

Occasionally there were isolated difficulties. For instance in 1854, because of the difficulty of obtaining an adequate staff of clerks at reasonable salaries, it was decided to establish a system of apprenticeship. Under this scheme 'respectable youths' of not less than sixteen years of age were to be taken at a commencing salary of £20 per annum, increasing to £30 and £40 in subsequent years.

The demand-supply position of labour seems to have begun to change in the late sixties and early seventies. One indication of this is in the waiting lists of applicants, which had been kept from the beginning but which became less useful. Whereas in 1840-41 men approved for future employment were usually subsequently employed, in 1868 numbers of them were not. In the six months October 1840 to April 1841 all the men on the Great Western waiting list for posts as policemen, porters, guards and clerks were subsequently employed. In the twelve months January to December, 1868, thirty-two men on the Great Northern waiting list for porters, clerks, vanguards etc. refused to join on being summoned to do so.

It was in the early seventies that 'the demand which exists for the class of men most suitable for railway employment' became a factor which the management felt necessary to take into account for its effect on recruitment and wages. That demand was then receiving attention in connection with a general agitation for increased wages. Comparison was made between railway and police wages and it was pointed out that whereas in forty years the police wages in London

---

1. *Hansard.* 23 July 1840.

had increased by 6s per week at the minimum and 9s per week at the maximum, the wages of porters had increased a mere 1s per week. The demand for 'the class of men most suitable for railway employment' does not seem to have been excessive.

Chapter 2

DISCIPLINE

The general adaptation of labour to the new industrial techniques and tempo of the early nineteenth century through a process of discipline had a special aspect in relation to railway labour. The peculiar nature of railway discipline arose mainly from the requirements of safety, the necessity of strict observance of time and the fact that all kinds of unskilled men were responsible for the safety of persons and property. Many of these men were labourers with only a brief and sketchy training. Even the early engine drivers were labourers.[1] Moreover in the early years of the railways the primitive techniques of operation allowed a great margin for human error. Regulations were frequently made as accidents showed the need for them.

There was no difficulty in finding labour. The difficulty was in finding a satisfactory quality of men capable of working to the minute, of consistent caution, and of resisting the comforts of drink and sleep under the burden of very long hours of work, frequent danger and the strain of responsibility. In default of a ready made supply of such men labour was hammered into shape by a discipline peculiar to the railways, which in turn had a deep effect on the character of the labour during the whole century. 'You might as well have a Trade Union or an "Amalgamated Society" in the Army, where discipline had to be kept at a very high standard, as have it on the railways', was the opinion of a railway general manager near the end of the century.[2]

The discipline system worked in different ways: through punishment by dismissal, by an elaborate system of fining and by the issue of cautions and reprimands; through reward in the form of gratuities

---

1. Report of S.C. on State of Communication by Railway, 1839. Evidence of E. Bury.
2. S. & B. Webb, *History of Trade Unionism*, 1920, p. 525.

for good work and conduct and for bereaved dependents, as well as pensions and payment of funeral expenses; through persuasion in the form of promotion of religious worship and education of both adults and children.

It was the use of punishment which gave the discipline its peculiar railway character. There was ample legal sanction for it. Quite apart from the Master and Servant legislation the railways had available the Act for Regulating Railways, 1840, and the amending Act for the Better Regulation of Railways and for the Conveyance of Troops, 1842, which contained the disciplinary clauses providing for the 'Punishment of Servants of Railway Companies guilty of misconduct'. In addition, the individual railway acts had disciplinary clauses. It is not surprising therefore that there is little evidence of the Master and Servant legislation being used and what there is, is before 1840. The following example, however, foreshadows subsequent conditions.[1]

'8 Feb 1836.

The Treasurer reported that on Wednesday last there had been a turn out amongst the old enginemen and firemen – Monday last several of the enginemen had given verbal notice that unless the firemen's wages were increased they would leave on Friday evening following. On Wednesday morning last, the Treasurer asked John Hewitt, one of the oldest enginemen whether he persisted in that notice, and Hewitt answering that he did, the Treasurer discharged him instantly. Upon this, the other enginemen refused to go with the trains, and some slight delay was experienced in despatching the coach trains. Other enginemen were however speedily engaged. Four of the old enginemen who had entered into written agreements with the Company, viz., Charles Callan, Peter Callan, Henry Weatherbury and George Massey, had been apprehended and taken before Richar Leyland and James Heyworth, Justices of the Peace, who investigated the circumstances of the turn out; and the breach of contract being proved, committed the said offenders to Kirkdale to be put to hard labour for one calendar month.

In respect of the enginemen and firemen who had conducted themselves so as to merit the approbation of the Directors the Treasurer was instructed to present each engineman with a Premium in the name of the Directors of from £3 to £5 according to circumstances and half that amount to firemen.

RESOLVED that a committee be appointed for making contracts of service with enginemen and firemen.
15Feb 1836.

---

1. Liverpool & Manchester Rly. Board Mins., 1836.

READ a letter from Charles Callan, Peter Callan, Henry Weatherbury and George Massey, now confined in Kirkdale Prison expressing sorrow for their offence and begging to be let out.

The Treasure to reply that the Directors had no power to liberate them from their confinement.

22 Feb 1836.

READ a letter from the Chaplain to the Kirkdale Jail, communicating the petition of the two Callans, Hy. Weatherbury and Massey to be relieved from the severe labour and fatigue of the treadmill, on which they were kept at work six hours a day. The Directors were disposed to mitigate the severity of their labour for the remainder of their term of confinement and Mr. Currie undertook, as Chief Magistrate, to recommend to the Governor of the Jail that the Directors' lenient disposition towards the prisoners might be attended to.'

The two Callans were subsequently employed on the London & Birmingham Railway and awarded gratuities of £5 each for good conduct. They at least, seem to have learnt their lesson.[1]

The disciplinary sections of the 1840 Railway Act, as amended and improved in 1842, which 'gave Justices of the Peace summary powers of dealing with railway servants guilty of misconduct' [2] were as follows. They were the legal basis of the system erected by the railway companies in the subsequent decades. For instance, they explain, to some extent, the heaviness of the fines imposed by the companies in the forties and fifties.

> 'Punishment of Persons employed on Railways guilty of Misconduct.
>
> ..... it shall be lawful for any officer or agent of any Railway Company, or for any Special Constable duly appointed .... to seize and detain any Engine Driver, Waggon Driver, Guard, Porter or other person employed by the said or any other Railway Company, or by any other Company or Person .... who shall be found drunk while so employed upon the said Railway, who shall commit any Offence against any of the Bye Laws, Rule or Regulations of such Company, or shall wilfully, maliciously, or negligently do or omit to do any Act whereby the Life or Limb of any Person passing along or being upon such Railway or the Works thereof, shall be or might be injured or endangered, or whereby the Passage of any of the Engines,

---

1. London & Birmingham Rly. Return of Gratuities to Enginemen and Firemen, half year ending Dec. 1842.
2. Cleveland-Stevens, *English Railways: their development and their relation to the state*, 1915.

Carriages or Trains shall be or might be obstructed or impeded, and to convey such Engine Driver, Guard, Porter and every other such Person so offending, or any Person counselling, aiding or assisting in such Offence, with all convenient Despatch, before some Justice of the Peace .... and every such Person .... shall, upon the oath of One or more credible witness or witnesses before such Justice as aforesaid, in the discretion of such Justice, be imprisoned, with or without hard Labour, for any Term not exceeding Two Calendar Months, or .... shall for every such offence forfeit to Her Majesty any Sum not exceeding Ten Pounds ....

'Justices of the Peace empowered to send any case to be tried by the Quarter Sessions.

.... it shall be lawful for such Justice .... to commit the Person or Persons charged with such Offence for Trial for the same at the Quarter Sessions .... and to order that any such Person so committed shall be imprisoned and detained in any of Her Majesty's Gaols or Houses of Correction in the said County or Place in the meantime, or to take Bail for his Appearance with or without Sureties, in his Discretion; and every such Person .... shall be liable, in the Discretion of such Court, to be imprisoned, with or without hard Labour, for any Term not exceeding Two Years.'[1]

The argument for including these sections in the bills was provided by the Report of the Select Committee on Communication by Railway of 1839, and also by the individual railway acts to that date. The Report said:

'It is essential to the safety of the Public and to the maintenance of regular intercourse by Railroads that the Companies should have a more perfect control over their servants. Much concurrent testimony upon this point will be found in the Evidence; and where the lives of many persons depend on the good conduct and ready obedience of subordinate officers, and where the smallest irregularity may be attended with fatal consequences, a system of exact discipline should be encouraged, and powers should be given to the directors for the purpose of upholding their authority.'

The 'concurrent testimony' was to the effect that although the railway should have the power to inflict fines, punishment by the magistrates would have more effect provided it did not deprive the directors of the power of punishment. Lord Seymour, sponsor of the

---

1. 3 & 4 Vict. C. 97. Secs 13 & 14, amended by 5 & 6 Vict. C. 55. Sec. 17.

1840 Act, held that 'There should be a registry of servants employed on the railroads because he understood that at present it was by no means uncommon, when a servant was dismissed by one railroad for neglect or misconduct, at once to get employ on another railroad'.[1]

The specific mention of drunkenness in the 1840 Act is worthy of note in view of its frequent occurrence later as a cause of dismissal. There was, not unnaturally, some preoccupation with the dangers of intoxication. The Select Committee of 1839 wanted to know what provision was made to ensure that the driver of a train did not go out intoxicated. On the Great Western they believed in trying to ration the supply of liquor. The licensees of two public houses were allowed to send in beer to men in Paddington station during two hours of the day, subject to not supplying any man with more than one pint or any spirits.

As an example of the individual railway acts as a source of disciplinary powers the Great Western Railway Act of 1835 laid down a fine of between ten shillings and five pounds for drunkenness.[2] The Company's own regulations in 1838, were sufficiently stringent. They provided, inter alia, that 'no instance of intoxication will be overlooked and that any man so dismissed will be liable to a fine by the magistrate'; that incivility or rudeness would be 'instantly punished'; that 'each person will be liable to immediate dismissal for disobedience, negligence or other misconduct'.

The Acts for Regulating Railways were implemented throughout the following decades and the companies included the disciplinary clauses in their rule books. The following rules, issued by the London & Birmingham, Eastern Counties, Great Western, Manchester, Sheffield & Lincolnshire and London & North Western companies made the intention clear:

'The non-observance of any of the foregoing Regulations will subject the Offender to Fines and to prosecution under Lord Seymour's Act for the Better Regulation of Railways.'

'No instance of intoxication will be overlooked and any man dismissed from the Company's service for that offence will be liable to a fine by the magistrate.'

'Ordered that in every case of infringement of Rules or departure from them the persons offending be immediately suspended and reported to the Directors so that in case of grave offence the parties may be discharged or prosecuted.'

'Before any person is employed he shall be required to sign these regulations and for disobedience of which he will be

---

1. Hansard, 23 July 1840.
2. Great Western Railway Act, 1835. Sec. 201.

punished as for an offence against his Employers and against the Law.'

'Enginemen are informed that instructions have been given to immediately arrest and convey before a magistrate, any engine driver or other person who shall disobey the Stopping or Caution Signals.'

'No instance of intoxication on duty will ever be overlooked, and besides being dismissed the offender will be liable to be punished by the magistrate.'

The practice is equally clear from the following short list of cases on the Great Western, London & Brighton, Sheffield & Manchester, London & South Western, South Eastern, London, Brighton & South Coast, and Manchester, Sheffield & Lincolnshire railways.

1841
Policeman. One month's hard labour for being asleep on duty.
Engine driver. Convicted and fined for being drunk on duty.
Switchman. One month's imprisonment. Drunk on duty.
Engine driver. Taken before magistrate. Drunk.
Police Constable. Taken before magistrate. Absence from duty.

1842
Fireman. Two month's hard labour. Drunk.
Engine driver and fireman. One month's and twenty one days' imprisonment respectively. Accident.
Two Guards. Two months' hard labour each. Drunk.
A 'party'. Taken before magistrate. Leaving rails, laying on the line 'in an improper manner'.

1847
Engine driver. Convicted. Error liable to cause accident.
Engine driver. One month's hard labour. Collision.
A request by the L. B. & S. C. that the S. E. R. should prosecute two engine drivers for disobeying signals.

1848
Signalman and Ganger. Fine of £3 or one month's imprisonment each. Causing risk of collision.

1849
Gatekeeper. Convicted. Neglect of duty.
Engine driver. Fine £2. Collision.
Proceedings ordered against an engine driver as soon as he recovered from serious injury. Collision through disregard of signals.

1850
Gateman. One month's hard labour. Negligence.
Engine Driver. Summoned before magistrate. Collision.

1851
Engine driver and guard. Fine or two months' imprisonment.
Fireman. £3 fine or two months' imprisonment.
Signalman. £1 fine or one month's imprisonment. All for neglect causing danger of collision.
Several men charged before the magistrate. Acquitted on a legal technicality. (Neglect causing danger of accident).
1865
Fireman. Taken before the magistrate. Quarrelling with the driver and taking the train on himself.
Switchman. Taken into custody and fined £10. Asleep on duty, resulting in an accident.
Gangers. Prosecuted. Error liable to cause accident.
1866
Policeman. Charged before magistrate. Drunk.

The offences were those most likely to endanger safety and the man most prosecuted was the engine driver. Men convicted were invariably dismissed but occasionally re-employed in an inferior position.

On the basis of this legal sanction the companies built up their own disciplinary system. A starting point was the legal power to punish any man committing any offence against any railway bye-law, rule or regulation. In the 1820s the bye-laws of the Stockton & Darlington provided for fines for neglect, the directors 'being determined to enforce power given them by Parliament for preserving order and regularity'; similarly with the Canterbury & Whitstable in 1830. Bye-laws of other companies in the forties provided that any engine driver or fireman neglecting his fire was to be fined a maximum of £5; that any engine driver allowing another person to ride on the engine was to be fined; that immediate dismissal was the penalty for taking any gratuity or fee. The plea of ignorance was not accepted but 'will be considered rather an aggravation'.

In general, the wide powers of legal punishment, including as they did any breach of railway regulations, not only enhanced the authority of such regulations but also diminished the likelihood of any objection to the companies' punishments which, however heavy, were at least less severe than the statutory ones.

We may look first at the use of dismissal, its causes and frequency and the relative seriousness of different offences. The intention is clear enough in the companies' rules and regulations. On the Great Western in the early forties dismissal was the penalty for all grades for disobedience of orders, negligence or misconduct, for taking any fee or gratuity, and for any policeman absent from duty 'even for the first time', except in sudden emergency. On the L. & N. W. in 1856 it was the penalty for disobedience, negligence, misconduct, incompetency, intoxication, improper language, cursing or swearing, and the taking of gratuities. On the Taff Vale in 1855 'not an instance of intoxication, singing, whistling or levity, while on duty, will be overlooked, and besides being dismissed the offender will be liable to punishment'.

A fairly exact assessment of cases of dismissal from the railway minute books is possible because there is little doubt that in the early years at least all such disciplinary cases were dealt with individually by directors. On the Stockton & Darlington in 1840 Charles Tennison, an engine driver, was dismissed for speeding; he drove a distance of 40 miles in 4½ hours. On the London & Brighton during the period March 1841 to September 1843, there were fifty-nine dismissals out of an estimated total staff of two hundred, approximately 12 per cent per annum. The line was opened throughout to Brighton in September 1841, and the men were being collected and were learning the work. The offences and number of each were: drunkenness – 16, absence from duty – 13, neglect of work – 13, theft – 6, insubordination – 2, misconduct – 2, asleep on duty – 1, breach of regulations – 1, unknown – 5. The Great Western line was opened throughout to Bristol in June 1841. Between August 1840 and July 1841 there were seventy-nine dismissals out of an estimated total staff of seven hundred. The offences and number of each were: drunkenness – 20, absence from duty – 18, theft – 10, insubordination – 8, misconduct – 8, neglect of work – 6, taking gratuities – 5, asleep on duty – 4. Absence from duty often meant the temporary absence for sometimes only an hour or two of, for example, a policeman, i.e. a signalman. The predominance of drunkenness and absence from duty is clear. The proportion of dismissals to labour employed was high, involving a considerable turnover; but there was no difficulty in replacing men from the large number kept as supernumeraries.

A similar result, though a less exact one, is obtained from the minutes of other companies in the 1840s. The same offences occur though the order of frequency varies. The general order of frequency was: neglect of work and errors in work, drunkenness, insubordination, theft, misconduct, absence from duty, incompetence. Punishment was used unhesitatingly and determinedly for any offence involving danger to life or property. It was also used conscientiously. The procedure of establishing guilt was often careful, corroboration by numerous witnesses was required and sometimes cases were deferred for further evidence. But the necessity of making an example was always remembered.

Twenty years later the conditions for the use of dismissal had changed. Not only had the labour force more than doubled but the level of operating technique had risen and standards of conduct and discipline had settled down. Two examples come from the L. B. & S. C. traffic department. In the years 1858, 1859, 1860 there was an average of ninety-two dismissals out of a total staff of approximately seventeen hundred, or 5 per cent per annum. The cause of most of these is not given but of those that are the offences and the average number of each were: neglect − 13, misconduct − 8, insubordination − 7, drunkenness − 4. For the period August 1862 to December 1863 there were one hundred and three dismissals. The main offences and the number of each were: absence without leave − 23, neglect of duty − 15, drunkenness − 15, theft − 12.[1] The practice on the Great Western and the Great Northern is indicated in the summary of cases of dismissal.

Table IV

	G. N. 1858	G. W. R. 1865/66	G. N. 1868	G. W. R. 1869/70
No. of cases	63	115	124	160 (per annum)
Period	six mths.	twelve mths.	twelve mths.	
Causes of Dismissal				
	%	%	%	%
Absence	24	14	31	18
Neglect and Error	11	29	14	25
Drunkenness	14	22	21	20
Theft	38	20	11	6
Misconduct and Insubordination	13	15	23	11
Other	-	-	-	25

On the Great Western in 1869/70 the proportion of all dismissals to total staff was about 3 per cent per annum. The proportion of porters dismissed to those employed in 1858 was also about 3 per cent.

The conclusion is that the frequency of dismissal diminished considerably with the need for it. Men were not so often punished for accidents as in the forties when the causes lay more in the

---

1. London, Brighton & South Coast Staff Book, 1861. Black Book, 1862/63.

absence of regulations and of equipment. Regulations were no longer so often made after the event. The reliability of labour had increased. Accepting tips was no longer an offence. Drunkenness and absence from duty, though still common, had lost their clear predominance over other offences.

The second main method of discipline was the fining system as indicated by the evidence given by railway managers to the Select Committee of 1839: 'The great point is to furnish a strong pecuniary motive to pay the utmost attention'. It was desirable to give the companies general powers to inflict fines which, except by special arrangement, they did not possess. Fines were the most effective form of punishment. Police and porters usually signed an agreement which provided, inter alia, for their being punished by fine. But the enginemen (strong in the excess of demand over supply) refused to do so. The men were fined twice in amounts ranging between 2s 6d and £1, and the third time were discharged. Enginemen were fined for carelessness, negligence, for 'loitering on the road, excess of speed, refusing to start; if the night is unfavourable, and the trade demands a spell and the man refused to go, he is fined'. Although sometimes there was no power to fine, fines were imposed and there was no difficulty in enforcing them.[1] This was the voice of experience.

As in the textile industry, the fining system, which began almost as soon as the railways and continued up to the end of the century, became an essential part of conditions of work. On the Stockton and Darlington in 1840 Thomas Snowden, engine driver, was fined 20s for speeding at twelve miles per hour. Seven other enginemen were fined 10s each by Joseph Pease for refusing to take their engines out when ordered to. Joseph Pickering was fined 10s in 1829 'for carrying passengers on his tender contrary to the bye laws' and John Fardon was fined 8s in 1830 'for furiously driving whilst coming down the run'. At the New Shildon locomotive works the rules said: 'Any workman leaving his work without giving notice to the clerk or the foreman to be fined 1s. Any workman swearing or using abusive language to a shopmate to be fined 1s.' In 1841 regular scales were drawn up. All drivers arriving three minutes or more before time were to be fined. Fines for exceeding the speed limit were laid down at 5s for the first offence, 10s for the second. Even the officers fined themselves 5s if they were five minutes late for a meeting without a good excuse and it was not unknown for directors to do the same

---

1. Report of S. C. on Communication by Railway, 1839. Evidence of Chas Saunders, Joseph Pease and E. Bury.

thing. Twenty years later a system of fines and rewards to give 'a direct interest in punctuality' was in full operation.

The records make it possible to compare the practice of the sixties with the forties on the London & Brighton where sixty-one fines were imposed between March 1841 and September 1843. The offences and number of each were: neglect of duty 14, breach of regulations 8, errors in work 8, damage to company's property 7, absence from duty 7, asleep on duty 5, misconduct 3, insubordination 3, drunkenness 3, unknown 3. The amounts were frequently considerable, the average being 17s 1d. The relative seriousness of offences may be judged from the average amounts of the fines for each type of offence. They were absence from duty − £1, drunkenness − 17s, neglect of work − 17s, breach of regulations − 16s, asleep on duty − 15s, errors in work − 12s, misconduct − 12s, insubordination − 10s, damage to company's property − 10s. On the Great Western between August 1840 and July 1841 forty-nine fines were imposed. The offences and number of each were: errors in work 13, breach of regulations 11, absence from duty 10, neglect of work 5, misconduct 3, insubordination 3, asleep on duty 2, theft 1, drunkenness 1. The average amount was 19s 6d. To this must be added in some cases loss of pay during suspension from duty for periods up to fourteen days. The relative seriousness of offences, judged by the average fine imposed, was: breach of regulations − 33s, neglect of work − 33s, drunkenness − 20s, errors in work − 17s, asleep on duty − 15s, insubordination − 13s, misconduct − 12s, absence from duty − 12s, theft − 10s. Evidently the tariff was rather higher on the Great Western. Payment was usually made in weekly instalments.

Other railways provide ample evidence of a similar system. The most frequent offences were neglect of work and errors in work. There were, of course, variations. On the London & South Western the fine was a stoppage of wages ranging from one to fourteen days. In general, however, the heavier fines are attributable to either the cost of the offence to the railway, which was sometimes included in the fine, or to a particularly serious danger of accident.

Offences were considered individually and carefully by the directors. For instance, in the case of a police constable who was fined £1 payable in eight weekly instalments for being asleep on duty, the chairman of the board noted down the extenuating circumstances that 'he had exerted himself extremely during the night'. As yet there was little evidence of resentment towards the system. In one case it was challenged by a porter who, having been fined one shilling for neglect of duty, issued a summons in the county court against the company, for which further offence he was duly dismissed. There was also the platelayer, fined and later dismissed for failing to give a signal to an engine in time to prevent a collision, of whom the directors were told:

'The Superintendent reported that he said: "How the devil dare you Sir to suppose the engine could be stopped in twenty or thirty yards", to which he replied: "How the hell was I to know your engine was coming". I said I should have no impudence and gave him with my open hand a box on the ear, upon which he gave me a torrent of abuse.'

There were also appeals against fines, but they were usually unsuccessful.

The fining system still persisted for the 1860s but had undergone several changes. A complete record of the disciplinary offences in the traffic department of the L. B. & S. C. is contained in its Black Book for the period August 1862 to December 1863. There were 482 fines imposed on a total staff of approximately 1800, or one fine to every five men employed per annum. The fines ranged from 1s to 5s. The average amount was 1s 9d. The offences and the number of each were: errors in work 135, late on duty 107, neglect of work 105, damage to property 73, breach of regulations 31, misconduct 27, insubordination 4. The relative seriousness of offences, measured by the average fine for each type was: damage to property — 2s 10d, insubordination — 2s 7d, misconduct 2s 4d, neglect of work 2s, errors in work — 1s 8d, breach of regulations — 1s 6d, late on duty 1s 1d. In 1865 and 1866 on the Great Western a record of major fines only shows twenty-three such in twelve months, with the high average amount of £1 14s. They were mostly imposed on drivers and guards for serious errors which resulted in accidents.

The discipline of the switchmen or signalmen tells a different story and was indeed a special case. On the Great Western in the two and a half years ending July 1870 1039 men were fined an average of 4s 5d for irregularities in their work. They were 42 per cent of the total number of that grade and 6 per cent of the total traffic grades. A fine disqualified a man for the customary bonus for good conduct. On the same line there was a special class of fine which was imposed for accidents caused by alleged carelessness. In connection with 247 such accidents in 1869, 105 men were fined, 14 were dismissed, 5 were reduced in grade and 123 were reprimanded. The fines averaged 15s 2d; they were probably influenced by the scale of damages awarded against the companies. This was the opinion of a railway witness before the Select Committee on Railways (Compensation) in 1870.[1] It is certainly borne out by the cases in which men were

---

1. Report of S. C. on Railways (Compensation) 1870. Evidence of H. Oakley.

ordered to pay the cost of repairs to property, a procedure which was called fining.

The main change in the period of twenty years seems to have been that although the frequency of fining increased the amounts became considerably smaller. There was a great number of petty fines and the system seems to have become a routine. Fining had become a far more common punishment than any other. Errors and neglect of work remain the most frequent offences. Drunkenness, sleep on duty and insubordination have sunk into the background, if not disappeared, at least in these examples. The most serious offences are no longer breaches of regulations, neglect and drunkenness but damage to railway property, insubordination and misconduct. It has become a question of maintenance of discipline rather than imposition of it.

Whether the men knew the use to which the proceeds of fines were put, or whether the knowledge would have been any comfort to them, is not known. The suggestion made to the 1839 Select Committee was that there should be a fund to which men should contribute the sums they forfeited for misconduct. In fact, the fines were often credited to companies' benevolent funds, provident societies, sick funds and compensation accounts throughout the period.

After the imposition of fines the next most common punishment was the caution, which was given for lesser offences. While for more heinous acts men were sometimes suspended with loss of pay or removed to another station. The following monthly punishment list shows the high proportion of cautions and also, incidentally, illustrates the publicity given to misconduct.

London, Brighton & South Coast Railway Circular to the Line

STAFF

The following cases of neglect of duty, misconduct, and other irregularities, on the part of certain Officers and Servants of the Company during the past month, have been recorded, and are hereby notified to the Line by order of the Directors:

An Inspector cautioned for incivility to a Passenger.

A Booking Clerk dismissed for not accounting for excess fares.

A Booking Clerk cautioned for erroneously booking a Passenger through ignorance of the Train Service.

A Booking Clerk cautioned for general neglect of duty.

A Booking Clerk cautioned for not being at his Office in

time to book the first Morning Train.
A Parcels' Clerk cautioned for delay to a parcel.
An Excess Luggage Clerk dismissed for gross misconduct.
A Telegraph Clerk cautioned for delaying, and then carelessly despatching a message.
A Telegraph Clerk fined for violently using his instrument.
A Guard cautioned for running past Signals when at danger.
A Guard cautioned for annoyance to a Passenger.
A Guard discharged for opening the Company's letters given him for delivery.
A Guard cautioned for taking a portmanteau beyond its destination.
A Guard and three Lampmen cautioned for not reporting the fall of a roof lamp in a carriage and consequent injury to a Passenger.
A Head Porter dismissed for incapacity.
A Head Porter cautioned in connexion with a train staff being carried beyond its limit.
A Ticket Collector cautioned for incivility.
A Checker dismissed for being absent without leave.
A Cloakroom Porter removed for carelessly performing his duty.
A Parcels Porter dismissed for being absent without leave.
A Porter fined for damaging a Passenger's box.
A Porter suspended for three weeks, with loss of pay, for quarrelling with the Outside Porter.
A Porter cautioned for carelessly holding the point handle, and throwing a carriage off the road.
A Porter cautioned for omitting to put a Passenger's bag into the luggage car.
Three Porters cautioned for incivility to Passengers.
A Porter discharged for intoxication.
A Porter fined for carelessly loading and sheeting goods.
A Lampman cautioned for being absent without leave.
An Engine Driver discharged for moving his engine without a signal, thereby causing a collision.
Five Engine Drivers fined for not making proper examinations of their engines.
An Engine Driver fined for running into and damaging an engine.
An Engine Driver fined for allowing a Passenger to ride on his engine.
An Engine Driver fined for not seeing that the tubes of his engine were cleaned out.

DISCIPLINE

An Engine Driver fined for allowing his Engine to get short of steam.

An Engine Driver cautioned for running past Signal when at danger.

An Engine Driver cautioned for allowing the water in his tender to get too hot to pass the pump and injector.

An Engine Driver cautioned for allowing his engine to get short of steam.

An Engine Driver cautioned for neglecting to report an accident at the time of its occurrence.

Two Drivers cautioned for not sending in their daily returns at the proper time.

A Fireman fined for depositing ashes from his engine alongside the carriage shed at Brighton contrary to orders.

Three Engine Cleaners discharged for neglect of duty and gross conduct to an old man whom they enticed into the shed.

An Engine Cleaner discharged for neglect of duty.

Two Engine Cleaners discharged for wilfully greasing the floor of the Engine Cleaners' Room.

A Hammerman discharged for losing time.

A Wagon Inspector cautioned for allowing a truck to leave a station without a side chain.

A Labourer severely cautioned for throwing a piece of wood from the roof of a station on to the permanent way.

Attention is also called to the following claims recently paid by the Company for losses and damage to goods, parcels, luggage, etc., arising principally through neglect and carelessness of the Staff:

Claim of £2 2s 0d paid for damage to some guttering in transit from London to Worthing.

Claim of £3 5s 0d paid for damage to some oil cake in transit from London to Pevensey.

Claim of £5 3s 2d paid for damage to a quantity of eggs in transit from Honfleur to London.

Claim of £2 19s 6d paid for damage to a quantity of lead in transit from London to Portsmouth.

Claim of £4 2s 9d paid for damage to cages in transit from London to Eastbourne.

Claim of £20 12s 1d paid for damage to furniture in transit from Brighton to London.

NOTE - In any case of claim arising from damage or loss, where neglect is traceable to any of the Servants, they will be held individually responsible for the amount of the claim.

General Manager's Office   (By order)   J. P. Knight
London Bridge Terminus, August 1872   General Manager

The complement to punishment was reward for good work and conduct. This was one of the many things which bound the men to the companies. Everything which attached men to the railway service 'by as many ties as possible' was in the interests both of the public and the companies.[1] There were two kinds of reward, firstly the gratuities given regularly to encourage correct or economical work by particular grades important for safety or cost, and secondly the ad hoc gratuity for individual meritorious action.

The first kind was, from the beginning, regarded by the companies, and no doubt by the men, as part of wages, conditional on good behaviour.

> 'It has been the custom in the Company to make a portion of the most important part of our working establishment - I mean the engine drivers, switchmen and policemen - contingent on their good behaviour.'[2]

On that line £358 4s 0d was given in gratuities to engine drivers and forty-five firemen in the half year ending December 1842, in amounts of £5 and £3 respectively. But this was offset by £42 9s 6d representing fifty-one fines, the most usual fine for drivers being £1 and for firemen, 12s.[3] On the Great Western fixed annual premiums of £10 and £5 were granted at the discretion of the directors to enginemen 'deemed entitled for faithful and approved service during one year'. Elsewhere in 1841 six enginemen received £10 and four received £5 for a year's service 'without offence'. A week's pay was granted to drivers, firemen and guards whose conduct was satisfactory. Economy in fuel was also rewarded; in 1849 on one line twelve drivers received £5 each, twenty £3 and eight £1 each. And this was replaced four years later by a half yearly gratuity for good conduct. Fuel premiums or bonuses were continued elsewhere up to 1870. Conversely enginemen were dismissed for wasting fuel.[4]

The other particular grade which was similarly encouraged was the switchmen or signalmen. Those with one year's service 'without any

---

1. Report of S. C. on Communication by Railway, 1839. Evidence of Capt. Moorsom.
2. London & Birmingham. Report of Annual General Meeting, 1842.
3. London & Birmingham. Return of gratuities to Engine drivers and Firemen. Half year ending Dec. 1842.
4. Report of S. C. on Railways, 1870. Evidence of J. Grierson.

neglect of duty or other cause of complaint' were entitled to an annual premium of £5. In 1841 twenty-one such rewards were given on one line, one being forfeited through the man having been fined once for negligence. On the same line twenty-five years later, during a period of twelve months, 277 men were given bonuses of £5, 13 of £3, 2 of £3 10s 0d and 19 of £2.

Rewards were also distributed more generally among the grades. In 1853 wages paid staff on the L. B. & S. C. with more than two years' service were granted one week's wages, those with one to two years' service were given half a week's wages, and salaried staff 5 per cent of annual salary. This amounted to £879 18s 8d. Again in 1856 the bonus was one week's pay to wages staff and two weeks' pay to salaried staff with two years' service, and half a week's pay to all staff with one to two years' service. Those who had been punished were excepted as were those on 'individual bonus', a system in which officers received bonuses in proportion to the dividends. Again nine years later, in order to improve the punctuality of trains, a system of rewards and fines for drivers, firemen and guards was introduced. The fines were to be a moiety of the rewards. The second kind of reward - that for single meritorious actions was too various and general to have any special significance. Gratuities were given generally and throughout for special vigilance, for extra work, prompt action in accidents, prevention of accidents, special care of a company's interests.

Punishment for unsatisfactory work and rewards for good work were the most direct forms of discipline. But there were many other practices conducive to the same result, creating, as it were, the atmosphere of discipline, rather than imposing it. Such a practice, for example, was the swearing in of men as special constables. In the 1840s many grades were sworn in: policemen (and for wasting time in doing so three of them were fined a week's wages apiece), conductors, guards, porters, platelayers, gangers and foremen. The special virtue of honesty required, and received, special methods of ensuring it. This was the system in which security or guarantee was required from all who had to do with the companies' money. The men concerned were chiefly clerks but some other grades were also involved.

This arrangement, as with the forms of more direct discipline, had its statutory basis. The Liverpool & Manchester Railway Act gave compulsory powers for the taking of security from servants.[1]

'The said Company shall and they are hereby required to take sufficient security from every person, who shall hereafter be

---

1. Liverpool & Manchester Railway Act, 1826. Sec. 91.

appointed Treasurer of the said Company, and from the Receiver, Collector, or other Officer having the control or custody of any money received by virtue of this Act, for the faithful execution of his office before he shall enter thereupon.'

Similar provision was contained in other acts and it was consolidated in 1845 as follows:[1]

'Before any person intrusted with the Custody or Control of Monies, whether Treasurer, Collector, or other Officer of the Company, shall enter upon his office, the Directors shall take sufficient security from him for the faithful execution of his office.'

The canals had already initiated this practice and lock keepers were required to give security equal to two years' salary.

On this basis railway policy developed, varying slightly from company to company. A special general meeting of the Leicester & Swannington was called in 1830 for the purpose of taking security from the treasurer. Depot agents on the Stockton & Darlington were required to give security for sums received. In 1840 on the Birmingham & Gloucester all persons receiving money were to give security equal to one year's salary although a little later this was altered, in order to avoid legal expense, to the obtaining of letters from parties willing to become sureties. In 1842 on the London & Birmingham all officers and clerks in receipt of money were required to furnish adequate security. In 1843 on the London & Brighton forms of bond for servants were ordered to be prepared and used 'on all occasions'. In 1846 on the Midland every servant who had charge of money was to give security.

The effects of this varied. Although officers and clerks were mainly affected so too, early on, were guards, ticket collectors, booking porters and police in charge of stations. The amounts varied considerably on different lines and according to the liability incurred, between the extremes of £10 from an under-guard to £1,000 from a clerk in charge of an important station. The practice is summarised in the following table:

---

1. London & Birmingham, Grand Junction, Manchester & Leeds, Midland Railways Acts.
Railway Clauses Act, 1845. Sec. 109.

Table V.
Security required from Employees

Grade.	Security £	Salary or Wages.
1840.		
Booking Clerks	50 - 100	£60 - £90
1841		
Clerks in charge	Min. £20	£60
Station Clerks	200	£60 - 100
Guards	40	25s.0d.
1842.		
Clerk in charge	1,000	£160
Ticket Collector	40	25s.0d.
1843		
Clerks	500	£50 - 150
Under Guards	10	25s.0d.
1844		
Head Guards	£80	30s.0d.
Booking Porters	50	25s.0d.
1845		
Clerks	200	£120
Clerks	100	£75
Clerks	500	Over £100
Clerks	300	£100 & under
1846.		
Clerk in charge	300	£150
1848.		
Clerks	100	£60 - 80
1849		
Clerk	500	£75
1850		
Clerk	200	£90
1860		
Clerk	500	£90
1866		
Clerks	300	£70 - 150

Railway servants arranged security, before the railways established their own guarantee funds, in one of two ways. They either obtained two respectable citizens to act as sureties for the amount required or took out a policy with one of the guarantee societies or an insurance society. The more simple method of merely putting down a deposit was used only in the beginning when the guarantee was small; in 1843 guards deposited £10 as security, while police in charge of stations were required to sign a letter of guarantee. In the forties station clerks particularly and indeed all clerks having charge of the receipt of money were required to provide the 'personal security of two respectable individuals'. Some of the occupations of these respectable persons were those of surgeon, commercial traveller, publican, carrier, solicitor, grocer. Enquiries were made as to their respectability and sometimes this proved necessary as on the occasion when, following a clerk's defalcation, a surety agreed to pay £100 down and to give three promissory notes for £50 each at one, two and three years.

At the same time the guarantee societies were used increasingly as they were approved by the railways. The relations between the two were sometimes fairly close as when the railways bore the cost of the premiums. This was the practice on the L. B. & S. C. in 1850 for instance, in cases where the salary was less than 25s. per week or the security required was more than one and a half year's salary; and on the Great Northern when the salary was less than 25s. per week or 20s. per week with lodgings or when the security required was greater than two years' salary. The guarantee society was preferred by the railways to the private suretyships for the obvious reason of greater security, and because of the 'moral influence which a public company exercises over those whose honesty may be guaranteed by it'.[1]

In some cases the guarantee business was conducted by a general insurance society such as the European Assurance Society, established in 1859, which was approved by the L. & N. W. in 1860 'to compete for the guarantee business of the company'. The cost of guarantee policies before 1860 was 12s 6d per cent for whatever amount. This society reduced the ordinary premium to 10s. per cent and, in order to cater for lower grades, to 5s. for policies for L. & N.W. men. The average guarantee was £91 2s 9d. and the average premium 9s 1d per annum, but a large proportion of the policies were for £50. Life assurance was also offered at cheaper rates if taken with a guarantee policy and this was accepted by at least some station masters.[2]

---

1. Correspondence, Secretary of L. & N. W. R. and Chairman of European Assurance Society, July and August, 1864.
2. European Assurance Society. Correspondence with L. & N. W. Rly, 1864.

The evidence indicates that the companies' policies were generally enforced and that their effect, in sifting out the best among a section of railway servants, was considerable. Not only were enquiries made into the respectability of sureties, but the guarantee societies also made, in the words of one of them, 'independent and searching inquiries into the character and antecedents of applicants'. Checks were made periodically by the railways to ensure that proper securities existed. When a guarantee society declined to give security for clerks they were discharged. Bonds of fidelity had to be produced before salaries were paid and when defalcations occurred the guarantee society always prosecuted if there was any likelihood of conviction.

It is not possible to say clearly how honest or financially reliable were the men working under this control. The European Assurance Society about 1860 had found it necessary to prosecute in every possible case in order to check a large number of cases on the Lancashire & Yorkshire and the South Eastern railways. But out of the six hundred policies held by that society among L. & N. W. men there were only fourteen defalcations in the four years 1860 to 1864. There had been a great advance by the time the railways came to establish their own guarantee funds in the seventies. When that happened deductions from pay for the guarantee fund became a normal condition of service, whereas before the finding of security had been a pre-requisite of appointment.

Proposals for a system of mutal assurance were long discussed by railway managements without result, although this method was used in Government departments in the forties. In the mean time the practice of taking out policies with guarantee societies involved some hardship for the lower paid men. One obstacle to the establishment of railway guarantee funds was the alarm felt at the danger of 'unlimited liability' by the subscribers to the funds. It became clear however that the small number of claims in relation to the number of value of policies would reduce any risk to a very acceptable level. In fact a satisfactory level of honesty had already been reached. A more important consideration leading to the establishment of the funds was that 'a higher tone generally in the service' would result, as it allowed men who resigned to receive back their subscriptions, provided they had not incurred any liability. When the railway guarantee funds were established, for example the L. & N. W. fund in January 1870, all persons who had access to the companies' money were required to give guarantee through them. The rules of these funds showed some improvement over the earlier methods from the men's point of view. The contribution for securities of £50 was still 5s 0d but for those of £50 to £75 it was reduced to 7s 6d. The minimum salary of any man required to pay a contribution was raised to £55 per annum. When the guarantee exceeded the annual salary the company paid contributions for the excess.

The degree of risk to the companies for dishonesty rapidly diminished so that the contributions were reduced by 25 per cent, in 1875 and again in 1882. This trend developed further until by 1915 the funds began to be maintained by the companies' contributions alone, without any from the men. On some lines however the payment of premiums continued even then. Financial reliability had thus fully developed but it is clear that for forty years the requirement of guarantee of honesty was a considerable influence on the character of this section of railway labour.

Three aspects of the discipline system may finally be considered: coercion, concession and persuasion. The first means punishment, the giving of security for honesty, the tied cottage. The second refers to welfare generally, provident funds, pension, gratuities to dependents, payment of funeral expenses, travelling privileges. (These matters are dealt with in Chapter 9.). The third refers to rewards and gratuities.

The system had a twofold significance. Firstly it was a factor in labour efficiency. Punishment was then the most effective way of improving efficiency; the way to prevent unnecessary shunting was to punish the men at fault. Perhaps it would have been otherwise if a suggestion to the Select Committee of 1839 had been adopted, that the men should maintain discipline themselves through their own committees for 'examining and awarding punishment'. Secondly it was an essential piece of the fabric of the men's lives and, in the absence of any appreciable evidence to the contrary, it was accepted as necessary.

Chapter 3

WASTAGE

Wastage of labour is here considered in its two main aspects: the turnover resulting from the rate at which men entered and left the railways, and the loss of labour resulting from occupational injury and sickness. Both have an important bearing on the effective use of labour by the railway companies.

There was on the railways a high turnover of labour along with a rapid expansion of employment. A preliminary indication of a link between these two features is given by the age distribution of labour. The following Tables VI and VII give the age distribution of all grades except artificers on the L. B. & S. C. in 1871 compared with other occupations, and the percentage of young persons under twenty years.[1] The latter have been excluded from the totals used as the basis for the figures in Table VI.

As can be seen from Table VI railway labour shows a remarkably high percentage of persons in the younger groups of those under the age of thirty-five. It is clear from Table VII, however, that this cannot be wholly attributed to a high proportion of young persons. It must be mainly explained by the rate at which men left the occupation and the rate of recruitment.

There is ample evidence that the flow of labour into and out of the railways was large. Reference has already been made to the volume of dismissals and to this must be added resignations. A rapid turnover is suggested by the character of the membership of the Euston Friendly Society between 1840 and 1860. This was a small society but typical in so far as it embraced most traffic grades at Euston. The membership in 1840 and 1856 was nearly the same size, 950 and 1015 respectively. But of the original 950 only 110 remained in 1856 and in the interval 3187 new members had joined. The annual average intake in the 1850s was 145 without any noticeable increase in total membership. The official estimate was that less than 5 per cent of the members would remain with the company until sixty years of age, a figure which cannot be explained by a high rate of mortality and incapacitation. It was the 'fluctuating character of the service' which produced such a large number of

---

1. London, Brighton & South Coast. List of Staff in All Departments, 1871. Census Report, 1871.

Table VI
Age Distribution of Persons Age 20 & Over in 1871

Occupation	Age Groups					
	20-24	25-34	35-44	45-54	55-64	65 & over
	%	%	%	%	%	%
L.B & S.C.R.	19.2	44.1	21.8	10.7	3.5	.7
Agricultural Labourer	12.3	21.7	20.1	18.2	14.4	13.3
General Labourer	14.3	25.2	21.5	17.2	12.0	9.8
Coal Miner	22.1	32.7	22.5	13.2	6.5	3.0
Seaman	18.7	33.3	21.4	13.8	7.2	5.6
Carrier	16.6	30.8	22.8	16.4	8.9	4.5
Domestic Servant (M)	26.7	31.2	18.1	12.0	6.8	5.2
Plumber, Painter, Glazier	19.1	32.1	22.6	15.0	7.7	3.5
Carpenter, Joiner	18.0	29.2	20.0	15.9	10.6	7.3
Engine & Machine Maker	22.5	35.5	21.8	12.9	5.4	1.9
Railway Grades						
Station Master & Clerk	31.9	37.9	17.9	7.8	4.1	.4
Supervisory	2.5	33.3	38.4	22.2	2.4	1.2
Enginemen	26.9	37.8	21.7	12.0	1.4	.2
Traffic Grades	18.5	48.5	21.3	7.6	3.3.	.8
Permanent Way Men	10.7	44.2	23.8	15.9	4.6	.8

discontinuing members.[1] The general picture is that of a simultaneous pressure of labour to get employment on the railways and an outflow, both of those who wished to better themselves and of those who did not reach the required standards of discipline or efficiency.

---

1. London & North Western Euston Friendly Society, Correspondence, 1856. Casualty & Benefit Cte. Report, 1856.

Table VII

Percentage of Persons under Age 20 in 1871

L.B. & S. C. R.	10.4
Agricultural Labourer	21.4
General Labourer	16.3
Coal Miner	27.8
Seaman	16.0
Carrier	13.1
Domestic Servant (M)	37.4
Plumber, Painter, Glazier	16.9
Carpenter, Joiner	15.1
Engine and Machine Maker	18.6
Railway Grades	
Station Master and Clerk	30.4
Supervisory	-
Engineman	10.1
Traffic Grades	7.1
Permanent Way Men	2.4

There was a continual movement of men who joined the railways to better themselves and of those who left for the same reason.

The rate of turnover of labour can be indicated with some accuracy by a comparison of the number of resignations and dismissals with the numbers employed. Resignations and dismissals, as recorded, do not give the total outflow but they do represent a very great proportion of it since they frequently include men who left because of incapacity, through accident or sickness A secondary indication of turnover is given by the length of service of the men who left. The examples of turnover which follow relate very largely to traffic grades and clerks. Data for enginemen and permanent way men are scarcer.

In 1843 the London & Birmingham was losing porters, policemen and clerks at the rate of seventy-six per annum. The number employed is not known but on the basis of the L. & N.W. figures for 1847 the turnover was about 4 per cent per annum The total rate must have been much higher. In 1844/45 the rate of resignations for clerks alone on the Eastern Counties was approximately 3 per cent per annum. In the 1850s the outflow continued and at a higher rate. Over a period of six years on the L.B & S.C. resignations alone of station masters and clerks were occurring at the rate of 3.5 per cent per annum. To this should be added the number of dismissals. The average length of service of these men also was quite short, in fact not more than nine years. The accounts of the L. & N.W. Superannuation Fund from 1853 to 1870 show conclusively a considerably higher rate of turnover. An average of 10 per cent of the members, who were officers, clerks and station masters, left every year.

Table VIII shows fairly exactly the rate of turnover on the L.B. & S.C. for 1858, 1859 and 1860. The figures refer to eight grades - station master, clerk, ticket collector, guard, switchman, porter, policeman and gatekeeper, that is most of the traffic grades.

Table VIII
Turnover on the London, Brighton & South Coast 1858-60

Year	Number leaving through resignation & dismissal	Appointments	Estimated number employed	Rate of Exit	Rate of Entry
1858	171	226	1,320	13%	17%
1859	184	235	1,454	13%	16%
1860	176	238	1,634	11%	15%

The number of appointments refers to permanent staff only; the number leaving includes temporary grades such as vanguard in which the turnover was particularly high. It is thus seen from the table that the turnover of the traffic grades was quite high. The figures in Table VIII can be split up so as to show the result for each grade separately, as in Table IX. In those grades (station master, guard, signalman) where rate of exit exceeded rate of entry new entrants were not usually appointed but appointments were made from inferior grades. In any case the number of station masters concerned is probably too small to have any significance. The other figures, however, show that the men who had acquired some skill or technique had the lowest turnover. The high figure for porters is partly explained by the inclusion of some temporary grades such as vanguard, carriage cleaner, etc. The low rate of exit for gatekeepers may be due to the fact that some of them were wives of platelayers, etc.

Table IX
Turnover of Grades on the London, Brighton & South Coast, 1858-60

Grade	Number Leaving	Rate of Exit %	Number Appointed	Rate of Entry %
1858				
Station Master	1	17	1	17
Clerk	23	7	35	15
Tkt. Collr.	7	19	11	29
Guard	7	6	2	2
Signalman	10	9	9	8
Porter etc.	124	21	139	23
Policeman	2	5	2	5
Gatekeeper	5	6	26	21
1859				
Station Master	6	90	-	-
Clerk	35	9	43	12
Tkt. Collr.	6	15	14	35
Guard	5	4	-	-
Signalman	6	5	5	4
Porter etc.	123	19	156	24
Policeman	3	7	5	12
Gatekeeper	6	7	12	12
1860				
Station Master	1	2	-	-
Clerk	32	8	31	8
Tkt. Collr.	5	9	9	18
Guard	8	5	1	1
Signalman	5	4	1	1
Porter etc.	129	17	176	25
Policeman	5	13	10	24
Gatekeeper	5	5	9	9
Average for 1858 - 1860				
Station Master	3	36	.3	6
Clerk	30	8	36	12
Tkt. Collr.	6	11	11	27
Guard	7	5	1	1
Signalman	7	6	5	3
Porter etc.	128	19	157	24
Policeman	3	8	6	10
Gatekeeper	5	6	16	14

The second example of turnover in the 1850s is from the Great Northern for six months of 1858. Dismissals and resignations of the traffic grades give the results in Table X. Information on the rate of entry is not available.

Table X
Turnover on the Great Northern, 1858

Grade	Number leaving through resignation & dismissal per annum	Number employed	Rate of exit per annum %
Clerk	62	675	9
Guard	12	175	7
Signalman & Policeman	16	118	14
Porters etc.	162	1,509	11
Total	252	2,477	10

The rate for signalmen and policemen is doubtful since the Great Northern did not include in its parliamentary return the numbers of signalmen employed. The number of policemen and watchmen has therefore been used as the most appropriate. Apart from that, and the low rate of exit for porters, the average rate for all others is similar to that on the L.B. & S.C. It should be noted in relation to this second example that although it was customary for all resignations and dismissals to be reported to the directors, some may well not have been and the rate of exit was therefore, if anything, slightly higher than 10 per cent.

For the late 1860s an analysis of the Great Northern for the twelve months ending December 1868 shows the following result:

Table XI
Turnover on the Great Northern, 1868

Grade	Number leaving through resignation & dismissal	Number employed	Rate of Exit per annum %
Clerk	53	845	6
Guard	14	217	6
Signalman & policeman	26	290	9
Porter	249	1,641	15
Total	342	2,993	11

The number of staff employed in the above table is a very approximate figure. It is an estimate, made by increasing the latest known figure, for 1860, in proportion to the increase in mileage open. A second example for the late 1860s is from the L.B. & S.C. Table XII refers to the whole of the traffic grades on that line for the years 1865 - 1869.

Table XII
Turnover on the London, Brighton & South Coast, 1865-9

Number leaving through resignations and dismissals per annum	Number of Appointments per annum	Average number employed	Rate of Exit per annum %	Rate of Entry per annum %
394	294	2,434	16	12

The figures given above are averages for 1865 - 1869. It should be noted that resignations and dismissals include temporary and supernumerary men such as van guards, whose rate of turnover was high, whereas appointments refer only to permanent staff. Comparison with the figures on the same line ten years earlier shows a distinctly higher rate of exit and lower rate of entry. The figures may give an impression of shrinking employment but in fact in 1865-9 they include a much higher proportion of temporary staff. The figures in Table XII can be split up to show the rate of exit for each grade separately as in Table XIII.

By comparison with the figures of ten years earlier the rate of exit has increased for clerks, guards, signalmen, ticket collectors and policemen, and fallen for station masters, porters, and gatekeepers. Little significance can perhaps be attached to this fact, except that any differentiation in the turnover of skilled men as compared with unskilled men has diminished.

More significance may be attached to the length of service of these men before they left on account of dismissal or resignation. This is shown in Table XIV which is based on sample cases of the more important grades in Table VIII.

By this measure the higher turnover of the more unskilled grades such as porter, carman, vanguard as compared with the more skilled, guards, signalmen, shunters, is more evident. The policemen may

Table XIII
Turnover of Grades on the London, Brighton & South Coast in 1865-9

Grade	Number leaving through resignation & dismissal per annum	Rate of Exit per annum %
Station Master	4	9
Clerk	80	19
Inspector	2	10
Foreman	2	10
Tkt. Collr.	12	21
Guard	22	22
Signalman	14	10
Switchman	4	17
Head Porter	4	12
Shunter	7	10
Porter	143	14
Policeman	4	15
Carriage Cleaner	6	18
Watchman	5	19
Lampman	2	18
Gatekeeper	6	4
Messenger	5	7
Carman	26	31
Vanguard	33	36
Truck Horse Driver	6	20
Stableman	5	19
Sheeter	1	14
Checker	.4	8
Warehouseman	.4	12
Labeller	.4	12
Total	394	16

appear an exception but by this date, having become differentiated from traffic grades, their functions were similar to those of civil police and a correspondingly greater permanence of employment was to be expected.

The outstanding fact, even after allowing for the effect of the inclusion of vanguards who were mostly temporary lads and of carmen, many of whom were temporary, is that the average length of employment of nearly 1000 cases was a mere 2½ years. Another

Table XIV
Turnover on the London, Brighton & South Coast, 1865-9

Grade	Average Length of employment Yrs. months		Number of cases
Station Master	12	7	8
Clerk	3	1	189
Foreman	7	0	6
Tkt. Collr.	3	11	32
Guard	6	5	80
Signalman	5	11	21
Switchman	6	6	10
Shunter	3	1	9
Porter	1	7	331
Policeman	9	0	7
Watchman	3	4	6
Gatekeeper	4	6	2
Messenger		11	16
Carman	1	10	106
Vanguard	1	0	156
Truck Horse Driver	2	5	14
Total	2	7	993

analysis of the Great Western in 1870 shows in Table XV the numbers leaving employment through dismissal and resignation as a proportion of the number employed for the year ended 31 July.

Table XV
Turnover on the Great Western, 1870

Grade	Number Leaving	Number employed	Rate of exit per annum
Station master and clerk	206	1309	16%
Porters, police, etc,	471	3833	12%

Porters, police, etc. includes switchmen, guards, carmen and checkers and the rate of movement in this example corresponds roughly to those given for the late 1860s on other railways.

A further point remains - what were the reasons and motives for this movement? The evidence suggests that movement was more voluntary than involuntary. It was due rather more to a desire for betterment on the part of the men than to their expulsion by the companies. This conclusion is reached by a comparison between the relative importance of resignations and dismissals as factors in the rate of movement away from the railways. The two factors are not completely distinct since resignations were sometimes enforced as a mild form of dismissal, but the broad distinction remains since the great majority of resignations were voluntary. In the main the volume of resignations was rather greater than that of dismissals, and increasingly so in the later years. Movement was becoming more voluntary. This may be illustrated in two ways. Table XVI shows resignations as a percentage of those leaving through resignation and dismissal. Table XVII shows how the volume of resignations was increasing faster than that of dismissals on the G.N. and L.B.S.C. between 1858 and 1868

TABLE XVI

Year	Railway	Resignations as % of men leaving through resignation & dismissal
1843	London & B'ham	37%
1858	L.B. & S.C.	39%
1858	Great Northern	57%
1859	L.B. & S.C.	51%
1860	L.B. & S.C.	51%
1865-9	L.B. & S.C.	55%
1868	Great Northern	64%
1869	Great Western	65%
1870	Great Western	58%

TABLE XVII

Railway	Increase in No. of Resignations per annum 1858-68	Increase in No. of Dismissals per annum 1858-68
L.B. & S.C.	161%	84%
Great Northern	46%	10%

The main motive for this mainly voluntary movement was undoubtedly the desire for betterment, on the part of both men entering the railways and men leaving them On the L.B. & S.C. in

1858-9, out of thirty-one applications for employment examined, nineteen explicitly stated as their reason for leaving their previous employment 'to better myself'. On the Great Western in 1869 out of a total of 286 resignations the motive for 64 per cent was stated as self-betterment; in 1870 out of a total of 391, the proportion was 60 per cent.

So far this analysis of turnover has related to traffic grades and clerks. As regards enginemen the assumption would be that since they, or at least the driver, were more skilled and better paid, they were less likely to leave. This is confirmed by the only evidence available.

The number of enginemen resigning from the Great Western may be calculated from the reports of that company's Enginemen and Firemen's Mutual Assurance Society. Membership was compulsory. The amount of contributions actually returned to members leaving, the rate of contributions and the proportion of a man's contributions which was returnable, are known. Possibility of error in the calculation arises because the length of membership of men resigning is not known. Two figures are therefore shown: one on the assumption that membership of all the men concerned dated from the establishment of the society (1865), the other on the assumption that on the average their membership dated from halfway between establishment of the society and date of resignation.

TABLE XVIII
Resignations of Engine Drivers and Firemen

Year	Number Employed	% of Members resigning on basis of whole period membership	% of Members resigning on basis of half period membership
1869	1118	0.2	0.4
1870	1168	0.7	1.4
1871	1220	1.0	2.0
1872	1497	0.6	1.2
1873	1593	1.4	2.8
1874	1697	0.5	1.0
1875	1756	0.3	0.6
Average	1436	0.6	1.2

From this it appears that taking resignations only into account the outflow of enginemen was very small. The rate of dismissals is not known but it may be assumed that it was not higher, and probably lower, than for the traffic grades. The turnover of enginemen was small, their standard of living was in any case well above the poverty line and their security was relatively high.

Occupational Risk and Injury

Risk existed for various reasons: long hours of work, unpunctuality and carelessness, indifference of the companies arising partly from lack of publicity and of compulsion to report accidents, and expressed in inadequate safety regulations and devices.

Contemporary opinion was definite enough although it might differ as to the causes. 'The railway system comprised an entirely new era in the history of mankind but no class of men in the entire community were exposed to more constant risk to life and limb in the public service than railwaymen.... The risks to which railwaymen were exposed were far greater than those of ordinary workmen.'.... 'Railway Servants have been shown to be liable to sickness, injuries and accidental death much beyond the average ratio: to diminish the causes of these to the utmost extent is a clear duty of the employers. Granted that they fulfil it as far as in their power, the result still shows the unmistakeably hazardous nature of the employment.'[1]

The chief inspector of railways of the Board of Trade, giving evidence in 1858, stated that many accidents arose from men being overworked since the tendency of the companies was to overwork their men generally. He was naturally contradicted by railway company witnesses.[2]

The degree of risk is difficult to state accurately. In 1840 the chairman of the London & Birmingham referred to a 'certain degree of hazard' inseparable from railway employment.[3] The same vagueness characterises official statistics until after 1870. On the basis of the Board of Trade returns of accidents the calculation for certain selected years shown in Table XIX may be made. There is, however, ample evidence that these figures are valueless until after 1871 and misleading thereafter. 'The returns of accidents to servants of companies or of contractors cannot be looked upon as complete, as many railway companies, not being required by law to do so, do not report to the Board of Trade every accident which may have occurred to that class of person.'[4] One may notice the remarkable

1. Reports of Railway Benevolent Institution, Sir William Fairbairn, 1865. W. F. Mills, *The Railway Service*, 1867.
2. Report of S.C. on Accidents on Railways, 1858. Evidence of Col. George Wynne R. E.
3. London & Birmingham. Chairman's Report, 1840.
4. W. F. Mills, The *Railway Service*, 1867.

change in the figures between 1870 and 1875. It was not until 1871 that the companies were obliged to inform the Board of Trade of every case of death or injury of servants.

Table XIX
Risk of Death and Injury

Year	Killed & Injured	Number Employed	Proportion of killed and injured to employed
1847	189	47,218	1 in 250
1852	212	67,601	1 in 319
1857	166	109,660	1 in 661
1860	189	127,449	1 in 679
1865	205	150,000 c.	1 in 750
1870	244	220,000 c.	1 in 1,125
1876	1,946	280,000 c.	1 in 167

The Casualty Fund of the Railway Benevolent Institution, gives a far more reliable picture. In 1866 that fund gave relief to 139 cases of injury or death on duty out of a total membership of 8450, or 1 in 61, whereas the parliamentary return for the previous year gives a proportion of 1 in 750. Even the figure of 1 in 61 does not represent anything like all injuries. In 1871 the risk of injury or death, according to this source, had risen to at least 1 in 37 (793 cases relieved out of 29,220 members).[1] It may have been that those who joined this fund (at twopence per week) were those who ran the greatest risk. However, the last figure is similar to that of roughly 1 in 40 mentioned by the general secretary of the Amalgamated Society of Railway Servants at the Trades Union Congress in 1875.

The Board of Trade figures of deaths by accident are probably far more useful than those of injury. There is the difficulty of definition of injury; did it mean permanent or temporary disability? Almost certainly the former. 'Many railway companies do not report all the accidents which may happen to this class of person, and a much larger number of persons are temporarily disabled by personal accidents which do not acquire public notoriety.'[2] A L. & N.W. parliamentary return of 1870 refers to the number of permanently injured, the figure being 6 out of a total strength of 32,000. A Great Western injuries figure of 1 in 184 in the traffic department, most prone to accidents, can only refer to permanent injury. No wonder

---

1. Railway Benevolent Institution. Annual Reports, 1866, 1871.
2. Leone Levi, *Wages and Earnings of the Working Classes*, 1867.

that a Great Western report of 1870 stated that 'stricter investigation of every kind' was admitted as the explanation of an increase in the incidence of accidents to company's servants of from 1 in 107 to 1 in 64.

Differentiation of the incidence of risk by grades would be more useful than a figure expressing risk for all servants. Here unfortunately the only guide is the Board of Trade returns shown in Table XX.

TABLE XX
Proportion of Killed to Employed

Year	Engine Drivers	Fireman	Guards	Porters
1841–45	1 in 210	1 in 184	1 in 130	1 in 546
1846–50	" 229	" 112	" 92	" 672
1851–55	" 274	" 228	" 192	" 683
1856–60	" 458	" 297	" 249	" 1103
1861–65	" 573	" 389	" 333	" 1937

These figures have no great value as an indication of risk of death by accident, though the latest figure for engine drivers corresponds quite closely to another of 1 in 546 given in 1874 by the Great Western Enginemen & Firemen's Society, which may be taken as close to fact. They are given here to indicate that the order of risk descended from guards to firemen, drivers and porters. Figures of the proportion of injuries to employed, by grades, can also be given but 'the returns differ so materially from the experience of the friendly societies' that they are of little value. The absurd conclusion is indeed sometimes reached from them that the liability to injury was less than the liability to death by accident.

Two further indications of risk may be given. They must, however, be partly accounted for by the high incidence of sickness which is discussed later. In 1869 it was estimated that the assurance premium required to give a railway servant £50 at death and 15s per week in sickness was £2 15s 4d per annum whereas to give 'the professions, merchants, shopkeepers, gentlemen and farmers' £100 at death and 15s per week, only 10s per annum would be required.[1] In 1853 the mortality rate of railway servants was shown to be higher than that of members of friendly societies in general, as is shown in Table XXI.[2]

---

1. Railway Benevolent Institution. Report of Annual Dinner, 1869.
2. Report and Table by Actuary of National Debt Office on Sickness and Mortality among members of Friendly Societies, 1853.

Table XXI
Mortality Rate at different Ages

Age	Railway Servants	All Members of Friendly Societies
25	.52	.71
30	1.18	.77
35	1.00	.83
40	1.56	1.03
45	1.63	1.21
50	1.74	1.50
60	5.50	2.61

Sickness, Natural Death and Old Age

An indication of the fact that 'liability to sickness among persons employed on railways is very great' was given in 1853 by the Actuary of the National Debt Office. Comparison was first made with two categories for insurance premiums: light labour and heavy labour, as in Tables XXII to XXIV.[1]

Table XXII
Percentage of Sick Members of Friendly Societies.

Age	Light Labour	Heavy Labour	Railway Servants
20	22.83	23.35	31.00
25	20.06	26.22	33.06
30	18.71	25.28	33.93
35	18.59	25.30	34.11
40	19.48	26.43	32.33
45	20.28	27.48	32.10
50	22.65	29.05	30.43
60	27.41	34.87	41.76

Table XXII shows clearly the high liability to sickness of railwaymen. Table XXIII emphasises the same point. Table XXIV might appear to indicate less severity of illness among railwaymen but any

---

1. Report and Tables by Actuary of National Debt Office on Sickness and Mortality among members of Friendly Societies, 1853.

Table XXIII
Average Amount of Sickness per annum to each Society member in days

	Light Labour	Heavy Labour	Railway Servants
20	6.42	7.10	8.00
25	5.97	7.34	8.63
30	5.98	7.57	9.93
35	6.13	7.92	8.89
40	7.16	9.10	10.91
45	7.94	10.58	12.15
50	10.40	12.48	15.23
60	16.15	21.42	15.45

Table XXIV
Average Amount of Sickness per annum to each member sick in days

20	28.12	25.03	25.00
25	29.75	27.99	26.10
30	31.97	29.93	29.25
35	32.98	31.30	26.06
40	36.73	34.43	33.85
45	39.13	38.49	37.85
50	45.91	42.96	50.06
60	58.92	61.42	37.00

apparent modification of the position revealed by Tables XXII and XXIII is probably explained by the higher proportion in Table XXII. A notable feature in Tables XXII and XXIII is the sharp decline in the amount of sickness of those aged over fifty compared with the other two categories. This may be accounted for by the higher death rate at over fifty years as shown in Table XXV

Table XXV
Mortality Percentage

Age	Light Labour	Heavy Labour	Railway Servants
50	1.59	1.42	1.74
60	2.79	2.43	5.50

Comparison was next made between railway servants and other dangerous occupations which were often excluded from membership of general friendly societies, as in Tables XXVI to XXVIII

Table XXVI
Percentage of sick Members of Friendly Societies

Age	Mariners	Colliers	Miners	Painters	Police	Railway Servants	Average
20	16.89	36.44	23.23	24.82	23.91	31.00	26.05
25	15.61	34.94	20.90	22.72	24.50	33.06	25.29
30	17.96	34.98	28.65	21.49	31.33	33.94	28.66
35	18.86	35.39	32.50	22.40	29.10	34.11	28.72
40	17.89	35.21	28.92	24.98	30.03	32.23	28.21
45	20.51	38.96	37.56	29.54	35.81	32.10	32.41
50	22.27	38.80	36.87	34.20	36.51	30.43	33.18
60	28.00	50.52	58.62	31.63	-	41.76	-

Table XXVII
Average Amount of Sickness per annum to each Society member in days

Age	Mariners	Colliers	Miners	Painters	Police	Railway Servants	Average
20	5.24	8.85	8.22	7.58	7.42	8.00	7.55
25	5.21	8.92	6.43	6.48	5.64	8.63	6.89
30	6.59	9.63	11.00	7.16	8.47	9.93	8.80
35	9.02	10.31	11.68	6.42	8.17	8.89	9.08
40	7.99	11.53	11.97	8.46	9.98	10.91	10.14
45	11.41	14.91	19.46	14.78	19.85	12.51	15.43
50	13.41	21.03	21.04	16.83	27.95	15.23	19.33
60	24.55	26.49	44.40	18.34	-	15.45	-

Table XXVIII
Average Amount of Sickness per annum to each Member Sick in days

Age	Mariners	Colliers	Miners	Painters	Police	Railway Servants	Average
20	31.02	24.30	35.39	30.54	31.05	25.00	29.55
25	33.38	25.55	30.76	28.54	23.03	26.10	27.89
30	36.69	27.52	38.39	33.31	27.03	29.25	32.03
35	47.84	29.12	35.94	28.67	28.09	26.06	32.62
40	44 69	32.74	41.38	33.89	33.23	33.85	36.63
45	55.63	38.26	51.80	50.05	55.42	37.85	48.17
50	60.19	55.49	57.08	49.30	76.57	50.06	58.10
60	87.68	52.44	75.74	58.84	-	37.00	-

Table XXVI shows that up to the age of forty the liability to sickness was greater for railwaymen than the average of all dangerous occupations. Table XXVII emphasises the same point. Table XXVIII shows, as in Table XXIV, less severity of illness among railwaymen than the average, heavily weighted as it is by miners and mariners, but this is again offset by the fact that more of them were sick than in other occupations.

Although the comparison with dangerous occupations does not show as great a contrast as with the categories of heavy and light labour, it does indicate that the railwaymen's liability to sickness was probably above the average of dangerous occupations. The actuary's suggestion was that 'possibly constant exposure to the elements bringing about, particularly in the case of railway servants, that condition known as weatherbeaten, has not little to do with the result'. While according to a medical officer of several companies in 1867 a driver could continue driving for twenty years. 'I know a driver aged 54 years', he wrote, 'who is still a very efficient man. Then generally they save enough to take an inn or buy a small piece of land.'

The foregoing tables must, however, be viewed with caution. They are based on Friendly Society returns which were scarce enough, particularly for the dangerous occupations, to make the results of doubtful value. However some confirmation is given by the experience of the Great Western Railway friendly societies as shown in Table XXIX.

Table XXIX
Sickness of Enginemen on Great Western [1]

Year	Number of Members	Percentage of Members sick during year	Av. Period of absence per sick person days	Av. Period of absence per member days	Percentage of possible working time lost
1869	1168	26	27	8	2.6
1870	1220	30	30	9	2.8
Sickness of Traffic Grades on Great Western [2]					
1867	3117	33	26	8	2.8
1870	4143	30	24	7	2.3

This table gives a complete picture of all enginemen and traffic grades on that line since membership of the societies was compulsory. The average periods of absence for all men are the very minimum

---

1. Great Western Enginemen's & Firemen's Mutual Assurance Sick & Superannuation Society. Annual Reports, 1869, 1870.
2. Great Western Provident Society. Annual Reports, 1867, 1870. Actuary's Report, 1871.

since the calculations for them were made on the assumption that all cases received full sick pay within the regulation period, whereas in fact some would have received half pay beyond that period. The actual average periods of absence were therefore certainly slightly longer. The Provident Society's actuary referred, not unreasonably, to the higher risk of sickness than in 'ordinary employment'. Another, more tentative indication is given by the records of the L. & N.W Friendly Society. The company's subsidy to the Society consisted of two weeks' sick pay at 12s per week to each member before he became eligible for society benefit. On the assumption that all sick persons had two weeks' pay the calculation may be made, given the total amount of sick pay allowed by the company, that 22 per cent of the members were absent sick during the year 1855. The assumption is, however, arbitrary and the percentage of men absent in this case must have been considerably higher.[1] In general the fuller details available from these societies confirm the liability to sickness suggested by the Actuary's Report of 1853.

As regards death from natural causes and the approach of old age, sufficient facts are not available to measure them with an exactness. It may, however, be argued from the liability to sickness that the heavy incidence of the one and the comparatively early approach of the other are beyond doubt.

The conclusion of this chapter is that turnover of labour was high among the traffic grades although much less so among enginemen and permanent way men. In the 1870s the actuary to the National Debt Commissioners stated that of the men in the traffic grades appointed annually on the Great Western about 25 per cent left within one year.[2] There was undoubtedly a large number of young unskilled workers who stayed with a company for only a short time. Turnover was higher among unskilled men than among the more skilled. Leaving the railway companies was more voluntary than compulsory and to that extent arose from a desire for betterment. Conversely a large proportion of the entrants were animated by the same desire. There was also a high rate of wastage from occupational risk.

What was the relation of wastage to labour as a factor of production, or to the efficiency and usefulness of labour? At first sight it might seem that the high rate of wastage must have been detrimental to efficiency. Probably it had some such effect. There are references to difficulty in obtaining a satisfactory type of individual

---

1 London & North Western Railway Friendly Society. Annual Report, 1855.

2. Great Western Railway Provident Society. Report of Actuary to the National Debt Commissioners, 1877.

as station master or clerk; promotion even was effected on rare occasions in order to retain men. On the other hand not only did the companies never have any difficulty in obtaining an ample supply of labour as a whole, but the amount of training required to qualify a man for a higher grade was not great. Signalmen, switchmen and guards were put through a course of instruction before appointment but the period of training did not exceed two to four weeks. [1] Organised arrangements for such training were on quite a small scale. The total economic effect of wastage was therefore probably not great. Its social effect on the lives of the men was considerable. The causes of wastage dealt with here are closely linked with the questions of advancement and security and these are dealt with in chapters 8 and 9.

---

1. Report of S. C. on Accidents on Railways, 1857; evidence of H.P. Bruyers. Report of S.C. on Railways, 1870; evidence of J. Grierson. London & North Western Railway Staff Regulations, 1874

Chapter 4

MOBILITY AND RATIONALISATION OF LABOUR

These two subjects are linked together in this chapter because of their inter-relationship and their common relationship to the effective use of labour by the companies. Any attempts at rationalisation, in the sense of eliminating waste in labour, could not be carried through without mobility of labour. The efficient use of labour required that it should be mobile.

Internal Mobility

It was clearly an essential and customary feature of railway labour that it should be moved about from station to station. Such movement was frequently necessary for promotion. Conversely, it arose from discipline: removal was sometimes an alternative to dismissal, and it was often necessitated by a reduction in grade. This aspect has already been discussed in chapter 2, but the following questions arise. What was the degree of mobility of different grades? How frequently did a man expect to have to move and how far? How far was a change in place of work and removal of home a normal part of a railwayman's life or how far was it exceptional? Was there, as a result, a lack of permanence in relationships between workmates and can it be said that this affected the existence of associations among them and thus the relationship between companies and their servants? There is some factual basis for answers to the first three questions; any answer to the last must be largely speculative.

The first and most obvious kind of mobility was that occasioned by the building of extensions and new lines. In the 1840s, more particularly, experienced men of all grades were continually being transferred to newly opened extensions. In 1840 and 1841 on the Great Western clerks, porters and guards were removed to new stations; in 1845 porters on the Sheffield & Manchester and many traffic grades on the L.B. & S.C. went to new lines; in 1849 station masters and clerks on the Great Northern and station masters, clerks and porters on the L. & S.W. were removed for the same reasons. Many of these removals were over a distance considerable enough to necessitate removal of a man's home. This process must have continued, at a somewhat slower rate, during the fifties and sixties. But the amalgamations of those decades widened the field of movement within any given railway system.

In the ordinary course of operation, apart from the effects of railway extension, station masters and clerks were probably the most mobile. Out of eighty-eight removals of these grades on the L.B. & S.C. between 1839 and 1861 more than half the men had moved two or three times before with an average interval of nine years between each move. Mention of individual removals, or of groups of individuals, in the directors' minutes was very frequent during the 1840s. A single minute of 1841 refers to the removal of six clerks.

This movement continued throughout the next two decades at an increasing rate. Removals of clerks for promotion alone numbered twenty-five in one year on the Manchester, Sheffield & Lincolnshire in 1868/9. In 1862 on the L. & S.W. station masters and clerks were being moved at the rate of seventy per annum, or one in five of those employed; more than half of them over long distances involving a change of home. Over the period 1865 - 1869 station masters on the L.B. & S.C. were moved at the rate of eleven per annum, or about one in every ten employed; clerks were moved at the rate of one hundred and thirty per annum or about one in every five employed. The conclusion is that the average station master or clerk could certainly expect to move his place of work and his home several times during his working life.

The mobility of other traffic grades was probably somewhat less on the average. Evidence of it is less plentiful, but it is clear that it was quite a common practice for foremen, guards, signalmen, switchmen, shunters, policemen and porters to be moved from place to

TABLE XXX

**Removals of Traffic Grades,
London, Brighton & South Coast
1858–60**

Year	Number of Removals	Removals as percentage of number employed %
1858	143	12
1859	178	11
1860	145	12
Average	155	11.7

place. An illustration of this in practice on the L.B. & S.C. in 1858-1860 is given by the above Table XXX. The figures are based on the movements of all traffic grades. They show that one in every nine men in each year might expect to be moved. For instance, Roger Langdon, the Great Western station master who acquired fame as an amateur astronomer, started as a porter at Bristol in 1850 and moved four times in Devon before settling at Silverton in 1867.

The degree of mobility on the same railway for the following decade can be shown for each grade separately, as in the following table. It shows a notable increase in mobility since the fifties. On the average of the grades shown, in each year one man in every six might expect to be moved. For some grades, the more skilled ones, the expectation was much higher.

TABLE XXXI

Mobility of Traffic Grades, London, Brighton & South Coast 1865-1869

Grade	Number Moved per annum Average of 1865-1869	Number Moved as percentage of number Employed %
Station Master	11	10
Clerk	130	21
Inspector	3	11
Foreman	2	6
Tkt. Collr.	13	20
Guard	29	14
Signalman	41	14
Switchman	5	23
Shunter	11	16
Head Porter	8	12
Porter	103	16
Policeman	2	6
Gatekeeper	10	14
Watchman	4	15
Lampman	.5	5
Carriage Cleaner	1	3
Messenger	8	11
Carman	2	2
Truck Horse Driver	1	3
Vanguard	3	3
Total	387.5	16

As to the question whether removal, involved a complete change of relationships at work and at home, it is possible only to estimate what proportion of removals were 'long distance'. For clerks and guards it is possible to divide removals into long and short distance; of the clerks about 30 per cent were long distance, and of the guards about 50 per cent. Many of the removals of signalmen, however, were of only a very short distance from signal box to box. Probably about half of the total were long distance removals. As regard locomotive and permanent way men, there is little evidence available. It may be inferred from this that the movement of these men was small since if it had been a matter of any importance, as in the case of the traffic grades, policy and practice would no doubt have been recorded in a like manner by the management. The enginemen worked from depots, fewer in number and larger than stations, at which there was normally an adequate supply of new drivers coming forward from the ranks of firemen and cleaners. Moreover, they had recognised arrangements for sleeping away from home, under which they were paid lodging allowances. Thus there was less organisational necessity for mobility in the sense of removal. Their operational mobility, arising from the nature of their work, meant a widening of relationships. As for the permanent way men, in the main there is little reason to suppose that they did not live and die on the same length of railway.

It is thus clear that internal mobility was an increasingly prominent feature among the traffic grades, but was least noticeable among enginemen and permanent way men. Station masters and clerks might expect to move both work and home several times. The general traffic grades might also expect to move their place of work at least two or three times, and this was more common for the skilled men than the unskilled. Probably about half these occasions meant a complete uprooting and removal of home as well. This factor was likely to produce an impermanence of relationships at work, which in turn may have had a discouraging effect on the formation of associations in the form of trade unions or friendly societies.

Such mobility was, on the other hand, essential to the efficient use of labour and it may be assumed that it was developed as far as was necessary for that purpose. There is no evidence of resistance to it, not that it was likely in so far as promotion was the reward. The only obstacle appears to have been housing accommodation, particularly at less populous places where the supply had continually to be increased.

Rationalisation

An analysis of railway statistics gives some general indications of changes in the utilisation of labour. The figures are given in appendix

1 to this chapter. The trends for the period 1847 to 1873 may be summarised as follows. The number of servants per mile of railway increased by 17 per cent. The amount of paid up capital per servant employed fell by 39 per cent. The gross investment (expenditure by the companies on plant, buildings etc. plus maintenance and renewal) per servant also fell, by 24 per cent. The revenue received per servant rose by 17 per cent, but between 1850 and 1873 it fell by 5 per cent. The number of passengers conveyed per servant rose 53 per cent and the tons of goods traffic per servant (between 1856 and 1873) also rose by about 11 per cent. If the profits of all British railways are divided by the number of employees in the United Kingdom the result is £96 per head for the year 1873. This figure is about double the average wage of railwaymen at that time. This might suggest a satisfactory state of affairs for the companies but the fall between 1850 and 1873 of the most significant ratio, the revenue per servant, indicates a far from successful or profitable use of labour.

In general, the necessity of maintaining services irrespective of the volume of traffic made it difficult for the companies to regulate the labour force economically. This subject is also discussed in chapter 9. Attempts were, however, made by the companies from time to time both to reduce the labour force according to fluctuations in traffic and revenue, and to rationalise labour so as to obtain greater productivity. These economy campaigns, usually arising from some financial stringency, were conducted sporadically throughout the period. Some examples follow.

In the 1840s, on the Newcastle & Carlisle approximately 6 per cent of the establishment was marked down to be dispensed with, the men being mostly porters and labourers. On the London & Brighton, 'reductions in the Force' (arising probably from a too liberal staffing on the opening to Brighton a year before) resulted in sixty-two men being dismissed in six months out of a total of about three or four hundred. Of these twenty-five were porters and twenty-five were policemen who may have become redundant with the completion of construction. The years 1848 and 1849 were remarkable for 'economical enquiries' resulting in not only reductions in labour but also in wages. The L. & N.W. ordered that all men whose services could be dispensed with should be discharged without waiting for the directors' sanction. The L. & S.W. reported that policemen had been dispensed with and their duties spread over to porters. A Great Western special committee appointed to enquire into a decrease in receipts (ascribed by it to the prevalence of cholera) reported that a considerable reduction in the number employed had been effected. Its decisions, which effected a saving of £1,010 per annum related mostly to policemen and porters. On the Manchester, Sheffield & Lincolnshire a similar reduction saved £894 per annum and another on the Eastern Counties, £960 per annum.

In the 1850s a semi-permanent Conference on Working Expenses on the Manchester, Sheffield & Lincolnshire attempted to reduce labour but was able to effect discharges of only about 3 to 4 per cent of the traffic grades.

In 1863 the Great Western had an enquiry into working expenses at ninety-seven stations in Middlesex, Berkshire, Buckinghamshire, Wiltshire, Warwickshire and Dorset. The proposed savings for all these stations was only £1,478 per annum out of a wages bill of £29,167 per annum, or approximately 5 per cent. The saving actually effected was probably less. But little of this was to come from dismissals, only eight porters and police could actually be dispensed with. Most of the saving was to be from the employment of juveniles instead of adults and from reductions in the grading of posts.

Another economy drive on the Great Western in 1868 - 1870 showed a saving of as much as £14,475 in two and a half years, effected by staff alterations among porters and clerks, but this was more than offset by promotions costing £18,407 in the same period. There may have been some reductions in labour but any saving was cancelled by increased expenditure. This particular campaign arose from the situation on that line in 1865 when an increase in labour costs at the rate of £50,000 per annum began to cause alarm. But in any case the tendency throughout was for the labour force and costs to advance rapidly and, in general, the attempts at reduction of labour seem to have been no more than ineffective rearguard actions against that advance.

Another possibility of rationalisation lay in the introduction of juvenile labour. In 1863, for instance, the Great Western approved the employment of boys as porters and clerks in order to reduce costs. The wages of boy porters were 6s to 10s per week and those of boy clerks, £20 to £55 per annum Over a limited area twenty-one boy porters were to replace men and two boy clerks to replace junior clerks. At Paddington 'stout youths' were to replace an unspecified number of porters and boys were gradually to replace junior clerks. By 1878 the salary of these boys had fallen to between £15 and £50 per annum. Earlier on in the fifties on the Manchester, Sheffield & Lincolnshire porters and clerks had been replaced by boys at wages varying between 8s and 12s per week. The employment of boys was by no means a new thing since on some railways, at least as far as clerks were concerned, boys were a recognised class from the beginning. But the proportion they bore to adults seems to have increased. The proportion of lad clerks in the Great Western traffic department had risen by 1870 to more than 50 per cent of the adult clerks and station masters, a high proportion which seems to represent a considerable increase. By contrast, the proportion of lad porters to adults was much lower, at about 12 per cent.

The practice of apprenticing boys as clerks for a term of years was another method of modifying labour costs. It appeared in the 1840s on some lines, and in 1854 it was introduced on the Manchester, Sheffield & Lincolnshire because of 'the difficulty of obtaining an adequate staff at reasonable salaries'. These apprentices were to be 'respectable youths of not less than sixteen years of age and of adequate education' and subsequently considerable numbers of them (forty-seven in twelve months) are recorded as receiving increments according to the terms of apprenticeship. Their salary was on a par with that of boy or lad clerks elsewhere. In return for being bound apprentice they had security and the opportunity of promotion to clerk. When apprenticeship was discontinued (on the L. & S.W.) weekly paid clerks who were subject to dismissal at one week's notice, were substituted for apprentices. On the other hand apprentices may well have displaced clerks, although there is little evidence of it. An inefficient clerk could be reduced to the status of apprentice. In any case this group lost significance in the 1860s, the practice of binding ceased and the term apprentice, though widely used in the 1870s, became synonymous with junior or assistant clerk.

Neither rationalisation nor a policy of relating labour to revenue seem to have been carried on consistently or continually. There were particular campaigns but with little permanent effect. Economy was more easily secured by resistance to claims for reduction of hours and for increased wages. A general incentive policy, covering all grades hardly existed except as noted in chapter 2. The chief concerns were punctuality and reliability which were secured by the discipline system There were some incentive schemes aimed at substituting the spirit of private enterprise for the stationary routine of a Government office but they were limited to officers and senior staff, as shown in chapter 6

Appendix I

Labour in relation to mileage, capital, investment, revenue and traffic conveyed.

The first rush of recruitment was followed by economy measures in the late forties. An increasing intensity of traffic is indicated in the sixties and the beginning of a reduction in hours of, for instance, signalmen and enginemen, may have been felt.

TABLE XXXII

Year	Servants per mile of railway in U.K.
1847	15
1850	10
1855	12
1860	12
1873	17
1884	20

TABLE XXXIII

Year	Paid Up Capital per Servant in U.K.
	£
1847	3,535
1850	4,006
1855	3,038
1860	2,732
1873	2,143
1884	2,179

(figures from Statistical Abstracts for U.K., 1847 - 1884)

TABLE XXXIV

Year	Gross Investment per servant in U.K.
	£
1847	2,416
1850	2,791
1855	2,200
1860	2,088
1873	1,825

(figures for gross investment from A. G. Kenwood, 'Railway Investment in Britain, 1825 - 1875' in *Economica*, Vol.XXXII, 1965)

The trend in Tables XXXIII and XXXIV is the increasing importance of labour in relation to capital. The railways became less capital intensive.

TABLE XXXV

Year	Revenue per Servant £
1847	180
1850	220
1855	220
1860	217
1873	210
1884	192

From 1850 there was an increase in the staffing without a corresponding increase in revenue and, in that sense, an increasingly unsuccessful and unprofitable use of labour

TABLE XXXVI

Year	Passengers conveyed per servant
1847	1,088
1850	1,215
1855	1,211
1860	1,283
1873	1,660
1884	1,890

TABLE XXXVII

Year	Tons of Goods Traffic per Servant
Y. E. 30. 6. 56.	627
1860	705
1873	696
1884	705

Tables XXXVI and XXXVII may indicate an opposite trend of some increase in the amount of work done per servant. But although it is clearly suggested in term of passengers it is not so in terms of goods traffic which provided the bulk of the revenue. The 1856 figure is probably too low since it refers only to general merchandise and minerals and not to livestock.

Chapter 5

INDUSTRIAL RELATIONS

The relations between labour and the companies in this period have a considerable bearing on both the standard of living and the effectiveness of the labour force. Peaceful relations would not necessarily mean contentment with material welfare; there were too many other factors involved - a discipline strictly imposed, disunity among the men, fear of insecurity, the pressure of labour supply. Nevertheless, they would be some indication of it. They would not, by themselves, demonstrate that the intangible side of the standard of living was acceptable - freedom, independence, self respect; but they would suggest some satisfaction with it. Such relations would, however, imply that operation of the railways was comparatively untroubled in so far as disruption by labour disputes was absent, and that it was not affected by undue acerbity between labour and capital.

The best available measure of relations is a record of disputes. The frequency and character of disputes depended on, amongst other things, the ways in which the companies' labour policies and the conditions of work secured the loyalty of their servants. These in turn had considerable influence on the success or failure of labour to establish its own organisations. These latter also serve as a pointer to the standard of living. The subject will therefore be discussed under the following headings: disputes between labour and companies; labour control by the companies; and labour organisations.

The term disputes is used in the widest sense of any disagreements between the two sides, in the form of strikes or in the petitions and memorials which remained at the negotiating level. The germ of all later disputes was present on the Stockton & Darlington in 1832 when the enginemen came to an understanding among themselves that they would run only one trip per day.

The record of strikes is a brief one. The following is a list, complete as far as can be ascertained.

STRIKES ON RAILWAYS: 1830-70

Year	Grade	Period	Proportion of Grade on Strike	Railway
1836	Enginemen	Few days	Most	Liverpool & Manchester

INDUSTRIAL RELATIONS

Year	Grade	Period	Proportion of Grade on strike	Railway
1845	Porters	Few days	Local	L. & S.W.
1848	Enginemen	Two weeks	Most in one division	L. & N.W.
1849	Goods Guards and porters	Two weeks	Most	Midland
1850	Enginemen	Few Weeks	Most	Eastern Counties
1853	Porters	Few Days	Local	E. Lancs., L. & Y., L. & N.W.
1854	Enginemen	Few Days	Few	L. & N.W.
1854	Porters and pointsmen	Few Days	Local	Midland
1866	Porters	Few Days	Few	Great Eastern
1867	Enginemen	Two weeks	Most	North Eastern
1867	Enginemen	Two Days	Most	L.B. & S.C.

There were only eleven strikes in a period of forty years. None of them lasted long, and most were very short. Although the list may well not be complete, it is unlikely that a complete search of every minute book would reveal a much longer one. The L.B. & S.C. directors could in 1867 justifiably refer, hopefully, to a past of twenty years' good relations. This was the experience common to most companies.

The list falls into two groups, the periods 1845-50 and 1866-67 with little between. These correspond with two waves of general labour agitation. They were also times of financial difficulty for the railways. In the aftermath of the railway mania the companies set about effecting economies. On the London & North Western, the dividend on ordinary shares was reduced from 9 per cent in 1847 to 7 per cent in 1848 and accordingly economies took the form of a reduction in the wages of the artisans in the locomotive, carriage and wagon shops and a new scheme of classification and wages of engine drivers and firemen. Under the latter it would take a driver twenty-five to thirty years to rise from 5s 6d to 8s a day, whereas previously he could do it in eight and a half years. In July 1848 nearly all the enginemen in the company's southern division struck and after a fortnight scored a victory. On the Midland the porters' wages had already been reduced by 1s in 1848 when the company announced another reduction in the following year. The porters at Leeds, Derby and Gloucester, Nottingham and other places came out on strike rather than accept 16s a week. They were joined by the guards whose wages were also to be cut, from 19s to 17s. The guards won, being not easy to replace, but the porters lost and had to go back at 16s because their jobs were being filled 'with cheap redundant agricultural labour'. The enginemen were again the target in 1850 in the Eastern Counties. The economy measures were linked with stricter discipline, both imposed by an unpopular superintendent.

Unreasonably heavy fines for minor damage to rolling stock provoked the men to strike for the removal of the superintendent. But they were replaced.

The second group of disputes in 1866/7 was also presaged by financial stringency and reductions in railway dividends. The bank rate was raised to 10 per cent in May 1866 and shareholders began to demand economies. On two lines this led to strikes in 1867. The L.B. & S.C. rejected the enginemen's demand for a ten hour day. Four hundred struck for three days and scored a partial victory; no guarantee of a ten hour day but a promise of better procedures for promotion. In the same year on the North Eastern Railway almost identical situations led to a longer and bitter strike of enginemen. But this time the men were completely defeated because the company was able to fill their places with men from other lines. These two companies had special financial problems. Five other large companies whose position was not so acute gave way to the demand for the ten hour day and payment of overtime, rather than face the losses feared from strike action. All the strikes except one were about wages. Seven strikes were for increased wages; two were against reductions in wages (in 1848 and 1849). Two of the former were also for reduced hours (in 1867). The exception, in 1850, was against disciplinary fines.

Most of the strikes were defeated. The exceptions were four: in 1848 the enginemen secured an 'understanding' that a new classification involving a reduction of wages would not take place; in 1848 guards were able to retain their existing wages; in 1853 the porters at Liverpool gained an increase in wages; in 1854 porters and pointsmen successfully resisted payment once a fortnight instead of once a week; and in 1867 the L.B. & S.C. enginemen obtained a partial victory, which was a compromise in the form of a right of appeal for promotion. Defeat was due to strong counter-measures by the companies. In 1836 it was possible to send the ringleaders to the treadmill. Later it was always possible to obtain outside labour or from other companies, as in 1850, or non-union labour, as in 1867 on the North Eastern.

The relative infrequency of strikes is attributable to too many causes - such as geographical and grade divisions, mobility, the enjoyment of security of employment - for it to be taken as any conclusive indication of contentment with the standard of living. On the other hand, a very great amount of discontent might have overcome the obstacles to labour organisation. The results of the strikes clearly did not materially affect working conditions.

From the aspect of labour efficiency, it is clear that both direct financial loss suffered by the companies and the indirect delayed loss arising from friction in labour relations were at a minimum. It is true that in some of the strikes the great majority of the grade concerned did leave work, but in almost all cases the strike was confined to one grade, and it was thus possible to continue operation with far less interruption than if it had affected several. Replacements were far easier to effect when guards could ride on the footplate to pilot strike-breaking engine drivers. Such replacements were not difficult even with engine drivers, less so with other grades. In the biggest strike, on the North Eastern in 1867, out of 1080 men who handed in their notice, only 174 were reinstated, according to the company. Replacements came from men on the same line, from other lines, from men discharged for disciplinary reasons, and from workshop artisans.

The strikes revealed most clearly the stresses in labour-capital relations, but in the background was a greater number of peaceful disputes, in the form of petitions and memorials. The right to petition the directors, acknowledged throughout the period by the companies, was established early on. Eight labourers employed by the Stockton & Darlington at the coal staithes at Middlesborough in 1838 petitioned against being fined 2s for taking half a day off to go to Stockton races, and took advantage of the opportunity to ask at the same time for their wages of 21s a week to be increased by 3s a week. The result is not known but in the same year the 'waymen', i.e. platelayers and lengthmen of the permanent way were successful. The committee considered their petition and resolved: 'the waymen of the 1st Division of the line, 43 in number, having applied for an advance in wages from 2s 9d to 3s per day, the Engineer is authorised to allow the same to such men as he may consider deserving'. In fact the wages of seventeen men were increased to 3s a day and of the remainder to 2s 10d a day.

The following list of petitions, though not complete, is representative. It is longer than for strikes, but not long in relation to forty years' operation. There are again the distinct groups of petitions in the late forties and late sixties, clustered round the strikes of those periods. But there is also rather more spread over the years than for the strikes. Again, most of the petitions were rejected. Of those that were accepted, the reasons for acceptance in most cases are fairly clear. Thus the protest of the enginemen against reduction of staff in 1849 was successful because all of them threatened to strike. The pointsmen in 1853 were only partly successful in that some classes were raised while others were not. The memorial from the L. & S.W. enginemen in 1854 came from only 'some of the first-class drivers of main line trains', i.e. the aristocrats. That of the L. & N.W. men in the same year was accepted only because it was based on a genuine misunderstanding of policy. The Great Western porters in 1865 were successful because the company thought that a strike was imminent, and in any case a similar increase in wages had been given by other companies. The porters of

1866 were successful only on condition that clothing was not supplied, and the gatemen only on condition that they did not occupy company's houses. The successes of 1867 were due to the threat of strike action and the unwillingness of most companies to pay the price of conflict. In that year the combination of men from a number of companies, unique in this period, was a portent of things to come.

RAILWAYMEN'S PETITIONS AND MEMORIALS, 1830-1870

Year	Grade	Proportion Represented
1838	Waymen	Most
1838	Labourers	Few
1838	Police	Most
1845	Porters	Local
1845	Enginemen	Most
1845	Guards	Very few
1846	Guards	Very few
1848	Enginemen	Most
1849	Enginemen	Most
1849	Guards	Most
1849	Enginemen	Local
1850	Guards	Local
1850	Porters	Local
1851	Enginemen	Local
1853	Pointsmen	Local
1853	All	Local
1854	Enginemen	Most
1854	Enginemen	Very few
1854	Enginemen	Most
1857	Enginemen	?
1858	Labourers	Local
1865	Porters and Carmen (2)	Local
1865	Labourers	Local
1865	Carriage Cleaners	Local
1866	Signalmen	Partial
1866	Signalmen (3)	Local
1866	Shunters	Partial
1866	Porters (3)	Local
1866	Gatemen	Local
1866	Clerks	Local
1866	Enginemen	Partial
1867	Enginemen	Most
1867	Enginemen	Most

Claim	Result	Railway
Wages	Accepted	S. & D.
Wages	Not known	S. & D.
Wages	Rejected	London & Greenwich
Hours & Overtime	Rejected	L. & S.W.
Wages	Partly accepted	Midland
Wages	Deferred	London & Birmingham
Wages	Deferred	L. & N.W.
Overtime	Rejected	M.S. & L.
Redundancy	Accepted under strike threat	Midland
Wages	Rejected	L. & S.W.
Hours & Wages	Rejected	L. & N.W.
Wages	Rejected	S.E.
Wages	Rejected	Midland
Not known	Not known	L. & N.W.
Wages	Partly accepted	L. & N.W.
Wages	Rejected	L.B. & S.C.
Hours	Rejected	Midland
Wages	Accepted	L. & S.W.
Contract	Accepted	L. & N.W.
Overtime	Rejected	Midland
Wages	Rejected	G.N.
Wages	One accepted under strike threat	G.W.
Wages	Rejected	G.W.
Wages	Rejected	G.W.
Hours & Wages	Rejected	L.B. & S.C.
Wages	Rejected	G.W.
Wages	Rejected	G.W.
Wages	One partly accepted	G.W.
Wages	Partly accepted	G.W.
Passes	Rejected	G.W.
Wages	Rejected	L. & S.W.
Wages & Hours	Partly accepted under strike threat	Midl., G.W., L. & N.W.
Hours & Wages	Rejected	N.E.

The significance of these petitions is further reduced by the fact that they were always limited to one grade (with one unimportant exception) and were frequently limited to one district or locality. Over a half were local in origin, and in some of these the locality was very small. It was not until after 1870, when a permanent trade union had appeared, that a memorial signed by all grades was presented.

In view of the comparative unimportance of disputes it is not surprising to find that there was nothing of the conciliation machinery associated with the names of Mundella and Sir R. Kettle in the 1860s. In any case, not only the organisational immaturity of labour but also the military character of the discipline would have been against it. Many years later, in 1892, the opinion of the general manager of the L. & N.W. in regard to the trade unions was: 'You might as well have a Trade Union or an amalgamated society in the army, where discipline has to be kept at a very high standard, as have it on the railways'. [1] Deputations of men were admitted from about 1850, but there is no suggestion of any diminution in the full sovereignty of directors until 1867, when the L.B. & S.C. Board expressed its willingness to submit any question in dispute for settlement by the Board of Trade. But this was the exception proving the rule.

There was, however, one modifying influence by the state, if a slight one, and that was from the Railway Department of the Board of Trade. That department was established in 1840 as a result of the Railway Act of that year. Because of its responsibility for safety on the railways and its function of enquiring into accidents the department became interested in labour matters and from time to time it was drawn into controversy between companies and employees. In January 1843 the department enquired into a fatal accident at Barnsley on the North Midland, following which the driver was convicted of manslaughter. The previous year an economy drive led by George Hudson, 'the railway king', had included the dismissal of some footplatemen. Men who refused to work a thirteen day fortnight with a compulsory daily run of 146 miles from Derby to Leeds and back were dismissed and their places were filled. But the company soon had to discharge most of the new men, in the words of the inspector general of the railway department, 'after a few days trial, on account of incompetence or misconduct, after having in several cases occasioned accidents. So far from having produced unexceptionable characters, at least six of the new men were discharged servants from other companies.' The driver at the Barnsley accident had been dismissed by both the London & South

---

1. Report of S.C. on Railway Servants (Hours of Labour), 1892, quoted in G.D.H. Cole and R. Page Arnot, *Trade Unionism on the Railways*, p.16

Western and the Great Western. The department then wrote to the company pointing out 'the inexpediency of sudden and sweeping reductions affecting the class of servants upon whose skill and good conduct the safety of the Passengers depends', that the directors' action had already compromised the safety of the public and that the new working conditions were 'too harassing for the men'. In reply the directors undertook to give what they called 'additional intervals for rest to the enginemen driving passenger trains'. Five years later the London & North Western enginemen on strike wrote to the Commissioners of Railways, the successors to the department and the railway board at the Board of Trade, stating that 'the public safety is endangered by the present state of things'. The Commissioners, suspecting that the strike was a factor in at least one accident, asked the company for information and were told that the company had taken proper measures to ensure safety and that it would keep them informed about the development of the strike.

The effect of hours of work on public safety was raised again in 1861 when a deputation of engine drivers visited the President of the Board of Trade to ask for a limit on their working day, but there was apparently no sequel. It was in the same year that the enquiry into the appalling accident in Clayton Tunnel on the L.B. & S.C. revealed that the signalmen who were involved worked a 24 hour day when they were on Sunday duty. Throughout the following decades inspectors of the railway department enquiring into accidents drew attention to excessive hours of work. All this did not amount to much at the time. It did however set precedents of intervention for the first steps towards state control of conditions of work and of industrial relations at the turn of the century.

Taking the period as a whole the disputes had little bearing on the relations between men and companies or the effectiveness of the labour force. There was no real interference with railway operation or efficiency, nor does there seem to have been any considerable degree of bitterness or hostility, with all the economic friction accompanying it. The number and nature of the disputes were, considered in isolation, some indication of either an absence of acute discontent with the standard of living, or of unsurmountable difficulties in expressing it. Strikes and petitions made little difference to working conditions until the late 1860s, when the enginemen won, inter alia, a ten hour day.

The relative peacefulness of labour relations depended, in part, on the ways in which contentment of labour and loyalty to the companies were secured. In the widest sense the important factor was those conditions of employment which either were favourable and which made railway employment preferable to others, or were deterrent to disloyalty. Of these there were, on the one hand, the security of employment, and on the other, the discipline system These subjects are discussed in other chapters. In some instances such conditions of employment were also a conscious method of labour control, as with the companies' friendly societies which are discussed in chapter 9. The promotion of porters to guards and policemen was 'one of the reasons why the South Western goes on so happily and so well with its servants'.[1] In this chapter the narrower sense of labour control is used, a definite policy having the purpose of encouraging loyalty or of defeating disloyalty. It may be divided into positive and negative aspects. Of the positive the most important were education and religion; of the negative the most important were the principle of 'divide and rule', combination among the companies, and intimidation.

Concern on the part of the companies with the education of servants and their children began early, in the thirties, when a decision was taken to establish a school at Wolverton. The following circular of 1847 shows a mixture of motives: the desire to obtain reliable labour as well as the realisation that 'property has its duties as well as its advantages'.[2]

LONDON & NORTH WESTERN RAILWAY
EDUCATION

To the Persons employed by the Company

General Order

To be Read by the Station Master to the Men and a copy to be given to each Married Person employed.

The Directors have encouraged the establishment of schools and are inquiring into the State of Education on all their lines. The Directors have relied on the co-operation of their Servants and they believe that the majority have made proper use of the opportunities provided. But in many cases where schools exist the education of children is much neglected.

When education can be had for a few pence per week there is no excuse for neglect. The Directors consider the proper education of young persons a matter of such vital importance that they cannot but look with distrust at the man whose negligence condemns a child to ignorance. They regard the performance of this duty as an additional proof of his trustworthiness and good character.

The Directors hope for special attention to the extension and

---

1. Report of S.C. on Accidents on Railways. Evidence of Hon. R. Dutton. P.P., 1857-8, Vol. IV.
2. London & North Western Railway. Circular 24 June 1847; report of half-yearly meeting, 12 Feb. 1847.

improvement of education among their servants; they trust that the L. & N.W.R. will be distinguished by the intelligence and morality of those engaged on it and be a pattern for other great establishments.

Educational policy was carried out in two ways: by the establishment of companies' schools, and by making donations or subscriptions to other schools attended by "companies' children". The following list of companies' schools is complete, as far as can be found, for the companies shown. Most of them were at the railway towns and were intended primarily for the benefit of enginemen and artisans. In fact there were only two, those at Euston and Camden which existed mainly for the traffic grades and enginemen.

Railway Companies' Schools

Place	Date of Establishment	Company
Wolverton	1840	L. & N.W. (L. & B.)
Crewe	1843	L. & N.W. (G.J.)
Swindon	1844	G.W.
Ashford	1848	S.E.
Woodhead	1848	M.S. & L.
Stratford	1850	E.C.
Euston	1852	L. & N.W.
Longsight	1855	L. & N.W.
Gorton	1855	M.S. & L.
Earlestown	1856	L. & N.W.
Camden	1857	L. & N.W.
Doncaster	1858	G.N.
Stantonbury	1859	L. & N.W.

The policy was not without opposition from short-sighted shareholders. One critic of an expenditure of £2,000 per annum on the L. & N.W. considered that half a dozen schoolmasters at £100 per annum was all that was necessary. [1] But on the whole it was well supported by shareholders' contributions. In fact the schools were partly financed from the companies' Sunday travelling funds. These funds were formed from a proportion of the revenue from Sunday trains, in response to the moral objections on the part of some directors and shareholders to Sunday travel. (In 1840 three directors of the

---

1. London & North Western. Report of half yearly meeting, 23 Aug. 1861.

Lancashire & Yorkshire resigned because of a decision to allow Sunday travel). The Sunday Travel Fund of the L. & N.W. amounted to £1,500 in 1850. The schools were not, of course, free. At the beginning it was laid down that education 'was not to be gratuitous, a kind of charity, but a reasonable charge was to be made', a charge which came out at about fourpence per week. At the school in Swindon, which was composed of houses built by the company, the fees in 1859 were fourpence a week for juveniles and twopence a week for infants. Later they were raised to sixpence, fivepence, or fourpence for boys and fivepence or fourpence for girls, according to their class in school, and threepence for infants. There were reductions for families; if more than four in one family were at school together the fifth and younger children were admitted free. Sometimes the fees were fixed in relation to the parents' wages. At Crewe the National schools provided by the Grand Junction Railway had an income from fees of £150 in 1848 when there were about three hundred children in attendance. Some schools, such as that at Euston, became nearly self-supporting.

The second part of the educational policy, financial support of other schools, depended on the number of 'companies' children' who attended them. The L. & N.W. assisted twenty to thirty schools, both Church of England and nonconformist, with sums usually in the region of £10 per annum, at one time or another over a period of twenty years. There were also subscriptions to the British and Foreign Schools Society. The cost of all this to the companies was not great. On the L. & N.W. the average charge per annum for companies' schools between 1848 and 1867 was £1,200; subscriptions to other schools came to about £200 per annum.

The policy on religion - that is, the provision of facilities for worship and the encouragement of it - cannot properly be separated from the educational policy. There was little distinction between spiritual instruction and education. At Swindon an attempt by the vicar of St. Mark's, the railway church, to make attendance at his services compulsory for the children attending the company's school caused some controversy and he had to be told by the directors that the matter should be left to the parents' discretion. The companies' policy originated during the construction period. Following, and in some cases before, the recommendation on this subject by the 1846 Select Committee on Railway Labourers, many companies spent money in implementing it to some extent. In 1845 the Chester & Holyhead Railway gave £300 to a fund for religious instruction of workmen; in 1846 the Great Western gave £50; in 1847 the Great Northern gave £400 and the South Eastern £200 for the same purpose; by 1849 the North Staffordshire had expended £1,100.

There were three aspects to the companies' policies: direct

SOMERSET & DORSET RAILWAY LOCOMOTIVE NO. 11 (NICKNAMED "BLUEBOTTLE") 1861

LONDON, BRIGHTON & SOUTH COAST RAILWAY PERSONNEL, 1881 (LEFT TO RIGHT: VAN GUARD, CARMAN, HEAD PORTER, GENERAL PORTER, CLOAKROOM PORTER, STATION SUPERINTENDENT'S CLERK)

provision of churches; financial support of other churches and organisations; and encouragement of religious observance among servants. The last was linked, from the companies' side, with the question of Sunday observance, and consequently, from the men's side, with Sunday work. The motives were probably mixed, as with education. A sense of responsibility for religious needs, consonant with the age, particularly in the new railway towns, was accompanied by a realisation of the value of well-behaved servants. The directors were 'like ordinary millowners bound to do for their population that which the millowners did', but they were also urged that 'the scheme deserved to be taken up in a worldly point of view, putting aside all Christian feeling . . . since it was calculated to exalt 'the character of the London and Birmingham'.[1]

Companies' churches were few and situated in the railway towns. There were probably not more than half a dozen, the most notable being at Wolverton, built about 1842; Crewe and Swindon in 1845; Doncaster in about 1858; and Stantonbury about 1860. At Swindon the cost of St. Mark's church of £6,000 was met by a legacy from a railway director and an appeal to the shareholders. The vicar's stipend of £120 was paid by the Great Western up to 1850. At Crewe, following a resolution of the Grand Junction Railway that it was 'the duty of the Company to contribute liberally towards the supply of spiritual instruction and education', Christ Church was financed by a contribution from the shareholders of £1,000 and the balance of £1,300 was made up from some of the directors' fees and the Sunday Travelling Fund. Under the directors' patronage, the church was endowed with £1,000 and a guaranteed stipend of £150. While it was being built a room in the coachmaking workshops was consecrated for divine worship. Nearly twenty-five years later, in 1869 the London & North Western opened a second church at Crewe, St. Paul's, Hightown. Financial assistance towards the building and maintenance of other churches and chapels was somewhat more frequent. Subscriptions were also made to city missions and for the services of scripture readers. The cost of this policy was often borne by the profits from Sunday travel.

The companies' attitude towards religious worship on the part of their servants was not so clear. In the forties they frequently received requests from bodies of clergymen to permit the men to attend church but their statements in favour of Sunday observance may be discounted to some extent. The author of a pamphlet published on behalf of the Early Closing Association in 1856 was moved to write: 'Amongst railway directors we see names of gentlemen who are distinguished for Christian principles and for benevolence. In the establishment of new

---

1. London & Birmingham. Report of Half-Yearly Meeting, 7 August 1840.

lines of railway we have looked to see whether they would try to stop Sunday traffic of passenger trains. But we have been disappointed. We see them making a faint protest against what they call "Sabbath desecration" but their trains run on Sundays'. [1] Certainly no other company expressed its attitude as clearly as the Taff Vale Railway in its rule book dated 1855:

"Rule 26. It is urgently requested that every person ... on Sundays and other Holy Days, when he is not required on duty, will attend a place of worship, as it will be the means of promotion when vacancies arise."

In the forties the clergy had been assured that the directors had arranged for their servants to attend to their religious duties, consistent with service to the public. In 1863 the following circular indicated the company's wish:

London and North Western Railway
Office, Euston Station,
London, 7th July, 1863

Circular

The Directors desire to remind the Officers and Servants of the Company that the arrangements made enable every man in their employ to attend Divine Service at least once on each Sunday, and they invite all the servants of the Company to avail themselves of the privilege.

By 1871, however, on the Midland the official opportunity for church or church going was reduced to every other Sunday, and in fact it is imrpobable that the 1863 statement was true, particularly in the case of station masters and signalmen, unless they were prepared to forgo completely their scanty week-end leisure. The men did not miss the opportunity to make use of the general feeling in favour of Sunday observance and the companies' declared policy when they petitioned for the abolition of Sunday work.

Before passing to the negative aspects of labour control brief reference may be made to a minor element on the positive side. This was the formation and encouragement of railway volunteer corps during the war scare of the early sixties. The existence of only four of these corps has been traced but it is quite probable that there were more. They were the Crewe, and the Swindon Volunteer Rifles, the Great Eastern Essex Rifles and the Montgomeryshire (Railway)

---

1. J. Fitzgerald, 'The duty of procuring for the labouring classes the earlier closing of shops and the Saturday half holiday', 1856.

Rifles. The Crewe Rifles were assisted by the railway company in the sixties with donations amounting to £400 and with accommodation, and the Swindon Rifles were helped in a similar way. For the most part these bodies seem to have been recruited from artisans since the traffic and locomotive men were prevented from joining by their hours of work.

On the negative side of labour control, the principle of 'divide and rule' was particularly evident on the railways because of the number and variety of grades, some of which could, in emergency, perform the work of others. The companies' purpose was to encourage division, not only between servants in different grades and on different railways, but also between militant and pacific in the same grade. They were helped in this by an extreme sectionalism amongst the men. The companies naturally dealt with each grade separately, but the men themselves acted as though each particular grade were independent of the rest. Petitions and memorials came always from a single grade; there is no instance of inter-grade fraternity. When the enginemen of the London & North Western struck in 1848 they made no attempt to get the support of the guards, with the result that the guards were used to pilot the new enginemen who had been appointed to replace the strikers.

'Divide and rule' was a routine method as well as one used with special force during disputes. The practice of using one grade as a check on the other was general. Orders issued in the fifties provided that guards were to report on the irregularities of signalmen; signalmen were to report engine drivers. From the forties onwards there are numerous examples of this in practice. Men of all grades were frequently dismissed or fined through the evidence of other grades. In fact the discipline system would not have been possible otherwise. The method is revealed clearly enough in the following evidence before a Select Committee in 1858: [1]

> 'J. Beattie (Locomotive Superintendent, L. & S.W.R.): Want of vigilance on the part of a man on duty may lead to accidents but other men are watchful and check the other. For instance if a man at a station neglects his signal, the guard and driver watch it and they report the case ... and the guilty parties are punished.
>
> Lord Alfred Paget: In fact there is no love lost between the engine drivers and the signalmen?
>
> J. Beattie: I think it would be a pity that there should be any; it would not be so good.'

---

1. Report of S.C. on Accidents on Railway, 1858. Evidence of J. Beattie. P.P., 1857-8, Vol. XIV.

The effective use of this method in disputes was made possible by this kind of sectionalism. Examples of the use of one grade against another can be seen in the strikes of enginemen on the L. & N.W. in 1848 and on the Eastern Counties in 1850, and in the strike of guards and porters in 1849. In the first of these the guards who piloted the strike breaking drivers were rewarded with a fortnight's additional pay. In the second, upper guards were given three guineas for the same service and under guards and porters £1 15s 0d each. In the third, guards were restored to their original wages since they were more difficult to replace, while porters, easily replaced from the ranks of agriculture labour, had the choice of reduced wages or nothing.

Men from one line were used against those on another. The Eastern Counties engaged drivers from the London & North Western and from the North British to break their enginemen's strike in 1850. During the strike of the North Eastern enginemen in 1867 the directors recruited drivers from the Midland, Great Northern, Lancashire & Yorkshire and London & North Western railways. In that year the London, Brighton & South Coast tried to do the same thing but found that very few could be spared.

Militants were split from pacifists in the same grade by giving gratuities to the men loyal to the companies as in the strikes mentioned, and by bringing from a distance men ignorant of the dispute, as in 1845. In that year the porters at the Nine Elms depot of the London & South Western suffered defeat by similar tactics. Working a sixteen hour day for 18s to 20s a week they petitioned the company for shorter hours or overtime pay. The chief clerk, travelling by special train for the purpose, obtained the signatures of the porters at each station right down the line to Southampton, to a new agreement which accepted the existing rates of pay and conditions.

He then presented it to the Nine Elms men with a demand for their signatures too. Thirty-nine of the London men refused and were dismissed. [1] In the 1867 strike of the L.B. & S.C. enginemen the company issued the following poster: [2]

London Brighton & South Coast Railway
Copy of a
RESOLUTION OF THE BOARD
Of Tuesday, March 26th, 1867.

That, in accordance with the recommendation of Mr.

---

1 *The Times*, 4 Nov. 1845.
2. P. S. Bagwell, *The Railwaymen*, 1963, p.160.

Craven and Mr. Hawkins, the Directors will with great pleasure give a gratuity of TWO GUINEAS to each DRIVER and ONE GUINEA to each FIREMAN who has not deserted his post this day, while so many are endeavouring to force the Directors to comply with demands which they consider unreasonable.

That any such Driver who was previously receiving a lesser sum shall at once be advanced to the first class and receive 7s 6d per day, and each Fireman 4s 6d per day, with the assurance that, come what may, the Directors will employ them at the above rates so long as they perform their duty.

That believing a large majority of those who are still out will (upon reflexion) regret having pushed matters to such an extremity they are willing to receive back into the service any of the old hands who may rejoin it not later than Thursday next. By Order

A. Sarle, Acting Secretary.

The technique of dividing the sheep from the goats may be visualised from the following extract from a verbatim report of proceedings between directors and a deputation of enginemen on the London & North Western in 1854.

"Chairman (of directors' committee): Is there anyone present who has not signed the memorial?
An Engineman: Most of us have signed.
Chairman: Just let those who have not signed separate themselves.
Committee Member: And those who have signed who wish to withdraw their names.
Chairman: Those who have signed go to my right. (The men did so, leaving a considerable number on each side.)"

While the deliberate employment of tactics to split the unity of men may be seen on the London & North Western in 1850. The engine drivers resisted contracts of three months' duration which had been introduced and asked instead for one month's notice on either side. The company presented them with 'the document' which demanded a signature from every man who wished to remain in its service under the existing regulations. When the men went to get their wages at Camden station, some were given fifteen minutes to sign the document, others were given half an hour, and the remainder had two days in which to think it over. [1]

---

1. *The Times*, 23 - 30 December 1850.

The men were divided, but the companies associated together. Combination among the companies arose out of their contiguity. If one railway altered wages it was necessary that it should be in line with others physically connected with it. In the early years, when precedents were rapidly being established and staff establishments were being settled, there was frequent reference between companies on labour policy and agreement was often reached between companies before a decision was taken. This occurred on the London & Greenwich in 1838. In 1842 such action was taken by the Midland Counties on a proposal to reduce enginemen's wages; in 1843 by the Sheffield & Manchester on rewards to enginemen; in 1845 by the London & North Western on a proposed increase in enginemen's and guards' wages These actions did not pass unnoticed; when the enginemen struck in 1848 they complained of combination against them. Three years later Charles Dickens, in the course of investigating railway unrest, referred to 'general talk (with a great deal of truth) of combination of capital against workmen' [1]

By the time of the disputes of the late sixties association between the companies had developed further. Combined action by the enginemen in 1867 was matched by consultation between the North Eastern, London & South Western, Great Western, Great Northern, and London, Brighton & South Coast companies. The value of this was apparent when the Great Northern permitted its firemen to go as drivers to the North Eastern to replace men on strike.

Since, however, labour disputes were comparatively infrequent over the whole period, association between companies was largely ad hoc. The minutes of the Railway Companies' Association (established in 1867 as the United Railway Companies' Committee), have no record of any labour question until 1869. Even when general applications for increased wages were received in 1871, the decision was that no general rule was applicable in view of the differing circumstances, and the companies were left to deal with the applications on their merits.

A certain amount of intimidation was unavoidably present within the discipline system and may be taken as a concomitant of the attitudes taken to discourage disloyalty. It appeared more particularly during disputes and the tentative labour organisations of the late sixties. Men who went on strike were required to express their sorrow and contrition before being taken back. Often they were not taken back. Men who gave notice of withdrawal of labour were told, not only that they would not be re-employed, but that steps would be taken to ensure that they found no employment elsewhere. In 1839 the Grand Junction asked the Stockton & Darlington not to employ

---

1. *Household Words*, 11 Jan. 1851.

enginemen it had dismissed, and promised to reciprocate. In 1850 the Eastern Counties issued a poster containing a black list of ninety drivers and eighty-seven firemen who had struck.

The precise effect of a labour control, such as described here, must be largely speculative, but undoubtedly certain dividends were obtained. The subscriptions to city missions were worthwhile even if they produced only tea parties for porters at which 'addresses of an encouraging nature were delivered'. [1] Benefits of this kind may have moved the directors on one occasion to suspend subscription because the scripture readers had neglected the enginemen's cottages at Camden. The benefit was greatest at the railway towns where the provision was most ample, and it was clearly expressed by the chairman of the London & Birmingham: [2]

> 'We are beginning to find more fully the economical result of the establishment at Wolverton. Attendance at the places of worship and the schools is most satisfactory and numerous. The result is more important than the mere comfort of the Company's servants there. It has a result which not only acts on our profits, but also most materially on the convenience and safety of the public.
>
> 'You will reap the benefit of this, for I am sure that there is not a single person attached to that establishment who would not willingly and gladly come forward and perform extra service, in order to meet occasional emergency.'

Four years later the Wolverton mechanics gave their help to the company during the enginemen's strike.

On the whole, the positive elements in labour control affected only the enginemen, artisans and a few traffic grades, but the negative elements concerned all the men. Both probably helped to form a certain humility, not to say servility, which might not be unexpected amoung those men who stood to gain from tipping by the public, but which was not absent even from the enginemen who, in their petitions, expressed their 'anxiety to do their duty faithfully and harmoniously' and 'their desire to respect their superiors'. What was perhaps the humblest petition of all arose from the very last dispute in this period. Some week after the collapse of the engine men's strike in the north east the following petition was sent to 'The Honourable board of directors of the Stockton & Darlington Section of the North Eastern Railway': [3]

---

1. The Beehive. 20 Dec. 1862.
2. London & Birmingham Reports of half yearly meetings, 10 Feb. 1843, 8 Feb. 1844.
3. P. S. Bagwell, *The Railwaymen*, 1963, p.42.

'We pray you to entertain the humble petition of your humble servants the engine drivers and firemen lately on your section. We have surrendered ourselves to William Bouch, esquire, and are now at his disposal. We had no quarrel with our employers; the course we took was to support the North Eastern men. We were betrayed into a false position and have acknowledged our error already. There were circumstances in the case we were not made acquainted with. We repent of what we have done and promise the act shall never be repeated."To err is human, to forgive is divine". We cast ourselves entirely on thy mercy. Hoping you will manifest towards us a true chivalrous spirit and have compassion on a fallen foe. And in proportion to your magnanimity, benevolence and humanity on the present occasion, will be our devotion, fidelity and obedience in the future. We petition you, gentlemen, to be so kind, so forgiving and condescending as to pay the money standing to our account. You will be aware, gentlemen, that most of the money was earned in the storm and tempest, whilst exposed to the howling wind and pelting snow.

P.S. Some of the families are now on the point of starvation. We hope, gentlemen, you will favour us with the money standing to our account. It is now sixteen weeks since we received any from you. And your humble servants will ever pray, etc.'

An account of labour organisations is soon told since there was no permanent trade union until 1871 when the Amalgamated Society of Railway Servants was established. The lateness of that event may be attributed to the conditions already described.

Each section of the men had a separate struggle. The enginemen were the most forward. They were the most clannish group. Their cohesion was strengthened by the self contained and almost invariable line of promotion from cleaner to fireman to driver. Their strong departmental feeling was expressed at different times in loyalty to a popular superintendent like Daniel Gooch of the Great Western, and in condemnation of an unpopular one such as J. V. Gooch of the Eastern Counties. The first definite mention of a trade union is in 1860 but there are several indications of it earlier. When the London & North Western enginemen struck in 1848 it was apparent that there was some organisation at work. At the strikers' meetings representatives came from at least four other companies. The charge of combination was bandied to and fro. It was denied by the men who, as proof, sent 'the rules of the Clubs' to the companies and to members of Parliament. It was asserted as a 'fundamental truth' by *The Times*, which referred to clubs and unions together and advanced the time honoured argument that the men were driven on by the threats of their leaders.[1] Three years later Charles Dickens alleged that the enginemen allowed others to do their thinking for them, they had 'deputy thinkers', who were not always the best workmen, sometimes not workmen at all, but 'designing persons who have enmeshed workmen in a system of tyranny and oppression'.[2] Again, the fact that in 1854 a company was asked whether the enginemen's solicitor could be present at a meeting suggests that some organisation existed. Although up to this point there is no evidence of a trade union, there was a strong friendly society. This was the Locomotive Steam Enginemen and Firemen's Friendly Society, which was established in 1839, had twenty-five branches by 1851 and at least two thousand members by 1862. It seems likely that it was active as a trade union. Its Camden Town branch met at the same place, the Railway Tavern in Hampstead Road, as the strikers in 1848, and both its Camden Town and Leeds branches had the same rendezvous as the first unions in 1860 and 1861.

An Enginemen's and Firemen's Association existed in 1860. In that year a certain Richard Dinnis applied on its behalf to at least six companies for a ten hour day. This was no doubt the same organisation as the one included in the London Trades Council Directory of 1861; only five branches are mentioned. It seems to have had a short life, perhaps because it was ignored by the companies. Very soon, in 1866, a more substantial successor appeared, the Engine Drivers' and Firemen's United Society with its own periodical, *The Train*. Contemporaries claimed that this union had sixty-four branches, fifteen thousand members, and £1,800 a year income.[3] But this must have been an exaggeration; the total number of enginemen employed in Great Britain was only 19,303 in 1873, and there were only 6221 members in the Locomotive Steam Enginemen and Firemen's Friendly Society in 1870. Whatever its size, the new union launched in 1867 a demand on all the companies for a ten hour day, over-time payment, time and a half for Sunday work and daily maxima of 150 miles' driving for main line drivers and 120 for local train drivers. As we have seen many companies gave way to this demand, at least partly, rather than face strike action. It was this union which successfully conducted the strike of four hundred enginemen on the London, Brighton & South Coast in that year but completely failed to assist or protect its members who struck on the North Eastern. It was probably this failure which brought about the collapse of the

---

1. *The Times*, 4 Aug. 1848 to 23 Aug. 1848.
2. *Household Words*, 11 Jan. 1851.
3. J. M. Ludlow and L. Jones, *Progress of the Working Classes,* 1867, pp. 200-205.

United Society within the new two or three years, in spite of the general success with the ten hour day. The enginemen did not make another move until they joined in the all grades Amalgamated Society of 1871.

Some other grades began to move in the same direction but their organisations were even weaker than those of the enginemen. A Railway Clerks' Association, formed in 1865, seems to have lasted only a few months. Its support was so limited to London that the companies could afford to ignore its demands. The following year some of the traffic grades came together in the Railway Guards, Signalmen and Switchmen's Society but it also was short lived. It sent memorials to the main line companies with demands for improving the signalmen's wages and hours of work but the companies would not recognise them. It was followed in the same year by another attempt, at a more general union under the guise of a friendly society, the Railway Working Men's Provident Benefit Society, but this suffered from victimisation while it was still small and expired very soon. All these were preliminaries to the Amalgamated Society of 1871. They may well have been stimulated by the contemporary ferment in the trade union world, the Master and Servant agitation, the struggle centred round legal status and the activities of the National Reform League in which there was some kind of railwaymen's participation.

Needless to say one factor in the weakness of trade union development was the strength of the companies' opposition, exemplified on the London, Brighton & South Coast in 1852, as follows: [1]

> 'The directors are in principle opposed to combination of any description for the purpose of interfering with the natural course of trade. They think that masters and men should be left in every establishment to settle their own terms and arrange their own differences, without foreign dictation or interference.'

The directors' opposition extended to any form of representation, necessary though it was found to be for the settlement of disputes. This may be seen from the following verbatim report of proceedings on the London & North Western in 1854. The enginemen were objecting to the contract method of payment.

> 'Chairman (of directors' committee): Wilson, have you any reason to suppose that you are in any way marked in consequence of your declining this?
>
> Wilson (an engineman): I do not know, we are in fear of being dismissed.

---

1. London, Brighton & South Coast. Circular, 9 Feb. 1852.

Chairman: Speak for yourself. Do not say "we".

Wilson: We are speaking for the body of men.

Committee Member: Speak for yourself and let the men speak for themselves.

Burtess (an engineman): I have no reason to complain.

Committee Member: He represents the Camden men here.

Another Committee Member: But let every man speak for himself.

Burtess: If men are on duty and are unable to attend we as a Deputation were authorized and wished by them to explain their grievances according to their wishes

Committee Member: Let every man speak for himself.

Chairman: He represents others and although his own particular experience may not be an illustration yet he has a right to speak of what he knows of others.

Committee Member: I think it is fair that every man should speak for himself.

Chairman: He represents the body.'

One can see the light of reason and the knowledge of necessity slowly dawning on this committee of directors.

An account of labour organisation would not be complete without reference to the two great political movements of this period, the Chartism of the forties and the reform campaign of the sixties. In the forties railway work was a new and expanding occupation for agricultural and general labourers, discharged soldiers and sailors and domestic servants and it is hardly surprising, with this background, that during the Chartist period railwaymen generally stood with the companies, on the side of law and order. During March and April, 1848, large numbers of them were sworn in as special constables in London, Liverpool and other places. The Eastern Counties enlisted porters under the charge of clerks, and the London, Brighton & South Coast enlisted their gangers. The directors expressed their gratification:

> 'In reference to the recent Chartist movement and the threatened Monster Meetings and Processions throughout the streets to the House of Commons, whereby Business would have been interrupted and the public peace endangered, the Directors have witnessed with satisfaction the readiness and zeal with which the Servants of the Company declared their determination to exert themselves for the maintenance of order and the Protection of Property.'

How far was it true that the men voluntarily came forward to help, and did they, as the companies claimed, 'cheerfully enrol themselves as special constables for the preservation of the peace'? The fact that for some years the men had been under an obligation to serve as constables paved the way. The companies' rules had included this stipulation for many grades, the purpose being not so much political as for the exclusion of trespassers and the protection of railway property. It was only, in fact, in the locomotive and carriage workshops that there was any problem at all, and there some pressure was necessary on the artisans. Although nearly five hundred workmen were sworn in by the magistrates at the Crewe works and the Edge Hill works at Liverpool also supplied special constables, the locomotive superintendent at Wolverton thought it necessary to make the workmen in his department sign a declaration of their willingness to serve as constables. There were signs of disaffection. At Crewe Nathan Crompton, George Lowe and John Waterton were dismissed for refusing to be sworn in and they were only taken back when they agreed to make 'a solemn declaration to serve as special constables to protect property and keep the peace whenever the magistrates shall require'.[1] At Watford the artisans, who were alleged to be 'confirmed Chartists', refused to sign a statement of loyalty unless it was limited to the protection of their own line, their bread and butter. These operative mechanics, 'the most dangerous class', were the only stumbling block. It seems true that the ordinary railwaymen 'willingly enlisted themselves on the side of order and expressed themselves anxious to be enrolled as constables'. After all, they were told that they were enrolled to protect the companies' property on which their living depended.[2] But by the late sixties the situation had changed and the railwaymen were at last reaching towards their own amalgamated society. What part they played in the Reform League is not known beyond the fact that the League demonstration on 11 February 1867 included a large group of them wearing their uniforms. They must have been traffic grades or enginemen, not artisans. It may be no more than coincidence that two years before the Reform Act the London, Brighton & South Coast Board resolved that it would not use any influence over its servants in the forthcoming election; that a year after it the Manchester, Sheffield & Lincolnshire Board resolved to be 'neutral' in the approaching elections and that the North Eastern issued the following poster.[3]

---

1. F.C. Mather, 'The Railways, the electric telegraph and Public Order during the Chartist Period, 1837–48', in History, Vol. 38, new series, Feb. 1953, No. 132, & correction June 1953.
2. B.T.C., L. N. W. Corres Anon to L. & N.W., 6 Apr. 1848; R. McConnell to. G. C. Glynn and R. Creed, 7 Apr. 1848; H. Booth J.H. Harrison and R. Madigan to R. Creed, 10 Apr. 1848; J. Trevithick to H. Booth, 17 July 1848.
3. P. S. Bagwell, *The Railwaymen*, 1963, p. 129.

North Eastern Railway
Darlington Section

THE ELECTIVE FRANCHISE

The Committee hereby inform the Officers and Workmen in their employ, that in Voting at the coming General Election, they are at liberty to act according to their own opinions, and that in doing so their position with the Company will not in any way be affected. The Committee also forbid Canvassing on the Railway Company's premises, by or on behalf of Candidates.

(Signed)
HENRY PEASE, Chairman
THOS. MACNAY, Secretary.

Railway Office, Darlington, July 22nd, 1868.

In conclusion, industrial relation were generally peaceful. Disputes and labour organisations were comparatively rare. This may be attributed to those conditions of work which encouraged satisfaction or loyalty to the companies, to the nature of railway work and to the methods of labour control. Chief among them were security of employment, prospects of advancement, strict discipline, the divisions between grades, and the practice of 'divide and rule'.

Chapter 6

INCOMES AND HOURS OF WORK

Money wages were, of course, the chief indication of the standard of living of railwaymen but there were other important and closely related factors. Some of these, such as opportunity for advancement, and security of employment, are dealt with elsewhere. Others, such as clothing, free travel and hours of work are dealt with in this chapter.

The wages of about fifty different grades are involved. The general level of wages for the different grades was broadly influenced by four factors. Firstly, the agricultural wage was a point of departure for the most unskilled railway labour, such as porters and permanent way men. 'In agricultural districts where wages were very low, fifteen shillings per week as a commencing wage for a porter enabled the company to obtain, without difficulty, as many men as they required.'[1] Secondly, there was the competitive pull of other occupations though this was not serious. Thirdly, the importance of the particular station in terms of traffic or operation decided the status of the work there. Fourthly, promotion channels sometimes affected differential wage rates.

The records of railwaymen's wages have hitherto been very deficient but a great deal of information is now available.[2] It is possible to distinguish between authorised scales of pay and the rates actually paid, and it is desirable to do this because the two by no means coincided. As a general manager said in 1879, 'In many cases the men were paid at wages lower than those authorised by the scale, it being generally understood that the wages therein stated were the maximum of wages to be paid in any case.'[3]

A summary of levels and trends for each of the more important grades is given below. Where figures in brackets are shown after the figure for wages actually paid they indicate the number of cases examined. With two notable exceptions the rates of most grades were

1. Great Western Railway. General Manager's Report, 1879.
2. A. L. Bowley, *Wages in the United Kingdom in the Nineteenth Century,* 1900.
3. Great Western Railway, General Manager's Report, 1879.

closely related in terms of promotion. Enginemen's and permanent way men's rates seem to have had little or no connection with the rates of other grades and there was very little interchange of personnel. The former were more related to the works artisans and the latter to the agricultural labourer.

Wage Rates of the Grades
Traffic Grades
Police

This was the original general grade from which were appointed the switchmen, pointsmen, signalmen, booking constables and clerks, until the residue became similar in function to the civil police. Employed first in the construction stage to preserve order on the works, they came to be responsible for hand signalling of trains. The more skilled of them were selected to take care of the switches and points and were paid a higher wage. During this time a distinction arose between 'police at the points' and 'strolling police'. Authorised scales were as follows: 1830s - 18s to 19s per week. Early 1840s - 16s to 19s. Late 1840s - 15s to 17s in the country, 16s to 18s in London. 1850s - 15s to 17s in the country, 17s to 19s in London. Early 1870s - the same rate as in the 1850s. It can be seen that there was very little change throughout the period. Rates actually paid were as follows:

	Average s d	Range s d s d	Cases
1830s	21 1	20 0 - 24 6	(7)
Early 1840s	19 3	18 0 - 21 0	(198)
Late 1840s	18 5	16 0 - 23 0	(24)
1850s	19 8	17 0 - 21 0	(11)
1860s	16 5	15 0 - 24 0	(136)
Early 1870s	19 1	18 0 - 22 0	(401)

Rates paid thus varied somewhat more than authorised scales, but again there was little change between the forties and the seventies. The differential between London and country rates appeared in the 1840s and continued throughout, varying from 1s to 2s per week.

Porters

This grade had a number of sub divisions in which men did rather similar work, though called by different names. The biggest group was the passenger porter, followed in turn by the goods porters, lad or junior porters, parcel porters, lamp porters, coal porters, signal porters (intermediate to signalman), office porters, and booking porters who were equivalent to clerks in charge or station masters at small stations. The last five of these were in small numbers.

For passenger porters authorised scales were: Early 1840s - 16s to 18s (country), 17s to 19s (London). 1850s and 1860s - 12s to 17s (country), 15s to 19s (London). Early 1870s - 15s to 18s (country), 16s to 20s (London). Rates actually paid were as follows:

	Average s d	Range s d s d	Cases
Early 1840s	18 7	15 0 - 20 0	(27)
Late 1840s	17 3	12 0 - 19 0	(28)
1850s	16 10	12 0 - 19 0	(427)
1860s	16 7	12 0 - 20 0	(167)
Early 1870s	16 6	12 0 - 20 0	(706)

Here again there is very little change, while the pay was several shillings a week better than that of an agricultural labourer.

Goods porters received a somewhat higher rate than passenger porters. Some rates paid were as follows:

	Average s d	Range s d s d	Cases
1840s	20 9	20 0 - 21 0	4
1850s	17 11	17 0 - 19 0	8
Early 1870s	19 6	17 0 - 21 0	1319

The rates for lad porters were of course much lower. Authorised scales were as follows: Late 1840s - 10s. 1860s - 6s to 10s. Early 1870s - 6s to 14s. Rates paid were as follows:

	Average s d	Range s d s d	Cases
1840s	7 6	5 0 - 10 0	5
1850s	8 6	6 0 - 14 0	36
Early 1870s	10 3	6 0 - 14 0	346

Here a slight upward trend is indicated.

Parcels porters received a somewhat higher rate than goods porters,

LONDON, BRIGHTON & SOUTH COAST RAILWAY PERSONNEL, 1881 (LEFT TO RIGHT: TICKET COLLECTOR, TICKET INSPECTOR, STATION SUPERINTENDENT, STATION INSPECTOR, GUARD, POLICEMAN)

LONDON, BRIGHTON & SOUTH COAST RAILWAY PERSONNEL, 1881 (LEFT TO RIGHT: LUGGAGE LABELLER, LAMPMAN, SIGNALMAN, TELEGRAPH CLERK, STATION MESSENGER, TELEGRAPH MESSENGER)

it reflected the higher value of consignment they dealt with. Some rates paid were:

	Average	Range	Cases
	s d	s d s d	
1840s	21 0	21 0	3
1850s	22 0	19 0 - 25 0	2
1860s	20 6	20 0 - 21 0	2
1870s	20 7	20 0 - 21 0	168

Lamp porters or Lampmen suffered a reduction in responsibility. Their rates declined from the 20s level to 13s 6d (average of 70) within a range of 10s to 18s. The booking porter or constable may come more properly under the heading of clerk. Some rates paid were:

	Average	Range	Cases
	s d	s d s d	
1860s	25 0	18 0 - 27 0	38
Early 1870s	24 3	23 0 - 30 0	209

Switchmen, Pointsmen, Signalmen

The terms are broadly interchangeable. The pointsman was called called a 'turner of points' in the 1840s. Both terms switchman and pointsman were used from the beginning when the best policemen were selected for their work. The term signalman does not appear until the 1850s and in fact switchman is the term used in parliamentary returns throughout. Authorised scales were: 1830s - 19s to 21s. Early 1840s - 21s to 24s. Late 1840s - 20s (country), 21s (London), 1850s - 20s to 22s (country) 20s to 24s (London). Early 1870s - 18s to 22s (country), 19s to 25s (London). It should be noted that a gratuity of £3 to £5 per annum for good conduct was paid throughout the period. Further reference to this is made in the part dealing with gratuities and bonuses. Actual rates paid were:

	Average	Range	Cases
	s d	s d s d	
Early 1840s	22 11	21 0 – 25 0	111
Late 1840s	22 0	17 6 – 25 0	20
1850s	19 11	18 0 – 25 0	34
1860s	21 4	17 0 – 27 0	82
Early 1870s	21 2	18 0 – 25 0	1586

There is a slight downward trend but the pay compares favourably with the average pay of a cotton operative.
Guards
There were two main groups of guard, passenger and goods, with different status, the former generally receiving the higher pay. Passenger guards were divided into head and under guards. There were also two smaller groups, mineral guards and brakesmen who acted as assistant goods guards. A fifth group, parcels guards, is sometimes met.

For passenger guards, authorised scales were as follows: 1830s - 24s to 25s. Early 1840s - 23s to 30s. Late 1840s - 23s to 40s. 1850s - 25s to 27s. Early 1870s - 20s to 40s. The dividing line between head and under guards remained constant at about 25s per week. Rates actually paid were:-

	Average s d	Range s d s d	Cases
Early 1840s	27 0	24 0 - 30 0	80
Late 1840s	24 6	21 0 - 30 0	13
1850s	25 2	18 0 - 30 0	41
1860s	26 0	24 0 - 28 0	29
Early 1870s	28 8	21 0 - 30 0	443

These figures point to a slight advance after a fall in the 1840s.

For goods guards authorised scales were:- 1840s - 19s to 28s. 1850s - 23s to 32s. Early 1870s - 21s to 36s. In the last period a differentiation between 'one home' and 'two homes' appeared and the higher rate of 30s to 36s for head guards was paid for 'two homes'. Rates actually paid were:-

	Average s d	Range s d s d	Cases
1840s	23 3	21 0 - 30 0	11
1850s	23 0	23 0 - 32 0	31
1860s	23 0	21 0 - 25 0	12
Early 1870s	26 0	21 0 - 36 0	1272

A similar advance to that of passenger guards is indicated.

Mineral guards appear to have been paid a somewhat lower rate than the ordinary goods guard. In the 1850s the rate paid was 21s 9d (average of 31) within a range of 21s to 23s.

Brakesmen were in general paid a similar rate to that of goods guard. Authorised scales were:- 1840s - 25s to 30s. Early 1870s - as for goods guards. Rates actually paid were:-

	Average s d	Range s d s d	Cases
1840s	18 0	16 6 - 24 0	13
1850s	18 0	18 0	2
Early 1870s	as for Goods Guards.		

For parcels guards only two mentions occur. The authorised scale in 1871 was 27s to 35s. In the 1840s the rate paid had been 27s. (25)

Shunters

These, whether passenger or goods, were more often than not promoted from porters and their pay varied at a definitely higher level. Their work was more skilled and certainly more onerous, although at the beginning they were called 'labourers in the yard'. No information on authorised scales is available until the early 1870s. The explanation is probably that shunters do not appear officially as a separate grade until 1875 and they were probably frequently included by the companies as higher paid porters or brakesmen. The authorised scale in 1871 was 19s to 23s. Rates actually paid were:-

	Average s d	Range s d s d	Cases
1840s	18 4	18 0 - 21 0	17
1850s	21 2	19 0 - 25 0	13
1860s	20 6	20 0 - 21 0	2
Early 1870s	20 7	20 0 - 25 0	539

Here there is an advance over the whole period.

Ticket Collectors

These were not a numerous grade; in 1860 there were only 400 of them in the United Kingdom. But their wages are worth mention because they give an example of a definite decline in the importance of a grade. Rates actually paid were:-

	Average s d	Range s d s d	Cases
1840s	27 11	20 0 – 40 0	15
1850s	21 0	18 0 – 26 0	5
1860s	21 8	18 0 – 25 0	6
Early 1870s	19 0	18 0 – 25 0	103

Gatekeepers

They had the simple, though essential, task of operating level crossing gates and sometimes they operated signals or points connected with them. They were one of the lowest paid grades though generally speaking the value of a rent free cottage must be added to wages. Sometimes the rent free cottage was the whole wage. In 1860 they numbered nearly 2000. Authorised scales do not appear to have existed. Rates actually paid were:-

	Average s d	Range s d s d	Cases
Early 1840s	13 5	12 0 - 21 0	22
Late 1840s	13 2	12 0 - 17 6	38
1850s	12 3	9 0 - 17 0	32
1860s	12 10	10 0 - 20 0	26
Early 1870s	11 2	10 0 - 20 0	319

Here there is a definite downward trend. The higher rates were for men who also did pointsman's duty.

Supervisory Grades (traffic)

The chief of these were Inspector, Sub Inspector, Foreman, and Head Porter, who was an inferior kind of foreman. Reference is here made to those men engaged on traffic work.

Inspectors

Authorised scales were:- 1840s - 25s to 30s. Early 1870s - 30s to 40s. Rates actually paid were:-

	Average s d	Range s d s d	Cases
1840s	35 8	25 0 - 60 0	12
1850s	44 7	30 0 - 60 0	7
Early 1870s	33 6	25 0 - 60 0	102

As can be seen, not much change is indicated.

Sub Inspectors

One authorised scale in the 1830s was 25s. Rates paid were:-

	Average s d	Range s d s d	Cases
1840s	23 0	24 0 - 30 0	9
1850s	31 7	30 0 - 40 0	8
1860s	30 0	-	1

Foremen

These were more numerous than inspectors. The first authorised scale, in 1871, was 20s to 25s (country), 21s to 30s (London). Rates paid were:-

	Average s d	Range s d s d	Cases
1840s	25 5	21 0 - 35 0	11
1850s	30 5	25 0 - 35 0	11
1860s	31 6	25 0 - 35 0	4
Early 1870s	28 0	20 0 - 30 0	322

Here there seems to have been a rise in the 1840s and 1850s but a considerable fall later.

Head Porters

Rates paid were:-

	Average s d	Range s d s d	Cases
1840s	23 0	20 0 - 25 0	7
1850s	21 10	20 0 - 22 0	16
1860s	21 1	20 0 - 23 0	24

Here there was a continuous fall.

Station Masters

There is no lack of figures on the wages and salaries of station masters but there is considerable difficulty in interpreting them. This arises from the fluid character of rates of pay. Pay was based primarily on the importance of the station in terms of either traffic or operational movement, or both; an importance which was continually changing relatively and absolutely in a period of rapid expansion of railway systems. Hence the pay for any station could change frequently from year to year. The station master sometimes had a house rent free but the tendency was for rent to be paid. Quite frequently, during the earlier decades, he was not the senior man at the station, this being the clerk in charge who sometimes received a higher rate of pay and who was responsible for the business side of the work, as the station master was for the operational. Only by the 1860s did the station master become the undisputed master of the station. Some station masters were paid on annual salary, some on weekly wage, this generally speaking according to importance but also partly according to the particular company's practice. On some lines considerable bonuses were given. These will be analysed later. For these reasons there were no authorised scales except on the Great Northern where £78 is referred to as 'the usual scale'. The following figures refer to rates actually paid per annum.

	Average £ s	Range £ s £ s	Cases
Early 1840s	62 10	45 0 - 100 0	20
Late 1840s	77 2	46 16 - 200 0	13
1850s		62 8 - 200 0	
1860s	107 16	52 0 - 250 0	151
Early 1870s	74 8	65 0 - 200 0	385

Here there seems to have been an advance in the 1840s but none thereafter. It seems probable, however, that the most important station masters became better paid.

Clerks

These were a very miscellaneous collection. The best division that can be made is between (a) clerks in charge of stations, (b) head office clerks and (c) others - the general run at stations and depots, who were sub-divided by function into booking clerks, goods clerks, relief clerks etc. The second two categories are found sub-divided by status and pay into junior clerks, experienced clerks, lad or boy clerks, and apprentices. Here also the difficulty in interpreting the figures arises from the same considerations affecting the pay of station masters.

Clerks in charge. They were sometimes superior to station masters in status and pay. This is particularly noticeable in the 1840s and 1850s but less so in the 1860s. It was, however, not a feature on all lines. On some, such as the Great Western, the grade does not appear to have existed; on others it existed only at small stations. Most of the men in this grade had a company's house, whether free or, more usually, rented. Authorised scales were as follows:- 1840s - three classes, viz. £80 to £100, £110 to £140, £150 to £200. 1850s - six classes, viz. £41 12s 0d to £52, and the other five up to maxima of £54 12s 0d., £65, £78, £120, £150 respectively. Rates paid were:-

	Average £ s	Range £ s £ s	Cases
Early 1840s	-	50 0 - 150 0	-
Late 1840s	64 19	48 8 - 150 0	59
1850s	70 6	48 8 - 150 0	73
1860s	84 6	65 0 - 120 0	16

Here there was a definite increase.
Head Office Clerks
Rates actually paid were:-

	Average £ s	Range £ s £ s	Cases
Early 1840s	96 0	60 0 - 150 0	16
Late 1840s	106 8	65 0 - 200 0	26
1850s	100 0	65 0 - 300 0	98

Clerks, General. The only authorised scales found are as follows: Early 1840s - five classes viz. £50 to £70, £80 to £100, £110 to £140, £150 to £200, £250 to £300. Late 1840s - three classes, viz. £70 to £100, £105 to £150, £150 to £250, and in four classes, viz. £50 to £76, £80 to £110, £115 to £155, £160 to £200.
Lad Clerks 1840s - £25 to £45. 1850s - £20 to £55.
Apprentices 1840s - £25 to £50. 1850s - £20 to £40. Early 1870s - £25 to £60.
Rates paid were as follows:-

Clerks, General	Average £ s	Range £ s £ s	Cases
1830s	-	48 8 - 91 0	-
Early 1840s	82 10	40 0 - 170 0	137
Late 1840s	70 9	47 0 - 150 0	98
1850s	69 4	50 0 - 175 0	178
1860s	65 5	50 0 - 140 0	40
Lad Clerks			
1840s	26 8	26 0 - 36 8	22
1850s	28 8	15 12 - 41 12	62
1860s	19 10	-	2

In 1871 the average salary of all clerks (628) on the L.B. & S.C. was £55 9s 0d per annum. The above figures suggest a downward trend.
Enginemen
Wages of the two groups, drivers and firemen, were closely linked through promotion. Payment was originally, in the 1830s, based on the trip, but came to be based on the day's work.
Drivers Authorised scales were as follows: 1830s - 1s 3d to 1s 6d per trip with 5 trips per day, and 7s per day. 1840s - 4s 2d to 8s per day according to service. The anonymous Veritas Vincit in the *Railway Times* and the *Railway Record* gives 7s as a general figure, though some companies paid 5s and 6s and some as little as 4s. 1850s - 5s 6d to 8s. 1860s - 5s to 7s 6d. Confirmation of this is

given by the demand of the Engine Drivers' and Firemen United Society in 1866 for a rate of 6s to 8s per day. Engine drivers were certainly paying income tax in 1860 and probably before that when the exemption level was lowered to £100 per annum in 1853. Early 1870s - As for the 1860s with certain modification, e.g. London Allowance of 2s 6d per week; shunting drivers who took the place of main line drivers received 6d per day extra. Some rates paid were:

	Average s d	Range s d s d	Cases
1840s	5 4	4 8 - 7 2	44
Early 1870s	6 6	5 0 - 7 6	197

A definite increase is indicated here. If a man was paid regularly for six days a week a weekly wage of up to 45s per week made him a good deal better off than a turner in an engineering workshop.

Firemen Authorised scales were: 1830s - about 5s per day. 1840s - 2s 9d to 5s per day. 1850s - 3s to 4s per day. 1860s - 3s 6d to 4s 6d per day. Confirmation is suggested by the demand in 1866 for a rate of 3s 6d to 5s per day. Early 1870s - same rates as in 1860s; if employed as shunting enginemen or turners they received 6d per day extra; if employed temporarily as main line drivers they received 1s per day extra. Some rates actually paid were:

	Average s d	Range s d s d	Cases
1840s	3 4	2 6 - 4 2	153
1870s	3 7	2 6 - 4 6	194

Here there was a slight advance.

A different system of payment peculiar to enginemen was introduced in the fifties On the Stockton and Darlington in the thirties drivers were paid by the trip or per ton mile, and they paid for their own firemen, coal and oil. The new contract system of the fifties under which men were paid by the mile was a return to piece rates. When it was introduced on the London & North Western in 1854 it aroused strong opposition. A deputation of men from Rugby Birmingham and Camden, under the impression that the new system was compulsory, claimed an increase in wages and complained of the long hours of work in which it resulted. The company replied that the system was optional and undertook to remedy the grievance on hours. The lack of enthusiasm on the part of the men may be explained by the fact that two years later out of one hundred and four men working on contract only twenty-five had earned payments above their normal wage rates. These payments were at the rate of £14 per annum. The contract rates of payment varied between 3¼d and 6¾d per mile i.e., for passenger trains from 3¼d to 4³/₈d per mile, for goods trains from 5½d to 6¾d per mile. The motive behind the introduction of this scheme was economy. The Manchester, Sheffield & Lincolnshire, feeling the necessity of reducing expenses in order to meet debenture interest and to increase the interest on preference shares, introduced a similar scheme in 1855. The company quoted the experience of the London & North Western and the Eastern Counties railways as well as the current high average cost of running per mile which it said was 4.11d per mile compared with 3.75d per mile on the other companies. In that year only nine drivers were working on contract but good results were confidently expected. The rates of payment were somewhat higher than on the London & North Western, ranging from 3½d for some passenger trains to 7d for salt trains. The next year thirty-one drivers were in the scheme and it was hoped to effect further saving. But by 1858 the number was 'much diminished', the reason being that far more men were adversely affected than were benefitted. Whereas the gains by the contracted men above their normal wages amounted to £91 in one year their losses were £349, a net loss of £258 per annum. The same system on the Great Eastern, which it inherited from the Eastern Counties, lasted somewhat longer, but only until 1866.

Permanent Way Men

There were three main grades: Gangers, Platelayers or Waymen, Labourers, and above them Inspectors and Sub Inspectors.

No authorised scales are to be found. Some rates actually paid are as follows:

	Per day		
	Average s d	Range s d s d	Cases
Gangers			
1840s	4 5	4 0 - 5 0	5
1850s	3 11	3 0 - 4 6	6
Early 1870s	3 8	3 6 - 5 0	190

Platelayers			
1830s	2 11	2 10 - 3 0	44
1840s	3 2	3 0 - 3 6	89
Labourers			
1830s	2 5	2 3 - 2 6	3
1840s	2 7	2 6 - 3 6	198
Early 1870s	2 10	2 6 - 3 6	653

The gangers' wages seem to have fallen whereas the labourers' have risen slightly.

For the year 1871 it is possible to give a complete picture of the average wage rates of all men in each grade on one railway, the London, Brighton & South Coast. The average wage rate of all men employed, excluding station masters, clerks, supervisory grades and workshop artisans, was 19s 10d per week. Compared with this a contemporary estimate, that of Leone Levi in 1867, of an average wage of 21s per week, excluding the same grades, was too optimistic. His overall average was based on the following grade averages: policemen 18s, porters 17s 6d, guards 20s, ticket collectors 20s, signalmen 20s to 26s, engine drivers 30s to 45s, firemen 18s to 24s, permanent way labourers 18s, platelayers 21s, gangers 21s per week. But he had overestimated the wages of the numerically large grades such as porter and labourer, and underestimated some smaller grades such as guard and ganger. [1]

Table XXXVIII
Average Wage Rates on the London Brighton & South Coast in 1871

Grade	Per Week s d	Number of which Average taken
Station Master	35 11	133
Clerk	21 4	628
Foreman	30 4	35
Inspector	30 1	33
Guard, passenger	25 5	150
Guard, goods	24 10	88
Signalman	23 0	316
Head Porter	22 5	67

1. London, Brighton & South Coast. List of Staff in All Departments, 1871. Leone Levi, *Wages and Earnings,* 1867.

INCOMES AND HOURS OF WORK

Grade	Per Week s. d.	Number of which averages taken
Timekeeper	22 0	7
Switchman	21 0	14
Shunter	20 9	65
Policeman	20 1	33
Booking Porter	19 10	5
Ticket Examiner	19 4	22
Office Porter	19 2	8
Ticket Collector	18 9	67
Watchman	17 2	24
Carriage Searcher	17 2	5
Porter	16 4	670
Lamp Porter	15 4	6
Waiting Room Attendant	13 7	11
Gas Man & lad	13 4	6
Messenger	13 3	24
Gatekeeper	10 9	68
Lad Porter	10 5	16
Train Signal Clerk	7 8	53

Goods Department

Grade	Per Week s. d.	Number of which averages taken
Horsekeeper	32 9	4
Steam Crane Driver	25 4	3
Hay Checker	24 0	1
Receiver	23 8	20
Warehouseman	22 2	7
Chaff Cutter	22 0	3
Billposter	21 3	2
Checker	21 3	15
Haulage Man	21 0	15
Lift Bridge Man	20 8	3
Loader	20 7	14
Coal Tipper	20 0	3
Carman	19 11	105
Sheeter	19 9	11
Packer	19 8	3
Stableman	19 1	21
Truck Horse Driver	19 1	23
Luggage Labeller	18 0	3
Scavenger	18 0	1
Coupler	17 4	3
Carriage Cleaner	17 1	13
Scotcher	16 0	4

Van Setter	14 0	3
Number Taker	12 8	3
Vanguard	8 2	38
Locomotive Department		
Foreman	89 5	4
Engine Driver	39 0	197
Shedman	26 7	7
Cokeman	22 6	24
Fireman	21 6	194
Firelighter	17 0	11
Cleaner	13 6	138
Permanent Way		
Ganger	22 0	190
Labourer	17 0	653
Ticket Printer	38 0	5
Detective	25 0	2

(Note. The above list does not include steamboat men and workshop artisans)

	20s & Over per week	Under 20s per week
All Grades (as above)	47%	53%
All men (except station masters, clerks, supervisory grades)	44%	56%

It is interesting to compare our averages, given above, with Levi's list of average wage rates of various occupations. His rate of 22s for cotton manufacture and coal mining comes fifteenth in order of size of wage. That rate was received by timekeepers on our list, the next nearest grade being head porter. His top rate of 30s for cutler, glass and boot and shoe manufacture is nearest to our rate 30s 1d for inspectors. His lowest rate of 14s 6d for agriculture was a good deal lower than our rate of 16s 4d for porters. If one takes G. H. Wood's average figure of 24s 2d (allowing for unemployment) for the industrial operative a 'hypothetical but not untypical' model, our nearest rate is that of the goods guard.[1]

---

1 G. H. Wood, 'Real Wages and the Standard of Comfort since 1850', in *Jnl. of Royal Statistical Society*, Vol.LXXII, 1901.

Other Earnings
Overtime Payment

The payment of overtime has two main aspects. It is firstly an indication of earnings as distinct from wage rates. Unfortunately it is not possible to say to what extent overtime increased earnings, but only whether it was paid, to which grades it was paid, and whether as an exception or as a matter of recognised principle or practice. On the other hand the mere existence of overtime was important for the implication that a certain length of working day or week was accepted.

As early as 1835 enginemen on the Newcastle & Carlisle were to be paid 4d per hour. In the 1840s the rate on that line was raised to 7d per hour and payment to enginemen was also recognised on the Eastern Counties. At the same time those on the Manchester, Sheffield & Lincolnshire complained of an attempt to discontinue overtime. Smiths, joiners and labourers also had overtime. Porters on the London, Brighton & South Coast were paid for extra time in exceptional circumstances. Clerks in the same period were less fortunate. Those at Manchester were ordered not to receive any and on the Grimsby & Sheffield the practice had existed but was ordered to stop.

Three years after the Ten Hours Act the principle of payment was recognised on at least one line. This was the Great Northern where the general practice of payment after a ten hour day was approved, the minimum period being a quarter of a day's work. On the London, Brighton & South Coast, however, lump sum gratuities were paid for extra work arising from the 1851 Great Exhibition. Practice varied considerably and it gave rise to complaint as in the case in 1856 of the porters at Hull who were paid while those at New Holland were not.

By the early 1860s overtime payment had evidently become general. Enginemen on the London & South Western were conceded an extra sixpence an hour when delayed beyond a certain time. The 'practice of paying for extra time to all classes of railwaymen paid weekly' was discussed. On the Great Western overtime in the traffic department was being paid at the rate of £24,140 per annum, equal to 1.5 per cent on the wages bill. It was not, however, accepted as a general principle and it was recommended that it should be paid only 'in special cases where daily hours were in excess of those usually required and only in exceptional circumstances as the Company's interests required'. [1] But the practice continued and by 1873 on the

---

1 Great Western Rly. Secretary's Report, 1863.

same line porters, guards and shunters were paid for time in excess of sixty hours per week in most cases. Shunting enginemen who lost their recognised meal time were paid extra for more than ten hours per week. Two years earlier porters, carmen and checkers at various places were receiving overtime by local agreement, viz. porters at Liverpool 6d per hour over 57½ hours per week, at Birkenhead 4d per hour over 10 hours per day, at Manchester payment for all over 57½ hours, at Bristol payment for over 10½ hours and in London after a 10 hour day; carmen at Birmingham, for over 12 hours a day including 1½ hours for meals; checkers at Birmingham, at the 'ordinary rate' for over 12 hours a day including 2 hours for meals. In the same year, 1871, some guards on the Midland were paid for time worked over 10 hours per day. Two years later shunting enginemen who did not get the recognised meal time off were to be paid overtime at the rate of 10 hours per day.

The essentially temporary character of agreements such as the above is shown by some of the economies in labour costs effected in 1879. Overtime payments in the traffic and goods departments of the Great Western were running at the rate of £22,116 per annum, equal to 1.3 per cent on the wages bill and averaging £2 8s 8d per head per annum. As the result of an enquiry the porters at Liverpool and Birkenhead were paid overtime at the ordinary rate of wages based on sixty hours per week instead of at a uniform rate of sixpence per hour; at Bristol the men apparently agreed to forego all overtime payment; in London overtime was to be paid only in very exceptional circumstances and then at a rate based on eleven hours per day.

To conclude, the evidence indicates a rearguard action by the companies. Until the middle of the century the prevalent view that a man might be expected to work all the hours that there were excluded any general practice of overtime. In the 1850s practice became fairly widespread, though without making any important addition to earnings. In fact some managements considered it preferable to increase the number of men employed. In the 1860s the addition to income became of considerable importance to at least some men in the traffic and goods grades, as well as to the companies in their search for economy.

Gratuities and Bonuses

Any review of wages is incomplete without reference to the system of granting gratuities of premiums and bonuses which, for some grades, meant a considerable addition to earnings. The incentive aspects of gratuities is dealt with in chapter 2. Here they are considered as part of wages sometimes as grants in lieu of increased wages. The grades concerned were quite numerous, being station masters, clerks, inspectors, foremen, guards, switchmen, permanent way men, porters, engine drivers and firemen, in different degrees.

Bonuses were on quite a different basis from gratuities or premiums. They were granted to station masters, clerks and inspectors; the gratuities, to all other grades named above. Bonuses were part of a system of payment by results in operation on some lines, in which the bonus was based on the size of the company's dividend. A payment by results system was advocated as early as 1840 but the first trace of one in operation is in 1850. In the 1850s such a system was certainly working on the Great Northern and the London, Brighton & South Coast and possibly on others. The chairman of the London, Brighton & South Coast described it as follows:-

> 'The object speaks for itself .... in short to substitute as far as possible the spirit of private enterprise for the stationary routine of a Government Office.
>
> 'This plan appears to me decidedly preferable to that of making the advance of salary depend on length of service and in adopting it we are only following the example of most of the large Contractors by whom Railways and other important undertakings have been successfully executed.
>
> 'I propose therefore, that the present salaries be adopted as a *minimum*, feeling satisfied that a comparison with those paid for similar services by other Railway Companies will show that no reduction on the present amount could be contemplated without injustice to the Officers and injury to the Company and that in future they be advanced at the rate of 25 per cent for every 1 per cent or 1¼ per cent for every 1s per cent of additional dividend.
>
> 'Thus the dividend for the Year 1849 having been £3 17s 0d per cent, if the dividend for the Year 1850 should be £3 18s 0d per cent, the salary of each Officer who came under the arrangement for the year 1851 would be raised £1 5s 0d for each £100.
>
> 'If the dividend should in the course of time reach £7 14s 0d per cent which would be the case if the traffic were to increase by about 50 per cent a contingency quite within the range of probability, if no unforeseen event should occur to prevent its development, his salary would be doubled.'

Subsequently the names of station masters, station clerks and chief booking clerks were added to the list of officers concerned.

The results are given in the following table based on the census of station masters and clerks. It will be seen that although the optimism of the chairman was not justified, the bonuses increased salaries by anything between 25 per cent and 40 per cent. About half the

Table XXXIX
Bonuses and Gratuities of Station Masters,[1] Clerks and Inspectors, 1851 - 1860

Averages over 10 years

Salary £	Bonus £ s d	Gratuity £ s d
Station Masters		
124	31 13 0	10 0
120	39 12 0	1 0 0
104	32 8 0	1 0 0
100	27 5 0	-
115	38 3 0	1 0 0
142	49 3 0	2 0 0
100	38 3 0	-
136	47 9 0	1 0 0
110	36 18 0	10 0
107	32 13 0	2 0 0
107	43 3 0	-
185	65 7 0	5 0 0
230	80 16 0	-
Station Clerks		
150	42 14 0	2 5 0
126	30 3 0	10 0
100	35 15 0	1 10 0
Inspectors		
147	52 14 0	1 10 0
131	41 12 0	1 10 0
114	33 6 0	2 0 0

station masters on this line benefitted and a small proportion of clerks and inspectors. In addition, as will be seen, most of them received much smaller gratuities averaging £1 to £2 per annum. Gratuities, based on one or two weeks pay or on 5 per cent of annual pay and conditional upon service and good conduct, were received almost regularly by many station masters and clerks. Some representative figures from the London, Brighton & South Coast are given below in Table XL.

---

1. London, Brighton & South Coast. Traffic department Census 1856 amended to 1861.

Foremen also benefitted, though not to the same extent. There are twelve cases of gratuities of from one to two weeks' wages between 1856 and 1861 on the same line. For passenger guards there are nine similar cases. The practice evidently continued elsewhere, for in 1871 on the Midland under goods guards had gratuities of £2 10s per annum and head goods guards gratuities of £5. These however, they had to surrender in return for being granted a ten hour day.

Table XL
Gratuities of Station Clerks, 1851 1860 [1]
Averages over 10 years

£	£	s	d
83	2	8	0
78	2	3	0
83	2	15	0
101	2	19	0
150	2	5	0
117	4	0	0
78	2	1	0
65	1	9	0
82	1	19	0
78	1	18	0
90	1	16	0
70	1	13	0
67	1	13	0
70	1	12	0

Switchmen or signalmen were a special case for encouragement, as noted in Chapter 2, and they generally and regularly had gratuities or premiums for good conduct up to £5 per annum. The Select Committee of 1839 reported bonuses of £3 to £5 being given and men who had four bonuses wore a red chevron on their sleeve. In that year such gratuities were in fact authorised by the Great Western and in 1843 forty men received £5 each. A few years later on the London & North Western there was a scale of £5, £4 and £3, subsequently reduced to £3, £2 and £1. In the 1850s on the Great Northern seventy-nine men each received the 'usual half yearly gratuity' of £2 10s in a period of three months. In the 1860s on the Great Western two hundred men each received £5 in a period of twelve months. In 1871 a scale of £2 10s to £5 was still operating on

---

1. London, Brighton & South Coast. Census, 1856 amended to 1861.

some lines, though abolished on others. Porters benefitted less than any of these grades. When they did it was usually from some general dispensation or exceptional circumstance. Only seven cases of bonuses of a week's wages are to be found in the 1850s and 1860s.

Engine drivers and firemen generally and regularly had premiums for safe driving, economy in fuel or punctuality. (See chapter 2). In the 1840s on the London & North Western drivers had £10 and firemen £5 per annum; likewise in the 1860s on the Great Western by agreement with the men. A little later on the London & South Western the system was discontinued but in its place a grant of £500 quarterly was authorised to be divided among the men who qualified.

Permanent way men benefitted only in the early years. In 1833 the Stockton & Darlington granted £97 14s to fifty men, 'those having their way in the best repair'. This was found 'very satisfactory in drawing forth the energies of the workmen' and in 1839 a further £70 was authorised.[1] There seemed, however, no further need to do this.

Gratuitous payments whether gratuities, bonuses or premiums, were, in general, a worthwhile increment for many grades and it may be inferred from a number of incidents that they were considered to be so. On the Great Western switchmen were placed on a flat rate of 21s per week in London and 20s in the country instead of a graduated scale of 20s to 22s per week with a premium. When pointsmen's premiums were abolished on the London & North Western in 1871 they were given an increase of pay in lieu. Engine drivers on the London & South Western who petitioned for an advance of wages in 1866 were to be given an annual gratuity instead, of £4 for drivers and £1 for firemen.

Other Monetary Income

There were certain other less important elements in income: allowances, private trading and sick pay.

Allowances

Various kinds of allowances were made to cover expenses incurred by servants; but it is doubtful whether these were any noticeable addition to income since in most cases they could only barely have covered expenses. In other cases wages were considered to cover such expenses. By the end of the period they had, in some companies, been stabilised and made subject to agreement.

The most important was the allowance made to men who had to sleep away from home. Lodging, or away from home, allowances were made to enginemen, guards and brakesmen. In the 1830s on the

---

1. Stockton & Darlington Railway. Sub Committee, 1833. Board, 1839.

Newcastle & Carlisle lodging money was prohibited; wages were to 'cover that charge'. But in the 1840s, on the London & Brighton, away from home allowance of 2s per night was paid to enginemen and guards. In the 1860s on the Great Western enginemen were paid 2s 6d for lodgings, but subsequently, because of the danger that they might profit from it, it was reduced to 1s 6d. In the early 1870s the pay of brakesmen on the London & North Western included any such allowances, but a little later the regulations provided for them to have 1s per night if no company's lodging house was provided. The scale at that time for other grades was as follows:- 1s 6d per day, 2s 6d per day and night; if continued beyond two days - 1s 3d per day and 2s per day and night. Lodging allowances of a different kind were also occasionally paid to clerks who incurred extra expense by removal. Removal allowances were rarely paid although removal was customary and frequent. Presumably effects were carried free by rail. Isolated examples do occur, such as the amount of £5 paid to the Newmarket station master in 1850. The allowance may, however, have become more general by the early 1870s for by then the London & North Western regulations provided that removal expenses were not to be paid, as a rule, to men *below* the rank of station master'.

Private Trading

Some station masters and clerks were able to trade on their own account by virtue of their employment and were allowed to. They could in this way add appreciably to their income. Other kinds of private trading were strictly prohibited. The matter was enquired into by the London, Brighton & South Coast in its traffic department census of station masters and clerks in 1856. Among the questions to be answered by the staff were these: (1) 'Is your income increased by any profits derived from any business *in connection with this Company's traffic* carried on by you as Commission Agent, or on your account? If so, state the nature and terms of such business, and say at what sum per annum do you estimate the profit to yourself derived therefrom.' (2) 'Does any man under your supervision, trade by Commission or otherwise, in connection with the Company's traffic? If so, describe his name and standing in the Company's service; and state the nature, terms and estimated profits to him of such trading.' In answer to the first question out of eighty-eight men thirty derived some additional income but of these only twenty-two had any considerable gain. These however had a profit, on the average, of £12 10s, which was worthwhile. Their trading was in coal, manure ('the London Dung'), sand, gravel and flints. The other eight received only the officially recognised commission on the sale of chalk from Brighton, which was quite small. In answer to the second question there were only four men and their gain was trifling. The station clerk in charge at Crawley (whose wages were 28s 6d per week including 3s 6d for rent) put in a strong plea to be allowed to continue this activity:[1]

'If I was not allowed to trade my salary would be insufficient to support my family and keep my payments up with the Company, as people, or 9 out of every ten, won't pay the carriage as they take their goods away. I have as much as £20 or £25 on Book frequently which I am obliged to make up to keep my account clear with the Company.

One remark I wish to make with regard to the Chalk you are sending from Brighton, that is you allow us to sell it at a small profit, as people won't pay for it as they take it away and some won't pay for 3 or 6 months but we have to pay redy (sic) money, which makes a very great difference.'

The point seems to have been taken, for when trading by station clerks was ordered to cease six years later a number of compensatory salary increases were granted.

The remaining item in other monetary income, sick pay, is left to be dealt with in the following chapter on security. The only grades for whom sick pay had any significance as a part of income were the station masters and clerks. In general, other monetary income had little significance for the main body of labour.

To complete the picture of incomes an estimate of the value of the various non-monetary additions to income is required. These were housing, fuel, clothing and free travel. Housing is discussed in detail in chapter 7. All that need be said here is that as an element in incomes, housing was not of great importance for the majority of men. Of all the men employed only about 10 per cent lived in company's houses. While the great majority of station masters had this accommodation, and for them it was a desirable perquisite, there was only one numerically large grade, the signalmen, of whom as many as one fifth were in company houses.

The main change in the provision of housing by the companies was from non-payment to payment of rent. This can be seen from the 'present regulation (of 1869) by which rent is charged to all persons in the service occupying Company's houses'. However, it would not be correct to infer that this change meant a reduction in total income. When payment of rent was substituted for non-payment a corresponding increase in wages was often given, as for example to the station masters at West Croydon, Three Bridges, Chichester and

---

1. London, Brighton & South Coast. Census, 1856

Ford Wharf in 1856. The complaint of the last named illustrates this point: [1]

> 'On my appointment to the station in 1847, it was stated that my wages was to be 24s per week and Rent Free, in 1851 my Wages was advanced to 27s per week and the 3s advance was put on as Rent, so that I did not receive any benefit from this Promotion.'

Conversely a rent free house was occasionally given instead of an increase in salary.

Rented houses were considered by the men as part of wages, for example, the station master who gave his wages as: 'wages 25s, and the House 3s 6d, total 28s 6d'. They were also considered desirable as such. Station masters and clerks applied for a station house if none existed. It might mean in some cases a definite increment, as in the case of the applicant on the London, Brighton & South Coast in 1856 whose housing was costing him in rent and taxes £25 per annum, far more than the average rent of a Company's house.

The provision of domestic fuel, either free or at reduced rates, must, however, be included in real wages. In the 1830s on the London, Brighton & South Coast an office porter had 21s per week wages with 'fire and candle found'. In the 1840s on the Newcastle & Carlisle twenty station masters, a clerk and a pointsman were supplied with 'a house and coals'. Probably free coal as a perquisite quickly disappeared but it was replaced by coal at reduced rates, and this was generally supplied until the 1860s at the latest. In 1866 it was customary for men on the Great Western to apply for coal at reduced rates. An indication of the value of this concession is given by the fact that in the 1870s Metropolitan Police were receiving fourpence per week for coal.

Clothing was probably the most valuable addition to wages and by far the most general one since it was supplied to practically all grades except clerks, and even to many station clerks. 'The Livery' was one of the first concerns of a company and received very careful consideration even before the line was open. Right at the beginning of the Great Western the traffic grades were fitted out in rifle-green cloth frock coat and waistcoat, Oxford mixture trousers and beaver top hat with leather crown and side stays. Even the porters had green plush or corduroy jacket and trousers and glazed top hat.

Clothing was regarded by both companies and men as a definite part of wages. In the 1830s an engineman on the Stockton & Darlington was given a suit of clothes as a reward for steady conduct. In the 1840s porters claimed shoe money, station clerks were

---

1. London, Brighton & South Coast. Census, 1856

supplied with clothing as a compensation for their wages being only 18s per week, porters requested, and were allowed to keep, their old clothes. In the 1850s the scale of wages for porters and police on the Great Western was criticised as too generous on the grounds that they were also 'clothed from head to foot at the expense of the company'. In the 1860s on the same line clothing was withdrawn from some porters in consideration of a wage increase. In the early 1870s a memorial from guards on the Midland for increased pay was met with the concession of 2s per week and an additional pair of trousers per annum. Clothing was generally issued free. One exception was the ten station masters on the Midland in 1847 who had 1s per week deducted from wages on account of 'livery'.

The actual value of clothing in terms of current prices can be shown from those tenders of clothing contractors which were accepted by the companies. The following table is based on the minutes of the London, Brighton & South Coast, Sheffield & Manchester, London & South Western and Great Northern companies in the 1840s and 1850s.

Value of Clothing, 1840s & 1850s

	£	s	d	£	s	d
Porters						
Jacket & trousers		14	8			
Cap		3	3			
Boots		7	6	1	5	5
Goods Guards						
Jacket & trousers	1	3	11			
Cap		5	9			
Greatcoat	1	18	0			
Boots		13	6	4	1	2
Passenger Guards						
Frock coat & trousers	2	12	0			
Cap		5	9			
Greatcoat	1	18	0			
Boots		13	6	5	9	3
Head Porters						
Jacket & trousers	1	17	0			
Cap		3	3			
Boots		7	6	2	7	9
Station Masters						
Frock coat & trousers	2	14	0			
Hat		12	6			
Greatcoat	1	18	0	5	4	6

	£ s. d.	£ s. d.
Ticket Collectors		
Frock coat & trousers	2 14 0	
Hat	9 6	
Greatcoat	1 18 0	5 1 6
Police		
Coat & trousers	1 14 6	
Hat	9 6	
Greatcoat	1 11 6	
Boots	10 6	4 6 0

Some other companies spent rather more on clothing, e.g. the North Staffs on which the following costs for new outfits were incurred in the 1840s: inspectors £7 11s 0d, upper guards £8 6s 5d, under guards £7 14s 2d, police £3 18s 4d plus boots, porters £2 8s 2d. The annual value was greater than the figures shown since although greatcoats were usually given only once in two years, most grades had two pairs of boots and trousers and porters had two jackets per annum. Enginemen's outfits were estimated at £3 3s, while in addition to the above, grades who were supplied with clothing included signalmen, switchmen, shunters, carmen, gatemen, watchmen and messengers. It may be noted that in the 1870s civil police had 26s to 30s per annum allowed for boots, but no doubt this was a special item.

Free Travel

This concession, which later became a valued and recognised perquisite of railway employment, was in this period on an occasional and tentative basis.

From the 1840s onward a 'pass along the line' might be given for leaves of absence. On the London, Brighton & South Coast it was the policy to grant station clerks free passes and the leave of absence to use them on 'all reasonable and proper occasions', that is when it was consistent with the requirements of traffic. Passes to London might be issued to the wives of clerks living within a radius of fifteen miles or if beyond, to the nearest market town, in order to cheapen the prices of shopping. Passes to the nearest market town were also granted more generally once a week to one member of servants' families. Subsequently a check to the practice was found necessary and it was laid down that the wives of clerks were not to have passes except for special urgency.

In the 1850s on the Great Northern passes were given to children of station clerks to travel to school, and to wives of officers, clerks etc. 'in any case considered expedient'. The 1851 Great Exhibition was an opportunity for greater generosity and the wives and one child of clerks, guards, policemen and porters were passed free to

London and back. The matter was defined as a privilege on the Great Western when it was resolved that 'occasional issue to clerks and servants be sanctioned as a reward for good conduct, provided that such indulgence be not granted to any individual more than once in six months'. It was put on a proper social basis by the rule on the London & North Western in 1856 that first class travel was for clerks on a salary of £100 per annum or above, second class for clerks on less than £100, inspectors, ticket collectors and guards, and third class for artisans, platelayers, porters, etc. The issue of free passes to men and families was still in 1865 an exceptional concession, granted in special circumstances. Its extension was dependent on the appearance of regular annual holidays. There is no trace of any connection between these two developments until 1870 and not until 1872 was the regular issue of free passes to men on leave clarified, although the practice may have existed some few years earlier.

Passes to travel to work were in a different category, they were mainly limited to suburban clerks in head offices. In the 1850s the principle of granting residential free passes to clerks to enable them to live in the suburbs was approved on the London & North Western and in the 1860s on the Great Western. Later in the 1860s those who had over a certain salary had to pay one quarter of the ordinary rate. In the 1860s one hundred and seven free passes were issued in one year to clerks at Euston to places as far distant as Berkhampstead and Aylesbury. Clerks in the Railway Clearing House had to pay half fare for season tickets.

In the same category as free travel was the rapidly established privilege of the annual works excursion. In the 1850s and 1860s the workmen in the Brighton locomotive and carriage department were allowed their usual trip in August. In the 1860s it was the usual practice for the 'Locomotive Servants of large companies' and, amongst others, the Doncaster, Stratford and Swindon men had their annual free trip.

In general, however, free or cheap travel was not yet a useful addition to income in this period for the great majority of men. To conclude this section it may be said that clothing and cheap fuel were the only significant items of non-monetary income for the generality but that these were of considerable importance

As regards the method of payment the general change was from the monthly to the weekly period for wages calculated on any period shorter than a year. At first on the Stockton & Darlington payment of all servants was monthly (and it was made on Friday instead of Saturday because of the complaint that the men spent several days in a disorderly fashion after being paid). In the 1840s on the South Eastern payment was ordered to be made weekly, two days wages being kept in hand. But it is doubtful if that practice was general at that early date; elsewhere the police, if not others, were paid monthly.

In the 1860s on the Great Western and elsewhere fortnightly payment for all, except clerks, seems to have been fairly general. It was not until the early 1870s that weekly payment was introduced on the Great Western following a strong demand for it. Even then the permanent way men continued on the fortnightly basis, on the alleged two fold ground that the men did not desire the change and that it would in any case cause inconvenience and expense. However, the enginemen on the London & South Western in 1872 presented a memorial for weekly payment and got it.

Hours of Work

In the early years hours of work were extremely long and left a bare minimum for sleep. There was no regular provision for Sunday relief or for holidays and the working week was normally a seven day one. By the end of the period there was a definite improvement with a corresponding advance in real wages. This development may be seen by the changes in the actual hours of duty and by the gradual advance to the ten hour day and six day week.

Throughout the whole period men complained about long hours of work. In the thirties men on the London & Birmingham complained of 'lengthened hours of attendance which forbid the enjoyment of either exercise or recreation and preclude them from the society of their wives and children'.[1] Thirty years later the Engine Drivers' and Firemen's United Society resisted a proposal from the London Brighton & South Coast for a sixty hour week, declaring:

> 'Under a system of working 60 hours a week they might have to work 15 hours one day and only 5 the next, or it might be possible to keep them on for 20 hours one day, and allow them to be off the next. The detriment to themselves and the risk to the public which were caused by that one day's overwork could not be compensated by the abstinence from labour on the succeeding day.'

There was a good deal of criticism too, from independent sources. The comments made by inspectors of the railway department of the Board of Trade enquiring into accidents have already been noted in chapter 5. From 1842 onwards they repeatedly returned to the theme of the danger to public safety of excessive hours of work. One of them, Col. George Wynne, stated in evidence to the Select Committee on Accidents on Railways in 1858 that many accidents

---

1. London & Birmingham. Memorials to Directors, 1838.

arose from men being overworked.[1] Four years later criticism came from quite a different quarter. The *Lancet,* which had appointed a special commission to enquire into the effects of railway travelling on the health of the public, published a report which showed that the real problem was the hours of work of the railwaymen. It noted that it was common for signalmen, guards and engine drivers to be on duty fifteen hours a day and made an eloquent protest:

> 'Suppose that men wearied out by long journeys and exhausted by fatigue and want of sleep are ordered, on pain of dismissal, to undertake immediately fresh duties for which they are rendered incapable by previous exhaustion of body and mind. Would it not then appear little short of miraculous if some accident did not result? The worn out engine driver nods, and a hundred lives are in jeopardy; the signalman, dazed by want of sleep, becomes confused, and in a moment the engines are pounding up human beings between them. The acute faculties of the guard are blunted by long unrest, the danger signal passes unnoticed, the brake does not second the efforts of the alarmed engine driver, and next morning there is recorded in the papers another railway accident.'

Nevertheless during the next few years the Board of Trade inspectors continued to point to excessive hours of work as contributory causes of accidents, such accidents for example, as those in Blackheath Tunnel in 1864 and near Daubhill on the London & North Western in 1865.

In the 1840s on the Eastern Counties the following hours were being worked in London. Porters 14 to 16 sometimes 17 or 18 including meal times, policemen 14 hours with 1 hour for dinner ticket collectors 12½ to 12¾ hours with 1½ hours for meals, switchmen 14 to 14½ hours with 1 hour for breakfast on the night turn, other meals being taken 'on the line'. In 1855 a conference on working expenses on the Manchester, Sheffield & Lincolnshire found that the average overall hours, including rest intervals, of thirty-one guards was 13 hours 8 minutes; the average of actual working hours was 9 hours 4 minutes. The conference was dissatisfied with this; the rest intervals were too great in proportion to the work done. Three years later its efforts produced an improvement: average overall hours were regulated at 13 hours 25 minutes, average actual working hours at 10 hours 2 minutes. Station masters had as long, if not longer hours, ranging from 12 to 16. Seventy-four of them on the London,

---

1 Report of S.C. on Accidents on Railways, 1858. Evidence of Col G. Wynne; P. S. Bagwell, *The Railwaymen*, 1963, pp. 36-39.

Brighton & South Coast in 1856 had an average working day of 14 hours, with very rarely any regular relief. The single-handed station master was often on duty even longer.

By 1871 the ten hour day was the criterion of advance. A few grades had reached it and even gone beyond and many others were appreciably nearer. There were still however very wide differences between grades and weekly hours ranged between 56 and 72.

Some of the goods guards had obtained their ten hour day or sixty hour week but only at the price of giving up their annual gratuity. Most had still an eleven or twelve hour day or seventy-two hour week, though even this was an improvement on the 1850s. Signalmen's hours also showed a marked improvement. On the North Eastern a maximum of twelve hours was laid down for junction working and this might be reduced when the 'active attention of men is almost constantly required'. On the London & North Western most of them worked eleven and a half or twelve hours but eight hour shifts were worked at the busiest places. Two years later, in 1873, on the Great Western there had developed a classification of signalmen into those working eight hour boxes, ten hour boxes and twelve hour boxes. Porters worked mostly eleven and a half or twelve hours but a considerable number worked only ten and a half or eleven hours. Within their ranks there were again considerable differences according, it would seem to locality and bargaining power. Thus goods porters at Liverpool and Manchester had a ten hour day with a fifty-seven and a half hour week (Saturday, seven and a half hours), at Bristol ten and a half hours, at Birmingham twelve hours including two hours for meals, and in London twelve hours including two hours for meals. Passenger porters had still an eleven or twelve hour day. Shunters had still mostly an eleven and a half hour or twelve hour day, in spite of the peculiar danger of their work.

The enginemen advanced first to the ten hour day, helped perhaps by the efforts of the engineering workers in the railway towns. In 1867 the enginemen agreed with the Great Western that 'ten hours was to be considered as a fair average of working hours for a week'. This was an improvement for according to a railway medical officer the average in the sixties for a goods driver was about thirteen hours per day and for passenger drivers about eleven hours. Their hours of duty had always been linked with mileage. If a man drove a goods train one hundred miles, with frequent and lengthy stops to pick up wages, it was reckoned that he could do a longer day than a man who drove a fast passenger train.

The extent to which the ten hour day had been reached by the traffic grades in 1871 and an outline of what happened afterwards is indicated by the following table, based on Great Western practice.

Table XLI
Hours per day worked by a 'Portion of Staff' [1]
in 1871, 1874, and 1879

Grade   1871

	10 & under	10½ & 11	11½ & 12	Over 12	Total Number
Shunters	16	17	78	1	112
Goods Guards	74	7	490	2	573
Signalmen, Switchmen & Policemen	5	122	757	59	943
Porters	139	597	838	56	1,630
Total	234	743	2,163	118	3,258
Percentage	7.2	22.8	66.4	3.6	

1874

	10 & under	10½ & 11	11½ & 12	Over 12	Total Number
Shunters	125	21	66	-	212
Goods Guards	630	14	50	-	694
Signalmen, Switchmen & Policemen	533	140	485	25	1,183
Porters	522	375	886	3	1,786
Total	1,810	550	1,487	28	3,875
Percentage	46.9	14.1	38.3	.7	

1879

	10 & under	10½ & 11	11½ & 12	Over 12	Total Number
Shunters	141	13	68	-	222
Goods Guards	664	108	29	-	801
Switchmen & Policemen	489	233	609	33	1,364
Porters	520	301	1,114	9	1,944
Total	1,814	655	1,820	42	4,331
Percentage	41.8	15.1	42.1	1.0	

---

1. Great Western. General Manager's Report, Feb. 1879.

Assuming that the company's figures were not likely to exaggerate the length of hours of work, at a time when the subject had been given a good deal of publicity, it is clear that the majority of the grades mentioned were working more than eleven hours a day, particularly those engaged in the movement of trains. Only a small minority, 7.2 per cent, had a ten hour day. The marked increase in the proportion of men having a ten hour day after 1871 may be noted. This was one of the first demands of the new Amalgamated Society of Railway Servants formed in 1871 and one of its chief arguments was the danger to safety arising from long hours of work. However, the advance since 1830 had been considerable.

Progress towards a six day week was essential if the men were to benefit from the gradual shortening of the working day. The other aspect of this development was the contention that Sunday labour was particularly onerous and therefore merited a special payment. The struggle for the six day week benefitted from the religious motive for Sunday observance. The seventh day was the day of rest. The special status of Sunday work was bound up with the early controversy about Sunday travel and also with the moral duty of railwaymen to attend divine worship. When in the 1830s the London & Birmingham was considering the question of continuing Sunday traffic, memorials signed by seventy men were received. They begged for its discontinuance on the grounds that 'they have not the least relaxation from their Labours, whereas if the Sunday was allowed them for rest, it would stimulate them to perform their Duties with Cheerfulness, and alacrity and more to the satisfaction of their employers'; that the 'Strict observance of the Sabbath wholly as a Day of Rest would no doubt in a Moral Point of View be attended with many beneficial results'; and also because 'such unintermitting application to business not only merits a higher remuneration than they have hitherto received but that no remuneration can compensate them for the physical injuries to which it will ultimately lead'.[1] The motives were mixed; they also compared themselves with the Metropolitan Police who did not 'sacrifice one Sunday in ten'.[1] On the Liverpool & Manchester at the same time some sort of special arrangements were made to enable enginemen and guards to spend Sundays with their families. In the 1850s Sunday duties on the Manchester, Sheffield & Lincolnshire were distinguished from week day duties by the fact that the working and overall hours of the guards on duty were much shorter. They were allowed some Sundays off, ranging from one in four to one in thirteen. Clerks had an easier time when the Saturday half day appeared. The Early Closing Associ-

---

1. London & Birmingham. Memorials to the Directors, 1838.

ation evinced from the London & North Western in 1856 a statement that at Manchester business finished at 1.0 p.m, in London over one hundred clerks finished work at 1.0 p.m, and at Birmingham 'we are reducing Saturday work very materially'.

Extra pay for Sunday work was practically unheard of except for the platelayers and labourers on the Newcastle & Carlisle in 1841 who were paid 2s to 'oversee' the line and the checkers on the Great Western in 1871 who were paid for Sundays at the rate of a ten hour day. In the same year guards on the Midland demanded that eight hours should be a day's work for Sundays but they had to be contented with a six day week of sixty hours. Other grades, however, on that line and on the Great Northern still had a seven day week of seventy-seven hours.

The position in the early 1870s was that some grades had the six day week and some did not. In 1873 guards, porters and shunters in the goods department of the Great Western had both a six day week and a seven day week with Sunday pay, whereas in the passenger department they had a seven day week without Sunday pay. Six years later seven days was still a week's work for signalmen, with relief being provided when possible. Thus the six day week was only partly secured. No doubt it still depended on the extent to which particular kinds of work had to be carried out on Sundays.

Chapter 7

HOUSING

The provision of houses for railway labour has always been a peculiar feature. The provision of a home as a condition of the job and often as part of wages, has been, to some extent, a bond with the companies, and an aid to loyalty. Broadly speaking, the housing was of two kinds: provision for those of the main scattered body of men who had to live near their work, and provision of large collections of houses for concentrated bodies of men at the locomotive and carriage depots and workshops in the railway towns, such as Swindon.

The origin of company housing was in the early period of railway construction. Dwelling houses were built for the enginemen of the stationary engines on the Stockton & Darlington. Contracts for two of them were accepted at a cost of £210 4s 9d. Houses at the weighing machines were also ordered. Cottages were leased from Stockton Corporation until houses could be built by the company. All this took place before the railway was actually opened while well before the Select Committee on Railway Labour of 1846 recommended that housing for navvies be provided companies such as the Sheffield & Manchester and the Manchester, Sheffield & Lincolnshire built cottages for the workmen, foremen and overlookers building the lines, in order to keep the men together. The cottages were let to the contractors and the rents were deducted from the monthly payments to them.

The necessity of providing houses was recognised by the companies from the beginning. By 1841 on the Newcastle & Carlisle, a line of sixty miles, thirty-five men, most of whom were station masters, were living in company's houses. On the Great Northern cottages were built for platelayers because of the difficulty of obtaining lodgings.

The motives were mainly economic and considerations of profit and loss were always present. It was thought that the return on the capital invested would be adequate. Disused property could be, and was, adapted and made habitable. It was a cheap way of securing attendance at level crossing gates; on the Eastern Counties and the London & South Western the wives of platelayers opened the gates in return for the use of a cottage. On the Manchester, Sheffield & Lincolnshire the shortage of accommodation affected recruitment and necessitated a search for single men and the removal of married men. Security of railway property was another reason for building porters' and workmen's cottages at or near stations.

No doubt, however, the companies were well aware of the other, moral, advantages suggested in a plan proposed by the *Railway Times* in 1840. It advocated, for the large concentrations of men, a system of large dwellings complete with public kitchen, hot water, gas, schoolroom, public eating and reading rooms; for the men scattered over the country, cottages with gardens. These would be a means of rewarding conduct and the result would be not only recruitment of the best class of worker but also 'a kind of local militia devoted to peace and order and opposed to the Chartists in the realisation that their own welfare depended on the security of railway property'.[1] The London & North Western chairman had the same idea in 1857, when proposing a vote of money for houses: 'Expenditure has been long postponed, it is now absolutely necessary to provide against demoralisation amongst servants which has taken place from the wretched and inferior class of lodgings which has brought them into contact with bad characters'.[2] The corollary of this was that if a man persisted in being demoralised he would not be housed by the company. In 1871 the London & North Western drivers realised this to their cost. Those who went on strike and lived in the company's houses at Camden Town were evicted.

The houses came, before long, to be regarded as customary and almost a right or condition of service. Part of the general provisions for staff made on the opening of a section of the Great Northern was that 'clerks in charge, station masters and gatekeepers have, in addition to their salary, Lodgings'. At the same time a list was made of men required and to whom 'Lodging was usually supplied by railway companies'. A little later the idea of entitlement appeared. On the Great Northern lodging allowances on a regular scale were given in lieu of the lodgings to which the men were 'entitled by the rules of the service'. A station master on the London, Brighton & South Coast was even given compensation for the loss of his garden when it was required by the company.

The grades of men whose standard of living was affected, to greater or less extent, by the provision of housing were quite numerous. Station masters, agents, and clerks in charge were the most important group. For instance in 1841 on the Newcastle & Carlisle only three out of twenty-two were not so provided. This proportion

---

1. *Railway Times*, 11 April 1840.
2. London & North Western Railway. Report of Half Yearly Meeting. 1857.

was not maintained at quite such a high level during the following decades. In 1871 on the London, Brighton & South Coast 27 per cent of station masters were housed by the company and by 1890 only 44 per cent of the stations on the Great Western had station masters' houses. Next, houses for gatekeepers, men or women, whether whole or part time, were very common. The Stockton & Darlington began it by ordering a gatehouse at Stockton Lane. Signalmen were in the same class from this point of view and on the opening of part of the Great Northern in 1848 houses were to be found for thirty 'gatekeepers or signals' out of a total new staff of one hundred and twenty-five. Inspectors, foremen, pointsmen, switchmen, policemen, porters, guards, ticket collectors, platelayers were all at some time and to different extents provided with houses as part of their remuneration. In addition there were the enginemen and mechanics at the depots. Though many grades were affected the proportion of them was small, except for station masters. For instance in 1861 only some 10 per cent of the traffic grades on the London, Brighton & South Coast were paying house rent to the company. These men would be the great majority of those for whom houses were provided.

The next point to consider is the relation between housing and wages. The practice as to whether rent was paid, and if so whether it was an economic rent or a nominal one, whether it was not paid but the value of the housing considered as part of wages, varied from company to company and from time to time. In any case the number of grades which had houses is sufficient to require that any consideration of wages must include reference to the value of housing provided. The general tendency during the period was from non-payment of rent to payment, i.e. from a net wage plus a house or rent allowance in lieu, to an inclusive wage from which rent was paid, or which included an element of rent.

There are four aspects of the relation between housing and wages: rent-free housing; payment of housing allowances by the companies; payment of rent by the companies; payment of rent by the men. Rent free housing occurred mainly in the 1840s. On the Newcastle & Carlisle in 1841 a complete list of staff of five hundred and fifty-six shows that of those receiving housing, numbering thirty-five, not one paid rent. On the London & South Western station agents' salaries were described as 'with no deduction for house rent'; the only payment of a rent (of £10) was to be absorbed at the next salary increase. Clerks, gatemen, wives of platelayers were all mentioned as being 'house free' on the London, Brighton & South Coast, London & South Western and South Eastern. But elsewhere, as on the

London & North Western in 1848, the policy was that all persons should pay rent.

Nearly all the allowances in lieu of housing occurred in the forties. On the London & South Western there was a regular scale of allowances for clerks in charge of stations; at chief stations it was £20 per annum, at others, £15. Those who were removed to a station without a house received an allowance in lieu. On the Newcastle & Carlisle a station master's salary of £94 included £10 in lieu of a house. On the London & South Western a station master on a salary of £100 received not only ten shillings per week allowance but also compensation for the crops at his previous station. On the London & North Western, London & South Western and South Eastern increases of salary were given in lieu of lodging. On the Eastern Counties a station master receiving a rent allowance was in future to have rent included in his salary.

Table XLII
Rent and Wages of Traffic Grades 1861, London, Brighton & South Coast[1]

Grade	Number paying rent	Average rent per week s d	Average Wage per week of those paying rent s d	Proportion of Rent to wages %
Station Master	38	4 3	32 11	13
Inspector	2	2 6	30 0	8
Foreman	4	3 6	31 6	11
Clerk	3	2 0	25 4	8
Guard	23	2 10	25 9	11
Tkt. Collr.	6	4 8	21 8	22
Switchman	10	3 4	21 0	16
Signalman	21	2 11	20 7	14
Tunnelman	3	2 4	20 4	11
Porter	30	2 10	18 10	15
Gatekeeper	2	2 3	18 6	12
Carter	4	1 10	18 3	10
Watchman	3	2 0	16 4	12
Labourer	1	2 6	14 0	18
Horse keeper	1	4 0	35 0	11
Total	151	3 3	24 7	13

1. London, Brighton & South Coast, Staff Book, 1861.

Payment of rent by the company was very exceptional and only isolated cases occurred. The change towards payment of rent by servants began in the forties where there were isolated examples of rent payments on most lines. These instances include some station clerks on the London, Brighton & South Coast who paid £10 per annum. By the sixties, however, the payment of rent had become more general. The regulation on the Great Western in 1869 was that rent was to be charged to all servants in company's houses. A complete list of staff in the London, Brighton & South Coast traffic grades in 1861 gives the number of men who paid rent and the wages for each individual. These are given in the above table. It shows that 151 persons were paying rent; this out of an estimated total staff of 1350 represents 11%. The following points may also be made. There were forty-eight station masters altogether. A few may not have been living in company's houses but of those who were, the great majority were paying rent. Most of the gatekeepers however must have been living rent free since there were ninety-seven of them altogether and most would be living in company's houses. Perhaps the most important fact emerging is that there is little, if any, correlation between rent and wages. In fact in the early days on the London & Birmingham, it was decided that rent should be based on the value of the property and on the 'pecuniary need of the class of person for whose use the houses were intended.'[1] Other evidence confirms the trend towards payment of rent. Plate-layers on the Stockton & Darlington in 1863 were paying a rent of 2s. 6d. per week. Considerably later, in 1890, two hundred and forty-six station masters on the Great Western, paid an average rent of 3s. 4d. per week.

Certain conditions for occupation of company's houses were, naturally enough, laid down. The men had to sign agreements to quit at seven days notice. Regulations were made, for cleanliness and repair, and if men did not keep their cottages clean and in proper repair they were liable to be dismissed. The taking of lodgers was another problem. On the Manchester, Sheffield & Lincolnshire no servants renting company's houses were to take lodgers or under-let without the directors' permission, and any such lodgers were to be railway servants themselves. The companies themselves sometimes incurred official displeasure. For instance, in 1851 the Great Northern was fined £50 for having built tenements without previous notice and approval as required by the Hitchin Local Board of

---

1. London & Birmingham Administration Cte., 1838.

Health. The same tenements were, however, subsequently approved without difficulty.

The general character of the housing did not vary much. The great majority of the houses and cottages were new buildings, either built by the companies themselves or by contractors. There were two exceptions. Firstly, when cottages were occasionally bought, as on the Great Northern in 1851 when eleven were bought for £562 10s 0d. Secondly when, more frequently, other buildings were converted and adapted in all kinds of ways. Railway arches were filled up, stables were converted, old houses, old stations, store rooms, tenements, were all adapted at different times. But these were a small part of the total. The emphasis was on cheapness. Cottages were built 'of the same plain cheap character for the police, porters and watchmen' on the Great Northern in 1850 and gatehouses were ordered as cheaply as possible. When possible old materials were used. If contractors were employed, the lowest competitive tender was usually accepted. The window tax also had some effect. Joseph Cubitt, engineer to the Great Northern, was required to report on the windows at stations which could be dispensed with in order to reduce taxation. By contrast, improvements were quite often carried out; for instance, on the London, Brighton & South Coast, switchmen's houses were improved by the addition of another bedroom and a scullery. Sometimes indeed the expressed wishes of the men for a minimum accommodation were met. A third bedroom was added to cottages as desired by the men on the Grimsby & Sheffield. On the South Eastern an additional room was given to a number of cottages in response to the request of the platelayers. All these were in the forties.

A complete picture of housing on one line, the London, Brighton & South Coast in 1871 is given by the following table.

Table XLIII
Housing on the L.B. & S.C. in 1871

Total number of company's houses occupied by servants (except workshop artisans & gatekeepers)	460
Number rent free	5
Total number employed (excluding above)	4,446
Percentage of servants in company's houses	10.3%

Grade	Proportion housed by company	Average Rent per week		Proportion of Rent to Wages
	%	s.	d.	%
Station master	77	4	9	14
Inspector	17	5	9	12
Foreman	27	5	2	14
Guard	11	4	6	16
Signalman	21	3	8	16
Head Porter	29	3	7	17
Porter	4	3	6	21
Carman	7	3	9	13
Engine Driver	11	4	1	10
Fireman	4	4	5	16
Ganger	26	4	1	16
Labourer	8	3	1	18

Average proportion of rent to wages for all grades   16%

Thus by the end of the period only a small proportion of servants were housed by the company. Signalman was the only large grade in which as many as one fifth had housing. Practically all paid rent. And while the rent was, for most, a moderate proportion of income, there is little evidence to suggest that it was much less than the economic rent. In general, therefore, housing was not any significant addition to the standard of living of the general body of men.

Chapter 8

ADVANCEMENT AND PROMOTION

The prospects of advancement must have an important place in any consideration of the standard of living of the railwaymen. How important, for instance, were they in relation to the contentment of the railwaymen and the fact that there was no permanent trade union until 1871, in an age in which the virtues and the possibilities of individual advancement were constantly emphasised? The following sentiments of a railway chairman were characteristic.[1]

> 'There is an old saying, "God will help those who help themselves" and if you have a hearty good will and try to do your best, and do that honestly, there is no station in life, however high, that is not open to many of you. Many of our greatest men have set out from small beginnings, and if you will only keep in the straight way and let not bad advice swerve you from it, there is no telling how high you may raise yourselves in the scale of society, not only for your own good, but for the comfort and happiness of those about you.'

Further, how important were those prospects in relation to the recruitment and retention of men on the line? That they were relevant is indicated by the remarks of a railway manager.[1]

> 'In agricultural districts indeed where wages were very low, 15s per week as a commencing wage for a porter enabled the Company to obtain, without difficulty, as many men as they required, especially as the chances of promotion afforded to the men a prospect of advancement far beyond what they were likely to attain in agricultural pursuits.'

An attempt to assess the prospects of promotion and what they meant to the railwaymen may go some way to answering these questions.

Prima facie, a rapidly expanding industry would provide good opportunities for at least the more energetic and fortunate men. Employment rose from a few hundred in 1830 to 47,000 in 1847 and 275,000 in 1873. Open mileage extended from about 500 miles

---

1. Manchester, Sheffield & Lincolnshire. Provident Savings Bank, Annual General Meeting, 1861.
2. Great Western Railway, General Manager's Report, 1879.

in 1838 to 13,500 in 1870. The expansion of employment was undoubtedly caused more by the extension of the system than by the spreading of work amongst those employed, at least in this period. It was therefore all the more favourable to the prospects of advancement. However, these prospects probably changed more favourably for some grades than for others. Reference to the statistics of the changes in the relative sizes of groups of men (see chapter 1) suggests that the chance of rising from the unskilled group to the skilled improved. On the other hand the promotion prospects of clerks probably decreased because of the lower proportion of managers. A similar conclusion for the skilled grades may be drawn from the inverse directions of change of them and of the supervisory group.

Official provision for advancement within the grade.

For Porters and for Police generally and throughout the period, wage scales provided for small regular increases after the first and second years of service but not thereafter. Thus in the early 1840s on the Great Western men started on 16s per week and received an increment of 1s per week per annum up to 19s. In the later 1840s on the London & North Western in the first year 18s was paid, in the second 19s and in the third 20s. In 1849, a year of reductions in wages, police in London were provided for as follows: first year 16s, second year 17s, third year 18s, and in the country 1s less for each year. Porters had the same annual increments but 1s lower in each case. In the 1850s, the following scale for porters was made on the L.B. & S.C.:

	1st year per week		2nd year per week		3rd year per week	
	s	d	s	d	s	d
Brighton	15	0	16	6	18	0
Lewes, Hastings, Worthing & Chichester	13	0	15	0	17	0
All other stations south of Reigate	12	0	14	0	16	0

On the Great Western a new but similar scale, introduced owing to the difficulty of getting suitable men at a lower wage, was, first year 15s, second year 16s, third year 17s, in London; 1s less in each case in the country. Two years later the level of the annual increments was raised to: first year 17s, second year 18s, third year 19s, in London; 2s less in each case in the country. In the 1860s junior porters on the London & North Western starting at age fourteen at 7s per week, had increments of 2s per week per annum until they received 15s a week at eighteen. Porters on the Great Western had successive rates of 17s, 18s and 19s in London and two shillings less in the country. Those at Paddington had increments from 19s per week in the first year to 20s in the second and 21s thereafter, but without clothing. In the early 1870s the same system of annual increments continued. Another scale of porters' wage rates was based on a classification of stations. On the Great Northern where there were six classes of station the maximum wage paid at district and first class stations was 21s, at second class stations 20s and at third, fourth and fifth class stations 17s 6d per week.

For signalmen, switchmen, and pointsmen there were similar scales of annual increments as for porters. In addition, towards the end of the period, there was division into classes according to responsibility; promotion went from class to class. In the 1850s switchmen on the Great Western received annual increments of 1s per week for the second and third years, both in London and the country. In the 1860s division into classes appeared. The 'best' signalmen on the L.B. & S.C. were paid 30s per week, a much higher rate than the average. Men were also reduced in class for disciplinary offences. The annual increments also continued in this decade. In the early 1870s switchmen on the Midland were grouped in three classes according to the number of operations performed, with wages ranging from 18s to 25s per week. Telegraph signalmen were also classified with annual increments within the class as follows:

	1st Year per week		2nd Year per week		3rd Year per week	
	s	d	s	d	s	d
1st Class	20	0	21	0	22	0
2nd class	19	0	20	0	21	0
3rd class	18	0	19	0	20	0

For guards, throughout the period there were both systems of annual increments and division into classes as the basis for promotion. This applied to both passenger and goods guards, two groups distinct in work and status.

In the early 1840s passenger guards on the London & South Western were divided into two classes receiving 25s and 30s per week. In the late 1840s on the London & North Western they were in five classes receiving 25s, 27s 6d, 30s, 35s, and 40s per week, according to whether they were under or upper guards and whether they worked local or through trains. In the 1850s the line of promotion on the Great Northern was from mineral guard through second class goods guard, second class passenger guard, first class goods guard to first class passenger guard. In the 1860s passenger guards on the Great Western and the L.B. & S.C. were still in five classes carrying wages of 21s to 40s; goods guards were in four classes. The latter had also the standard second and third year increments within the particular class, and the head guards had an extra increment after eight years' service. Head guards could be, and were, reduced to under guards. In the early 1870s, the division into classes according to whether main line or branch line work was done continued with promotion from the latter to the former. The annual increments for senior guards on the Midland were however slightly extended to the fourth year. Within the class rates the London and country differential also continued. An additional grade of inspector guard on the Midland provided another step in promotion. Although the division into classes was a well marked channel for promotion the system was not always welcomed by the men. A severe restriction on the numbers in the top class could be unfavourable to the general level of wages. In 1874 on the Great Northern guards asked for the different classes to be abolished, although without success.

Brakesmen, originally a separate grade but later merged into that of guard, were similarly classified for promotion. In the 1840s on the Great Western and London & North Western they were in three classes at 25s, 27s 6d, and 30s per week. By the late 1860s they were classified with goods guards. Some other traffic grades also had the annual increments or the possibility of promotion through classes at least by the early 1870s and quite probably before. The shunters on the Great Western and the Great Northern had the second and third year annual increments of 1s each year. They were helped by assistant shunters who had 1s less basic wage. Checkers and capstanmen also had the second and third year increments of 1s.

The development of the enginemen's system of promotion throws a light on the relative advantages to the men of the annual increment method and of the classification method of advancement. From the companies' point of view it was a choice between 'length of servitude' and 'wholesome competition' as the basis of promotion. This was linked to the important issue as to whether promotions should be based on length of service or on merit and ability, which is dealt with later on. There is little doubt, however, that in this case the enginemen preferred the 'unwholesome basis of length of servitude', as they showed unmistakeably in the strike of 1848 on the London & North Western. The main objection of the enginemen to the classification basis was that it gave no security of promotion since the companies could arbitrarily reduce the maximum numbers in the higher classes. This did not apply to the servitude basis which, although limited in scope, was conditional only on good behaviour. Similar considerations would apply to other grades and in fact they are specifically mentioned in relation to the guards.

In the early 1840s on the London & Birmingham the scale gave one wage increment of 3s per day for drivers and 1s 2d per week for firemen. In the late 1840s on the Eastern Counties there was a flat rate with increments after two years' service, of 10d per day for drivers and 6d per day for firemen. On the London & North Western there was a more elaborate method based on service as follows: Drivers - first year 4s 2d per day, second year 5s, third year 6s, fourth year 6s, fifth year 7s, and then 2d per day per annum up to 8s per day; Firemen - first year 2s 8d, second year 3s 2d, third year 4s per day. The company then attempted to introduce classification according to the type of train worked, as follows:

Drivers	Class	Max. Number in class	Wage per day s d
	Special	20	8 0
	First	40	7 6
	Second	30	7 0
	Third	30	6 6
	Fourth	20	5 6

For firemen - 20 men at 4s per day, 30 at 3s 9d, 20 at 3s 6d, 30 at 3s 3d and 20 at 3s. This attempt seems to have arisen in part from some discontent with the promotion prospects afforded by the service system as shown in a memorial from the men which requested, inter alia, a 'higher inducement for good conduct'. The system was however withdrawn as a result of the strike in 1848 of practically all the enginemen affected. The annual increment system still existed in the 1860s. In one agreement between the men and the Great Western in 1867 all drivers had the same increment of 6d per day per annum up to the fourth year, and thereafter another 6d per day after a further three years. Firemen had an increment of 3d per day per annum for the second and third years with another 6d after five years' service.

The general picture is of limited but secure advancement in wages, based primarily on length of service, and also on responsibility but only in so far as it corresponded, as it often did, with length of service and age. One minor modification of this was that in the 1860s shunting drivers were paid 6d per day less than train drivers.

For station masters and station clerks, the determining factor in promotion was the classification of the station according to revenue, traffic or operational activity. Although this gave definite opportunities of promotion from class to class it was not always to the advantage of the men who did not necessarily receive the 'pay of the place'. In one instance in the early 1870s twenty-seven clerks were advanced in salary because they had not been paid up to the class of station for some time.

In the 1840s on the London & North Western stations were

divided into four classes and the station clerks were classified according to their station, viz. first class stations numbering three at £175 per annum, second class numbering eight at £150, third class numbering ten at £125, fourth class numbering sixteen at £100 and those below fourth class at £80. Promotion from one class to another usually involved removal to another station and the prospects may be indicated by the number of stations in each class. On the London & South Western the clerks were divided into five classes and the class to which station clerks belonged depended on their station. In 1851 the stations on the Great Northern were divided into five classes and the rates of pay for the clerks in charge of them were similarly classified at 16s, 21s, 25s, 30s and 40s per week respectively. The possibilities of promotion from one class to the next may be indicated by the fact that there were five first class stations, eight second class, nineteen third class, twelve fourth class and thirteen fifth class. In the 1860s a new scheme of classification of stations and of the station masters or clerks in charge of them was produced on the London & North Western on the principle of 'responsibility as indicated by money receipts and labour and time indicated by the circumstances of the place'. In exceptional circumstances some stations were classified higher than the receipts warranted owing to extra responsibilities such as junction working, or competition with other companies. These stations numbered forty-two out of a total of three hundred. In the early 1870s on the Midland station masters were in eleven classes, their salaries ranging from 20s to 30s per week, with differentials of 1s to 3s per week.

The whole body of clerks, whether directly concerned with traffic or not, was divided into classes from an early date. In the 1840s on the London & North Western they were arranged in six classes ranging from £30 to £300 per annum with intervals of £10 between classes, a system which was subsequently amended to one of eight classes ranging from £60 to £250 with intervals of £10. On the London & South Western they were in five classes ranging from £25 to £200 per annum with intervals of £5 between classes. On the Midland they were in four classes ranging from £25 to £250 per annum without any interval except one of £20 between the third and fourth classes. All three schemes provided for annual increments, conditional on good behaviour, up to the maximum of the class, of amounts ranging from £5 to £10 per annum. It was understood that superior classes were filled from men in the inferior ones. There is little doubt that these promotion schemes were general and were retained. The first of the above three schemes was certainly recognised up to 1857 when it was replaced by a new one. And in the 1860s clerks on the Manchester, Sheffield & Lincolnshire were being granted advances regularly and in considerable numbers for 'increased efficiency and responsibility or attention to duties'.

The apprentice clerks on the London & North Western and the London & South Western had their annual increments of £5 or £10 according to the terms of apprenticeship and were normally promoted to the junior class of clerk at the expiry of their term. This practice began in the 1840s and continued, in some places, until the 1870s. Telegraph clerks were a group apart by reason of their distinct and somewhat new-fangled technique. They were not absorbed into the general clerical classification but they had their annual increments of £5 per annum from age fourteen to twenty-two.

In general therefore there were definite and clearly marked channels of advancement from class to class and by annual increments within classes.

Official Lines of Promotion between Grades

The lines of promotion from grade to grade were quite numerous as might be expected in an expanding occupation. They became quite clearly defined from three sources; the actual promotions made, reductions in grade for disciplinary reasons, and orders issued by the companies. The lines of promotion for each grade separately, the lines of reduction where known, based on some actual movements are given below. The same material from the following companies has been used in all cases, viz. Eastern Counties, Great Northern, Great Western, London & Brighton, London & North Western, London & South Western, London, Brighton & South Coast, Manchester, Sheffield & Lincolnshire, North Eastern, Sheffield & Manchester and South Eastern. The relative importance of each channel of promotion may be judged by its frequency.

Police

Grades to which promoted	Number of Promotions	Period
Switchman, signalman	23	1830s-1850s
Guard	16	1840s-1860s
Clerk	8	1840s 1850s
Ticket Collector	2	1840s
Head Porter	2	1840s
Station master	2	1840s
Porter	2	1840s
Sub-Inspector	1	1840s
Grades from which reduced	**Number**	
Switchman, signalman	11	1840s, 1850s
Gateman	4	1840s

In the early decades the main promotion was to switchman. Most of the switchmen and signalmen came, in fact, from police and police generally were instructed in the duties of signalmen. The distinction between a policeman in charge of a station and a clerk doing the same work was very faint and the uniformed man was not distinguished so clearly from the clerical worker as later on.

Porters

Grades to which promoted	Number of Promotions	Period
Guard	53	1830s-1860s
Clerk	16	1840s-1860s
Switchman, signalman	14	1840s-1860s
Policeman	7	1850s
Head Porter	6	1840s-1850s
Shunter	6	1850s-1860s
Foreman	4	1850s
Loader	3	1850s
Ticket Collector	3	1850s-1860s
Station master	2	1840s-1850s
Watchman	2	1850s-1860s
Carman	2	1850s-1860s
Bankrider	1	1840s
Caller Off	1	1850s
Booking Porter	1	1840s
Lad Porters promoted to Vanguard		1850s

Grades from which reduced	Number	
Guard	13	1840s-1860s
Switchman, signalman	12	1860s
Policeman	5	1840s-1860s
Shunter	4	1850s-1860s
Head Porter	3	1860s
Checker	1	1860s
Carman	1	1860s
Ticket Collector	1	1860s
Foreman	1	1860s
Loader	1	1860s
Caller Off	1	1860s

Porters had a large field of promotion, the most general line being to guard, clerk and signalman. Promotion and reduction correspond closely except in the case of clerks where there is no instance of reduction. A porter could make a useful clerk but not vice versa. In fact many of the clerks' disciplinary offences, were defalcations for which the punishment was usually dismissal. The most common promotion to guard, was through an intermediate grade of porter guard. The London & North Western stated in 1870 that guards 'were in many cases supplied from porters'. Most of these promotions to guard were in fact to the less exalted goods guard. Passenger guards, especially those on the main trains, were a dignified and important grade from which porters were excluded up to 1860 on the Great Western, and even later were only admitted in special circumstances. The promotion to signalman was also sometimes through the intermediate grades of porter signalman and porter pointsman.

This promotion was specifically safeguarded by the London & North Western and the North Eastern in the early 1870s by providing for a minimum differential between the wages of signalmen and porters in order to make the promotion. The outstanding point is perhaps the relative importance of the promotion step to clerk, many of whom were, in the earlier decades, in charge of small stations and thus equal or superior to station masters. Promotion from the wages staff to clerk was still provided for in the regulations of the early 1870s.

Switchmen, signalmen, pointsmen.

Grades to which promoted	Number of Promotions	Period
Guard	5	1840s, 1860s
Head Porter	3	1860s
Clerk	2	1840s, 1860s
Station master	1	1840s
Inspector	1	1860s
Police Sgt.	1	1860s

There were two reductions from guard in the 1860s.

Head Porter

Grades to which promoted	Number of Promotions	Period
Guard	9	1840s-1860s
Station master	4	1840s 1860s
Clerk	2	1850s
Foreman	2	1840s, 1850s
Ticket Collector	1	1840s
Warehouseman	1	1840s

ADVANCEMENT AND PROMOTION

There was one reduction from guard in the 1850s.

Ticket Collector

Grades to which promoted	Number of Promotions	Period
Clerks	10	1840s-1860s
Guard	7	1840s, 1860s
Station master	1	1840s
Foreman	1	1860s
Head Porter	1	1850s

The frequency of promotion to clerk is noteworthy

Guards

Grades to which promoted	Number of Promotions	Period
Station master	9	1840s-1850s
Clerk	9	1840s-1860s
Inspector	5	1840s-1860s
Head Porter	2	1840s-1850s
Foreman	1	1850s
Signalman	1	1850s
Booking Constable	1	1860s

There was one reduction from booking constable; again, the frequency of promotion to station master and clerk may be noted.

For the other grades, the lines of promotion were less frequent and may be more briefly indicated as follows. The promotions for each grade are given in order of importance.

Grade	Grades to which promoted
Clerk	Station master, inspector, foreman
Inspector	Station master, clerk
Foreman	Inspector, clerk
Shunter	Guard, foreman
Gateman	Porter, station master, clerk
Carman	Porter, stableman, watchman
Vanguard	Carman, stableman, clerk
Watchman	Guard, gateman, coal porter
Loader	Foreman

The permanent way men had their own hierarchy rising from labourer to platelayer, ganger, sub-inspector and inspector, with a clear wage differential between each. But the small number of gangers and inspectors in relation to other grades necessarily severely limited the prospects of promotion. Moreover, these men rarely went into traffic or other grades. They kept, or were kept, to themselves. Only occasionally did a platelayer become a gateman or a ganger become a signalman. It was not until the 1870s that a wage differential between platelayer and signalman was fixed on the North Eastern so as to indicate promotion. But this was probably unusual.

The position of the locomotive men was much the same. There were the recognised promotions from cleaner to fireman, driver, foreman and inspector; again, however, promotion stopped at driver for the great majority. They rarely, if ever, transferred outside the locomotive world; the only known exceptions were on account of disability through accident. A fireman on the London, Brighton & South Coast who became station master was the exception to the rule.

In general therefore, there were well defined if limited channels of advancement. Most grades had a definite, though strictly limited, scale of increase within the grade. For many grades, particularly traffic grades, there were also clearly defined lines of promotion to higher grades. The possibilities of inter-grade promotion were greatest for the lower grades Moreover they grew as the division of labour and the number of grades increased. But although a gradual increase in complexity of work might be expected to improve the possibilities within a given grade this was not necessarily so. It could be offset, and in fact probably was, by limitation of numbers in the higher classes in a grade.

Advancement and Promotion in Practice

So far the official channels for advancement have been indicated; firstly within the same grade either by scale increments or by promotion from class to class, secondly by the lines of promotion from grade to grade. It remains to assess the extent of the use of these channels in practice. How far did their existence correspond to the actual prospects of promotion? The following analysis is on the same lines as above showing advancement within the grades as well as promotion between grades, since some men had only one such promotion while others had both. Material is available from two sources to illustrate both means of promotion. From the one source it is possible to make a fairly exact assessment of promotion prospects, from the other it is possible to make only a general statement that a particular kind of promotion existed.

As regards advancement within the same grade some quantitative

ADVANCEMENT AND PROMOTION

indications are given below. Over the period 1856 - 1861 a London, Brighton & South Coast traffic department census shows that station masters, clerks, inspectors and foremen were receiving quite good advances of pay as follows:

Grade	Number	Average advance per annum %	Average Period years
Station masters & station clerks	41	5.4	9
Clerks	24	11.0	10
Inspectors	4	7.0	5
Foremen	3	3.0	6

In 1858 on the Great Northern there were the following scale advances during a period of five months.

Grade	Number	Amount of Advance		Estimated Proportion of Employed %
		s	d	
Clerk	55	1	0	
	6	2	0	
	2	3	0	
	63			22
Foreman	1	1	0	3
Signalman	17	1	0	35
Shunter	7	1	0	
Porter	101	1	0	16
Vanguard	18	1	0	
	2	2	0	
	2	3	0	
	22			
Loader	3	1	0	
Caller Off	3	1	0	
Carman	1	1	0	
	218			

During the same period the clerks also had nineteen inter-class promotions, in addition to the above scale advances. This decisively increases the proportion of clerks receiving advancement. The promotion of clerks in 1868/9 on the Manchester, Sheffield & Lincolnshire for a period of twelve months was as follows:

Advances in accordance with term of apprenticeship	47
Advances for increased efficiency, responsibility etc.	162
Promotions on removal	25
Advances in order to retain in the service	3
Total	237

Here the interval between advances seems to have been quite short. The average interval of twenty-seven cases was seventeen months, and three years was noted as an unusually long interval. In 1870 on the Great Western, clerks' 'special promotions without change of duty', i.e. scale advances, were being paid at the rate of £2,011 per annum to 171 men, an average of £11 17s 7d per annum. Porters' promotions of the same kind were involving expenditure at the rate of £2,819 per annum.

In addition to the above quantitative indications of advancement within different grades there were numerous scattered examples of station masters and clerks, from which a common practice may be inferred. Such advances were frequently made on the London, Brighton & South Coast and London & South Western in the 1840s. In the 1850s a single board meeting on the London, Brighton & South Coast authorised advances to twenty-one clerks; while in the 1860s on the London & South Western there were eighteen promotions to a higher class in a period of four months. It is fairly clear that the policy laid down early on that 'the intention is to reward merit and faithful execution of duty by promoting to vacancies gentlemen already in the company's employ' was generally carried out and it is evident that as regards advancement within the grade the official scales of increments and promotions by classes were not a formality but were in fact operated generally.

The available material regarding promotion between grades makes possible a fairly exact estimate of promotion prospects. The tables on pages 134-137 which are based on actual promotions give a prelimininary indication that the opportunities for men corresponded to the official schemes. A more exact indication is given by the following examples.

The London, Brighton & South Coast traffic department census referred to above shows that the great majority of station masters and station clerks between 1856 and 1861 began as lower paid wages grades:

Origins of Sixty Station Masters & Station Clerks

Original Grade	Number	Average period taken to reach station master years
Porter	18	5
Policeman	14	8
Clerk	12	5
Gatekeeper	5	5
Ticket Collector	3	3
Guard	2	5
Inspector	2	3
Sub-inspector	1	2
Station master or station clerk	3	

These promotions were quite rapid, the average interval between one hundred and thirteen inter-grade promotions being three years eight months. There were some outstanding instances of a rise in the world, for example, from policeman at 20s per week to station master, London Bridge, at £200 per annum in fourteen years; from policeman at 19s per week to station master at New Cross at £150 per annum in nineteen years; from gatekeeper at 15s to inspector at £175 per annum in fifteen years; from policeman at 21s to station master at £130 in fifteen years; in a sample of eighty-seven individuals from this census only four had no advancement and only one was reduced. The average rate of increase in pay for all these cases was 10 per cent per annum over an average period of eleven years.[1]

The following promotions were made for each grade:

Porters

Promoted to	Number	Average wait for promotion. Years
Station Master or Station Clerk	10	4
Guard	4	2½
Ticket Collector	3	6
Head Porter	3	2
Clerk	3	1
Switchman	2	3

---

1. London, Brighton & South Coast, Traffic Dept. Census 1861.

Promotion to:	Number	Average wait for Promotion years
Policemen to:		
Station Master or Station Clerk	6	5
Guard	4	3
Clerk	2	2
Switchman	1	3
Head Porter	1	1
Sub-Inspector	1	2
Head Porters to:		
Guard	3	1
Foreman	2	6
Station Master or Station Clerk	2	4
Ticket Collector	1	1
Clerk	1	3
Ticket Collectors to:		
Station master or station clerk	5	3
Clerk	1	2
Head Porter	1	2
Gatekeepers to:		
Porter	3	1
Station master or station clerk	2	2
Inspector	1	7
Switchmen to:		
Station master or station clerk	2	7
Guard	1	2
Clerks to:		
Station master or station clerk	13	3
Foreman	1	3

Promotion:	Number:	Average Wait for Promotion
Inspectors to:		
Station master	4	2½
Sub-Inspectors to:		
Station master	1	2
Inspector	1	1
Foremen to:		
Inspector	1	4

On the Great Northern in 1858 the following inter-grade promotions were made during a period of six months.

Grade	Number Promoted	Estimated Proportion of total Employed
Porter	39 }	
Head Porter	6 }	6½%
Shunter	3 }	
Policeman	8	7%
Signalman, Carman, Foreman, Loader, Caller Off, Clerk (one each)	6	
Total	62	

On the London, Brighton & South Coast in 1861 the following inter-grade promotions were made during a period of twelve months.

Grade	Number Promoted	Estimated Proportion of total Employed
Porter	40	8%
Ticket Collector	7	12%
Carman	7	-
Guard	5	3%
Switchman	2	1%
Signalman, Clerk, Head Porter, Vanguard, Shunter, Watchman	6	
Total	67	

As well as the above experience on particular lines there is evidence of inter grade promotions occurring frequently throughout the country at this period. Much the same pattern emerges of policemen becoming guards, switchmen and ticket collectors; porters becoming guards, clerks, switchmen and head porters; head porters becoming station masters; guards becoming station masters, clerks and inspectors; ticket collectors becoming guards, station masters and clerks; switchmen becoming guards.

In conclusion it may be said that there were good, various and real opportunities of promotion for the more energetic or fortunate men, although they could be taken by only a small minority of the total. There was also much more freedom of movement between the manual worker, unskilled as well as skilled, and the clerical and supervisory worker than there was in the twentieth century.

The conditions of advancement were of four kinds: expansion of the railways, mobility or willingness to move from one station to another, discipline or good behaviour whatever that may have meant, and ability or merit. A stimulus was undoubtedly given to promotion by the growth of the railway system. The examples given below all refer to the forties, although opportunities on a similar scale must have arisen in the sixties. On the extension of the Great Western and of the Bristol and Exeter in the early 1840s promotions to new posts were given to guards, porters and clerks. On the opening of the Sheffield & Manchester between Sheffield and Dunsford Bridge in 1845, porters and ticket collectors were promoted; similarly on the extension of the Great Northern from Gainsborough to Doncaster in 1849 there were promotions for station masters, clerks and porters. When the London & South Western opened its Windsor, Farnham and Godalming extensions in 1849 the new posts were filled by promotions of clerks in charge, apprentice clerks and porters. These promotions had, of course, repercussive effects on other grades.

Considering mobility as a condition of promotion, there is no doubt that in many cases the willingness to move his home was a pre-condition of a man's promotion, although this was more true of inter grade promotion than of promotion within the grade. The provision of a house by the companies in many cases made this condition less onerous. Out of one hundred and eighty-five inter grade promotions of traffic grades on the London, Brighton & South Coast between 1856 and 1861, 50 per cent involved removal to another station. Out of sixty-two inter grade promotions on the Great Northern in 1858, twenty-three involved removal. Out of twenty-one promotions in the grade of clerk in the same year on the same line, fourteen meant removal. During 1868/9 on the Manchester, Sheffield & Lincolnshire most of the class promotions of clerks seem to have involved removal. Other scattered evidence shows that mobility was essential to promotion throughout the period. It affected some grades more than others, notably station masters and clerks.

The other two conditions of promotion were linked, good discipline and ability. They were not always distinct since both might be covered by the words 'attention to duty'. In the 1840s the scale advances of clerks on the Midland and the London & South Western depended on their conduct being to the 'satisfaction of the Board', whatever that might mean. Discussion did in fact arise as to the meaning of the phrase and, as we have seen, a lengthy controversy continued throughout the period as to whether the emphasis in promotion should be on merit or length of service. In 1840 on the London & Birmingham the two qualifications were bracketed for purposes of advancement. But in 1848 and again in 1861 it was found necessary on the London & North Western to emphasise that scale increments up to the class maxima should depend 'rather upon ability and good conduct than on mere length of servitude without especial merit'. Merit was to be rewarded with scale increments; extraordinary merit, by promotion to the next class. In the late 1860s one hundred and sixty-two advances to clerks on the Manchester, Sheffield & Lincolnshire were all ostensibly for 'increased efficiency, responsibility and attention to duties'.

There were evidently repeated attempts by the companies to resist the danger of the promotion system becoming stereotyped. They tried to prevent a situation in which the pay, to use the words of the Manchester, Sheffield & Lincolnshire in 1868, 'will cease to be measured by the natural relations of supply and demand, and will be raised from time to time upon conventional feelings to a standard more than the market value of the services rendered'. The dispute whether ability or merit and length of service should be the basis for promotion extended to most grades. Recurrent investigations, undertaken in order to secure economy, quite frequently showed examples of men whose pay had been advanced for length of service, without relation to responsibility. In fact, generally speaking, the accumulating weight of the system of scale increments was too great to be shifted by considerations of merit. Any exact definition of the qualifications necessary for promotion to a higher grade was rare. One isolated dictum on the South Eastern in 1842 concerning the early station masters stated that they were to be from 'the better class of applicants, better trained, used to office or general business, better educated' but the subsequent practice could not be said to bear this out. Certificates of competency for signalmen appeared thirty years later when training establishments were set up on the London & North Western.

Control of advancement by good discipline alone was a simpler matter. On the Great Western in the 1850s it was ordered that porters should have their annual increments of pay only if there was 'no blot against them'. This proviso may have worked the other way - the promise to be good resulting in increased pay. There was, for instance, the case of engine driver Hyde on the London & South Western in 1867 who, having been suspended for neglect which damaged his engine, was reinstated following an application in which he undertook not only to obey all the company's rules but also not to belong to any trades union. Eighteen months later he had an increase of threepence per day and three years after this he was twice awarded gratuities for vigilance. Bad discipline or incompetence was often the cause of the reverse of promotion, reduction in grade. Again it is difficult to make a distinction between indiscipline and incompetence since errors in work, which were frequent and often punished by reduction, might have been due to either or both. The shortcomings were in fact pretty equally divided between the two. In the 1840s out of a collection of twenty-five reductions in four large companies, thirteen were for such disciplinary offences as absence without leave, neglect of duty, drunkenness; twelve for such a mark of incompetence as errors in work. In 1858, out of ten cases on the Great Northern, indiscipline and incompetence accounted for five each. In the 1860s out of a collection of forty-one cases in four companies, indiscipline accounted for twenty-three and incompetence for eighteen.

Finally, it is clear that there was continuously some degree of discontent with opportunities for advancement. For instance, the signalmen on the Great Northern in 1874 complained about the limited prospects of promotion. The volume of resignations from the railway service is, however, the best evidence. As has been shown in chapter 3 resignations were common, particularly those of the lower traffic grades and of clerks. All would not be due to discontent but probably most were. In 1869 on the Great Western out of 286 resignations of porters and police, 127 resigned explicitly to find a 'Better Place', 33 were 'dissatisfied', 11 went to take up business and 13 to emigrate, a total of 184 or 64 per cent discontented with their prospects. In the following year the proportion was 63 per cent out of the total resignations of 305. The total resignations of these grades was approximately 12 per cent of the number employed on that line. The resignations of clerks show that 50 per cent were due to discontent with prospects. In all, 7 per cent of the clerks employed resigned.[1]

Although it is not possible to say what proportion of resignations

---

1. Great Western General Manager's Report, 1870.

was due to discontent with prospects in the earlier decades, it may be safe to assume that it was not much less than that indicated above. It is known, however, that the volume of resignations was considerable. In 1856 the secretary of the Euston Friendly Society referred to the 'continual inflow and outflow' of men in the service.[1] In the same decade on the London, Brighton & South Coast 19 per cent of the station masters and station clerks resigned in the course of six years. On the Great Northern in 1858 about 5 per cent of the porters resigned in the course of six months, while in the London, Brighton & South Coast traffic department in the 1860s resignations were coming in at the rate of between 4 per cent and 8 per cent of the men employed. There was a continuous outflow of men discontented with their prospects, particularly in the traffic grades.

In conclusion, although it is not possible to give a precise answer to the question how important advancement and promotion were for the standard of living, there is sufficient evidence to show that there were definite channels of advancement which a minority were able to use successfully, sometimes with marked success. The advancement possible for most was limited, if secure, but there were real opportunities for the more ambitious. To that extent promotion was of considerable importance. Certainly the vast majority of workers who had worked their way up the ladder had started at the bottom. Experience, not apprenticeship or training, was required for promotion.

---

1. Letter from secretary of Euston Friendly Society to George Carr Glyn, 25 June 1856.

Chapter 9

SECURITY

Any assessment of the railwayman's standard of living must also take into account his security, or absence of it. It is a question not only of security of employment, important though that was at a time when insecurity was the general rule, but also of security against the hazards and risks of life and especially those peculiar to railway work. The security of the railwayman's dependants as well as his own must be included. Security in all these senses had also a bearing on the efficiency of labour. Those benevolent directors and shareholders who contributed to provision against the risk of railway employment were not unaware of this. In an appeal on behalf of the Railway Benevolent Institution in 1862 the Duke of Buckingham said: 'All parties, directors, shareholders and the public were interested in being served efficiently in railway management, but they could not be well served by men struggling with difficulties and who because of such difficulties, would be ever on the look out to better themselves in other employment.' On a similar occasion, four years later, the President of the Board of Trade, Milner Gibson, said: 'No doubt railway companies are primarily interested in the servants of the railway companies being satisfied with their conditions and not being constantly in a restless condition thinking they will leave their employment and look for something better.[1]

Security of Employment

So far the general assumption has been that employment was permanent and secure, conditional only on good behaviour; but how much is this supported by evidence? Some inherent permanence of employment may be inferred from two factors, the requirements of railway operation, and the various aspects of managerial labour policy. The nature of railway operation made it difficult to regulate the amount of labour employed in accordance with fluctuations in trade and traffic. The necessity of maintaining service meant that comparatively few grades could be dispensed with in times of bad trade, although this applied less to porters and clerks, particularly supernumeraries, who could be laid off more easily. There was a relative rigidity of employment which successive committees of

---

1. Railway Benevolent Institution Annual Dinner. Reports of Proceedings 1862, 1866.

enquiry tried to combat, without much success. Broadly speaking, therefore, any reductions in labour costs to keep in step with reductions in traffic were more often obtained in other ways. Moreover, taking into account the difficulty sometimes experienced in obtaining, not general labour, but really suitable and reliable labour, there was some reluctance to lose the more skilled and reliable men.

An assumption of permanence of employment is also clearly indicated by many aspects of labour policy. Increments were normally based on length of service. The promotion and maintenance by subsidy of friendly societies and of educational and religious facilities and the provision of houses were all part of that general assumption. Furthermore the form of application for employment required extensive information for future reference. The applicant on the London & Birmingham had to state whether he was married, widower or single, with or without family, the names of previous employers and length of service with them or whether in business on his own account, whether he had been abroad and if so, when and where. Applicants on the London & North Western frequently submitted elaborate lists of referees. One who applied for work as a policeman in 1862 appended the names and occupations of nineteen citizens ranging from the mayor of Coventry to a humble grocer. Another, applying for a porter's post, gave eleven referees.

The terms of employment laid down by the companies also have a bearing on this point. In general, the longer the notice of termination of employment required, the stronger the assumption of permanence. Such regulations varied considerably. On the Edinburgh & Glasgow in 1842, there was a scale of notice of termination of employment, nicely graduated according to the grade of labour, viz. superintendents and managers - three months, special agents and clerks - two months, general agents and clerks - one month, guards and enginemen - two weeks, porters and others - one week, such notice to be given by both parties Pay in lieu of notice was also to be given.[1] Compared with this, the Great Western in the 1840s required all grades of employees to give one month's notice without specifying any similar obligation on the part of the company, thus binding the servant without affording him security. On the Sheffield & Manchester, police constables had to give one month's notice. There was the special case of the enginemen on the Liverpool & Manchester in 1837 when the demand for them was temporarily considerably in excess of the supply and it was found necessary to bind them by a written agreement for three months, but this did not last long. By

---

1. Reports to Privy Council. Edinburgh & Glasgow Railway Bye Laws, 1842

the 1860s clerks on the London & North Western and the London, Brighton & South Coast had the benefit of one month's notice from either party and by the 1870s, if not earlier, all other servants were required to give and take one week's notice.

All security of employment was, of course, limited by the condition of good behaviour. The companies invariably and explicitly reserved the right of instant dismissal in case of 'fraud, neglect, disobedience of orders, or any act of insubordination'. It has already been shown in chapter 2 that those words were capable of wide interpretation.

The term, the average railwayman, has been used but a distinction must be made between the permanent employees who were on the authorised establishment and the temporary ones who were supernumeraries. The above remarks on permanence of employment apply, of course, only to the first group. The practice of having an authorised establishment, the maximum approved number to be employed in all grades, existed in the 1840s on the Newcastle & Carlisle.[1] The number and proportion of supernumeraries, the men who were outside the establishment, is not known until 1870 when it was probably in the region of 5 per cent. They included only a few grades, porters, clerks, permanent way men, among whom the two distinct causes of their temporary status, seasonal traffic and the imposition of certain physical standards, were most important. In those few, though large, grades they were, however, in considerable numbers and, differentiated by conditions of employment, came to be regarded as a separate section. In 1860 the Great Western was finding difficulty in maintaining a policy of having a regular establishment of goods porters instead of using a 'considerable supply of supernumeraries'. This seems to have been due to the physical standards required since at the same time the minimum height and the maximum age for entrants were lowered. Five years later orders were given for a 'large number' of supernumerary porters at Paddington to be placed on the establishment. But in 1869 and 1870 supernumeraries were again being employed in considerable numbers, viz. 6 per cent and 14 per cent respectively of all porters and police appointed in those years. In 1870 on the same line there were 385 supernumeraries in all grades of the traffic department out of a total of 7,249. On the Great Northern in 1863 there was an 'anomaly of a large supernumerary staff' among the cartage men, until it was removed by appointments to the establishment. That particular anomaly was removed but there still remained a distinct group of supernumeraries. Among the permanent way men on the London &

---

1. Newcastle & Carlisle Railway. Establishment Book, 1841.

North Western in the same year there was the general practice of recruiting 'extra men' from whom the permanent servants were later selected.

As well as lacking security these men also had inferior conditions of employment. In a dispute in 1871 supernumerary porters received a wage of 2s 8d per day without clothing whereas the permanent men had a scale of 16s to 18s per week with clothing and somewhat shorter hours. However, although the inferior conditions of these men must have exercised some pressure on the conditions of the permanent men, their numbers, though considerable, were confined to a few grades and do not seriously weaken the general assumption of permanence and security for the majority. Nor is it weakened by the companies' attempts to rationalise labour or to reduce the labour force, as shown in chapter 4. The relatively few men who were thus dispensed with were often given a certificate of discharge. However, their prospects of being re-employed by the railways varied considerably from company to company. With some companies the principle was that men, once discharged, were never re-employed, on others they were frequently taken on again. Even in one case, for a short time on the London & North Western, redundant clerks were placed on half pay until they were absorbed.

Supplementary to the general security of employment there is a secondary though important question of security of status or grade. If the railwayman could, in general, be fairly sure of keeping a job, could he be as certain of keeping his particular job? As always the discipline system impinges on this question. It has already been shown that reduction in grade as a disciplinary method was quite common. Insecurity might arise in two other ways - through economy measures, and through the introduction of juvenile labour. It cannot be found that there was much reduction in grade on the first score but juvenile labour was a more serious threat. Certainly more of it seems to have been introduced in the later decades, particularly among clerks and porters, as shown in chapter 4. But although the proportion of clerks under the age of twenty in 1871 was much higher at 30 per cent than for many other occupations, the proportion of all railway servants under this age, at 10 per cent, was lower.

A further indication of security would be given by the actual length of service but no adequate figures are available. On one line, the London, Brighton & South Coast, forty-six station masters had an average length of service of nineteen years, and sixty clerks had an average of eleven years. But these figures include all those who left for whatever reason, whether retirement, dismissal or resignation and it has already been shown in chapter 3 that the average length of service of men who left through the last two causes was quite short. Moreover, probably about 25 per cent of traffic grades left during the first year or two of their service. So far as they go therefore, these figures strengthen the general argument.[1]

In conclusion, the preliminary assumption remains largely unaltered, that security of employment, high as it was compared with conditions of labour in most other occupations, was an important element in the standard of living.

Security against Occupational Risk and Injury

Against the security of employment must be set the risk of death and injury peculiar to that employment, and against that in turn the provision against risk, made by the companies The question is how far security against occupational risk impinged on the standard of living.

The nature and degree of risk has been dealt with in chapter 3. Here it is sufficient to say that risk was peculiarly high among railwaymen. That there were 'numberless cases of misery and distress, often by unavoidable accident, sometimes by want of thrift and care' was the opinion of an experienced railway chief, granted the circumstances of an appeal for charity in which it was delivered.[2] Some security against this state of affairs existed. Various forms of ex gratia compensation such as payment of wages during disability and of medical expenses, donations to dependants, funeral allowances, were available; often companies contributed to hospitals, infirmaries, etc., and so compounded for any implied responsibility for individual misfortune; and provident societies and accident funds existed which were subsided by the companies.

All payments of compensation made by the companies were essentially benevolent; there was no question of any right to compensation either formulated by the men or admitted by the companies. The view in 1870 was that 'servants voluntarily undertook dangerous employment, servants injured on duty were treated as cases for charity, they had no legal claim'.[3] Similarly in 1854 it was stated that 'The directors have never held themselves liable to make compensation to their servants in cases of sickness or accident. Frequent appeals in such cases have been made to their liberality or

---

1. London, Brighton & South Coast. Traffic Department Salary Staff Book, 1864 - 1893.
2. Railway Benevolent Institution. Speech of Sir Daniel Gooch, 1872.
3. Report of S.C. on Railway Companies. Law of Compensation, 1870. Evidence of Capt. W. O'Brien.

compassion and they have been accustomed to yield to kind feeling what they might have refused to strict legal obligation.'[1] But some kind of responsibility was implied from the beginning. In 1840 the chairman of the London & Birmingham said that 'from the nature of the employment of many of these individuals the directors have deemed it proper to advance a small sum to compensate, *so to speak*, for that additional risk.'[2] The effect in practice of a compromise between these positions is shown below.

Firstly, as regards temporary disability from injury on duty, some companies seem to have begun about 1850 to pay wages, fully or in part, during absence. Other companies limited themselves to a gratuity in case of special distress. On some lines payment was linked to membership of the company's sick fund. Thus on the Great Northern it was usual to pay the difference between the company's provident society benefit and full wages. Forty-one such cases in 1868 refer to porters, guards, shunters, signalmen, foremen and inspectors; the duration of payment ranged from eight days to eight months and the amounts from 4s to 26s 8d per week. This was the practice after 1858 and probably before. Payment was also made to men who had not yet qualified as members of the society, and it was then for an amount equal to the difference between what they would have received as society members and their ordinary wages. On the Great Western the same practice was followed in some cases. It should be noted that in both these cases membership of the societies was compulsory for employees. Where there was no compulsory society half wages were paid by some companies as a matter of course. In quite exceptional circumstances such as meritorious service or extreme distress full wages might be paid. By the early 1870s the enginemen, the aristocrats of railway labour, were receiving half pay and 'Accident Pay' had become a recognised expense for all traffic grades. On the London & North Western in a twelve month period during 1865-66 ninety-three men of all traffic grades received accident pay for periods ranging between two weeks and nine months and this practice was continued throughout the sixties. Even so, the total paid out for all grades on that line in 1869 was only £1,023 7s 4d, a modest sum considered in relation to a staff of forty thousand. Such payments were quite often conditional, sometimes on discipline, sometimes on self help. Thus on the Great Northern in the 1850s a man might receive only part of the difference between friendly society benefit and wages if his injury was caused by a breach of the regulations. On the London, Brighton & South Coast

---

1. London & North Western. Casualty Fund Cte., 1854.
2. London & Birmingham. Report of Annual Meeting, 1840.

he might be, and was, refused assistance if, by omitting to join one of the company's funds, he encouraged a 'want of providence'; alternatively he was granted an allowance provided he joined such fund. A circular of 1854 stated that 'It is proper to remind you that the directors cannot entertain an application for assistance from persons who have neglected to make so easy and requisite a provision'.[1] This was one way of ensuring that men paid part of their own compensation.

As regards permanent disability from injury, the most usual way of discharging responsibility was a small lump sum The early method of financing it was by using the fines for disciplinary offences. The loss of a leg, a fairly common injury, was thus provided for, although it is fair to add that it was sometimes made good by a cork one. Edward Bell of the Stockton & Darlington, who had lost a leg in an accident in 1836, was supplied with a wooden one. When, after two year's service it became almost useless, the committee resolved: 'Agreed, to allow Edward Bell 20s out of the fine box towards the expenses of a new wooden leg'. In the 1830s on the Stockton & Darlington and in the 1840s on the Eastern Counties and the London & South Western the standard payment for the loss of a limb was £2. By the 1850s on those lines and the Great Northern the tariff had risen from £3 to £5, and by the 1860s on the Great Western and London, Brighton & South Coast, amounts ranged between £5 and £20. These sums varied, to some extent, according to grade: porters received £5 to £10, guards received perhaps £20. A guard's leg was evidently worth more than a porter's. In 1863, on the London & North Western, the 'practice of donations in case of serious or fatal accident' was ordered to continue but by 1870 donations had reached only the modest total of £660 per annum on that line. The law rarely entered into this but in those very few cases in which legal action was possible and those still fewer cases in which the injured man had legal advice, the man gained handsomely. Two such cases on the Great Eastern and Great Northern in 1867 and 1868 were settled for £250 and £245.

If the man was not completely disabled he was frequently found less active work. 'If the man is fit we try to keep him in the service.[2] But it was generally at a lower wage and with inferior status; it might be necessary for the Poor Law authority to solicit such action as on the Eastern Counties in 1845. The men often became gatemen or watchmen. For men who were completely disabled there was no general provision beyond the small lump sum, although a few

---

1. London, Brighton & South Coast. Traffic Department Circular.
2. Report of S.C. on Railways, 1870. Evidence of Captain O'Brien.

companies had benevolent funds from which pensions were given, in limited numbers. The London, Brighton & South Coast Benevolent Fund, established in 1851 for this and other purposes, gave pensions of one third wages. But the number given was very small; there are only four recorded in the twelve years between 1854 and 1866. Moreover they were to some extent conditional on the recipients supporting the companies' societies.

A further provision for permanent disability was the payment of medical expenses or free attendance by the companies' doctors. Sometimes surgeons' fees, of about £5, were paid, sometimes an artificial limb or a truss were supplied, as on the Great Western and Great Eastern. This practice started early, on the Stockton & Darlington. For the years 1870 - 1875 the average expenditure per annum on medical expenses on the London & North Western was £590, a modest sum. How far these payments extended to all men incapacitated it is not possible to say. It may however be inferred from the returns of servants injured that by no means all men had even this degree of compensation.

These various methods of discharging responsibility for men seriously injured were not necessarily alternatives, a man might receive a little compensation from each of them. Thus one labourer on the Great Northern in 1850 who lost his arm on duty was paid 10s per week for nine weeks, had a donation of three guineas, payment of surgeon's fee of seven guineas, and was re-employed as gateman at a lower rate of wages.

The dependants of men who met their death in accidents received some consideration. The practice of making donations became more or less standardised and in 1870 it was officially stated that 'the rule of the Company is to grant widows and children £10'.[1] In fact the actual amount was most often £10 although practice was not always the same and £5 was quite common. It varied between £3 and £25 and did not noticeably increase. The amount of donation seems to have depended on three factors - the man's grade, his dependants, and his responsibility for his own death as viewed by the companies. The higher amounts usually went to the senior grades and sometimes to widows with large families. On the other hand noticeably smaller amounts were given for men who were alleged to have lost their lives by breaking regulations or carelessness. In most cases which were brought to light a donation was made.

The custom of paying the funeral expenses of the men killed at

---

1. Report of S.C. on Railways, 1870. Appendix 2.

work was also widespread and continuous from the beginning. The amount granted was most usually £5 to cover expenses but when the exact cost was reimbursed it was rather more than less than that amount. A limit to the desire for respectable burial had to be set and one company made the maximum £5 after it had received a bill for seven guineas for burying a platelayer. More might be spent on superior grades, as in the case of the London Bridge station master for whom £30 was granted. It is probable that only a minority of cases were covered by these grants, certainly less than for men permanently disabled. The total of 'Funeral Expenses' on the London & North Western in 1863 was £75, in 1869 it was only £34, but the return of men killed on duty for 1877 gives one hundred and one on that line. The actual number killed ten years or so earlier would not be much less, and on the basis of £5 per burial it is clear that only a small minority of funeral expenses were paid for. And probably the grant did not fully cover the expenses. In one case on the Eastern Counties in 1850, in reply to an application for £10 the company at first offered £7 and only under the threat of legal proceedings settled for the full amount. Very occasionally a small pension for a few weeks was paid to dependants. Employment of the orphans, or occasionally of the widows, was also a principle of the companies, though only a few examples are to be found. Occasionally other minor forms of compensation are met. The bereaved son might have his wages increased or might be given a house rent free on condition that he supported the family, as on the London, Brighton & South Coast and the Midland in the forties.

The companies' practice of making annual contributions to hospitals and infirmaries may be regarded as a way of compounding for responsibility for individual injury. Although part of the motive was a feeling of obligation to the hospitals, part was the desire to obtain prompt treatment for the injured, and this can be regarded as giving a kind of supplementary compensation to the men. The subscriptions to hospitals were made in consideration of the large number of railway cases they received and were an acknowledgement of an important service rendered by them to the companies. In this way the companies had beds at their disposal. By 1872 the London & North Western was making contributions to forty-seven hospitals, infirmaries and dispensaries, totalling £443 per annum, in amounts ranging between three and twenty guineas.

A third and important form of security against occupational risk was the companies' friendly and insurance societies. They were complementary to the gratuitous donations and in fact provided for the companies a means of avoiding them. Their raison d'etre was that they provided the companies with 'a relief from the burden of maintaining servants disqualified by age or accident, or contributing to the support of families of persons killed in their service'.[1] Most of the big companies and some of the smaller ones promoted these societies. The first, the Great Western Railway Provident Society, was established in 1838; by 1850 there were about a dozen, and by 1870 there were at least fifty. A list, complete as far as can be ascertained, of those existing in 1871 is given in Appendix 1. There was considerable variety of benefits, contributions, membership and finance. Two peculiar features which were noted and strongly criticised by the Royal Commission on Friendly Societies of 1874, i.e. subsidies by the companies and compulsory membership, are dealt with later. The societies fall into four groups: friendly societies, insurance funds, widows' and orphans' societies, and superannuation funds.

Temporary disability was looked after by both friendly societies and insurance funds. A distinction was made between accident sick benefit and ordinary sick benefit. The friendly society provision against accidental injury was of two kinds. Firstly, in most societies, it was identical with ordinary sick benefit. This was of course a considerable burden on the financing of ordinary sick benefit; these societies found their funds threatened by the accident risk. Secondly, other societies had a separate and usually higher rate of benefit for accident disability as compared with sickness disability. In the Midland Railway Friendly Society the full accident benefit was 15s whereas the ordinary sick benefit was only 12s per week.[2] Insurance funds existed solely for the provision of accident benefit, and were limited to a few companies. In 1871 there were apparently only four, on the London & North Western, Lancashire & Yorkshire, London, Brighton & South Coast and North British railways. They were either an alternative to the friendly society or a means of separating the accident risk. Thus on three of the four above-mentioned railways there was no friendly society. Benefits from these funds ranged from 5s to 20s per week. Contributions were lower than those of the friendly societies but they were all subsidised by the companies.

There was much less provision for permanent disability. Only six societies or funds made any such provision in 1871, the Great Western Provident, London & North Western Insurance, Lancashire & Yorkshire Insurance, North British Insurance, North Eastern Provident, and North Eastern Permanent Way and Provident. Only one of these, the Great Western Provident, gave a weekly pension and it ranged between 4s and 10s per week. The rest gave lump sums ranging from £15 to £50.

---

1. Railway Clearing House Provisional Cte. Report, 1850.
2. W.T.H., *History of the Midland Railway Friendly Society*, 1928.

Death from accident was met by nearly all the friendly societies with a lump sum ranging from £2 to £25, and by all the insurance funds with a larger sum ranging from £35 to £100. A few societies had the differential rate between accident death allowance and ordinary death allowance of which the accidental was the higher, e.g. the Midland Friendly Society paid £25 and £12 respectively. Widows and orphans were rarely themselves provided for. The only notable examples were the Great Western Railway Enginemen's and Firemen's Mutual Assurance Society (Widows - 4s to 6s 6d per week), the Great Western Railway Provident Society (Widows - 4s, orphans - 1s and 6d per week), and the London & South Western Widows' and Orphans' Friendly Society (Widows - 2s to 10s per week).

The inadequacy of the security against accident provided by either of the two methods of gratuitous donations or subsidised friendly societies is illustrated by the work of the Railway Benevolent Institution, established in 1858, and particularly that of its Casualty Fund established in 1864. The Casualty Fund was set up in order to reduce the hardship of men injured at work, and of dependants of men killed. Its secondary purpose was to put a central organisation in place of the many and scattered collections from the public which it was the custom to make at the stations. Like the Institution itself it depended partly on members' subscriptions, partly, and to a much greater extent, on charity. It was a 'Provident Institution aided by benevolence'. The usual method of gaining subscriptions was to take an annual collection from railwaymen. Contributions of 1s and upwards gave entitlement to some benefit but the maximum in any one year was only £5. The need for such a fund is shown by the rapid increase in the number of men subscribing which rose from 9,000 in 1866 to 49,270 in 1876, and in the number of cases relieved which rose from 60 to 1,578 in the same period, or one in thirty of the subscribing members. The companies' support was lukewarm and slow in developing and in 1871 the general manager of the Midland complained that 'a great number of directors and officers' were still not supporting the fund. This was somewhat natural in view of the implied criticism conveyed by the Fund, of the companies' own provision for hardship.[1]

Security against sickness, natural death and old age

The liability to sickness is dealt with in chapter 3 where it is shown that it was a heavy one for railwaymen. As with accident risk,

---

1. W.F. Mills, *History of the Railway Benevolent Institution*, 1903; W.F. Mills, *The Railway Service*, 1867; Rly. Benevolent Instn. Annual Reports, 1858-1877; *Railway Times*, 10 May 1871.

the companies' provision for sickness was in two complementary forms - gratuitous allowances and the friendly societies. A distinction must be made, however, between the ordinary run of manual workers and the clerks and station masters.

As regards the manual workers, gratuitous sick allowances were unusual. 'No work, no pay' was the rule. Exceptions were rare, occasionally made for a man with unusually long service or for special supervisory grades. In a few cases also the company paid the differences between companies' friendly society benefit and wages. But the total amount paid by the L.N.W. in 1860 was only £620 and in 1856 the number of men thus paid was only seventy-five of whom the great majority were paid for less than three days. On this trifling scale the actual rate of payment was usually half wages. Thus the main form of provision was the friendly societies organised and often subsidised by the companies. The connection between the two forms of provision was close. The company's subsidy to the London & North Western society, which was 12s per week per sick person for the first two weeks, was the same amount as the sick pay made to the society members, and when the company withdrew its support from the society it also stopped all gratuitous sick pay to other men outside the society. The list of societies (see Appendix 1) shows great variety of sick benefit. The full benefit, which usually lasted for twenty-six weeks, to be followed by half benefit, ranged between 2s and 20s per week.

Provision against natural death was on similar lines, gratuities to dependants were rare, being made, if at all, from companies' benevolent funds and usually amounting to not more than £5 or £10. The friendly society benefits included, for the most part, a small death benefit, but it was rarely more than 'funeral money', ranging from £2 to £20. A notable exception was the Great Western Railway Enginemen and Firemen's Mutual Assurance Society which gave £60 or £100 according to class of membership, for death or permanent disability, and 4s or 6s 6d per week to widows.

For old age and retirement the provision was far more meagre but did exist for a small number. Gratuitous provision was almost nonexistent. An exception was the L.B. & S.C. Benevolent Fund, established in 1851 and entirely financed by the company, which gave pensions of one third wages to 'deserving men' who qualified by length of service and excellence of character. They were refused to men who started at a late age and could not qualify by service. But its restricted scope is shown by the fact that in 1871 there were only twenty-three men receiving such pensions. Only a few societies provided for old age pensions; the Great Western Railway enginemen had 7s 6d or 12s 6d per week, the London & South Western traffic grades had half of sick benefit, and the London, Brighton & South Coast traffic grades had from 9d to 12s 6d per week. In these cases practically all men were members. The small London & North Western society provided 5s per week pension but to only a small number and it ceased to be a company's society in 1863. But an exceptional example of liberal provision was the North Eastern (Darlington Section) Superannuation Society which provided pensions based on a percentage of the average wage, for manual as well as for clerical workers, and generous provision for the return of contributions to leaving members.

For clerks and station masters, the provision was quite different. They were much less often members of sick or burial societies, their term of engagement were longer and consequently they usually had sick pay from the companies. In 1868 the official policy of at least eight big companies was to give full salary for periods up to one month, followed by reduced pay for longer periods. This is confirmed by decisions made in individual cases and in fact full salary was quite often given for longer periods up to three months. This went back, at least in some companies, to the 1850s, though probably not beyond. For death there was little provision. Occasionally a gratuity would be given to a station master's or a clerk's family but unless the general friendly society included such men they were left to their own devices to effect life assurance. The evidence suggests that where they had the opportunity to belong to a railway society they took advantage of it. Of seventy-five station masters and clerks on the London, Brighton & South Coast in 1856, 68 per cent belonged to the company's provident society. Old age and retirement were, by 1870, better provided for through the superannuation funds. By that date there were already four of them, i.e. on the London & North Western, London & South Western, Great Western and Midland, established in 1853, 1864, 1865, and 1870 respectively. All, except the London & South Western fund, gave a pension at age sixty based on a percentage of average salary, which increased with years of contribution, and a lump sum to dependants if the member died before superannuation age. Superannuation might take place after ten years' contribution if there was disability through sickness. Contributions were 2½ per cent of salary, the companies' subsidy being an amount equal to the members' contributions. The London & South Western fund was in the form of a deferred annuity at age sixty. However, the majority of the salaried workers throughout the country were not in these funds and for them there existed only the companies' benevolence and those few friendly societies which both admitted clerks and had pension benefits. The benevolence might result in a pension of one third salary in a few cases or a gratuity of

£20. The societies might give a pension of 12s 6d per week or have special arrangements for life assurance with a commercial assurance company, as on the London, Brighton & South Coast and the Birkenhead railways.[1]

In the case of the clerks also the work of the Railway Benevolent Institution throws a critical light on the foregoing provision. This institution, originally established in 1858 for officials and clerks only, gave small annuities and gratuities to widows and distressed members and provided for the education of orphans. The need for it is indicated by the admission of a railway company's secretary that 'Railway boards are not always ready to support the families of employees', a studied understatement appropriate to a meeting attended by directors. Only one company's superannuation fund existed at that time. Annuities from the Benevolent Institution were on the modest scale of £10 to £25 per annum according to length of membership, but up to 1870 most were £10. Gratuities were £5 or £10. The number of beneficees remained small for some years, limited as it was by the slowness of directors and officials to give support, and by 1871 it included only fifty-eight pensioners, about two hundred recipients of small gratuities awarded during the preceding fourteen years, and twenty-six children put out to school. Yet the applicants for relief were many more than those whom it was financially possible to elect to it and the unsuccessful ones had to wait until another year. In 1867, for instance, a great increase in applications necessitated many claims being postponed. The membership too rose from six hundred to thirty-five thousand in thirteen years. Evidently, in spite of the uncertain nature of the benefits from the institution, the increased membership expressed a strong desire for greater security. Evident too, was a great need for charity to supplement the inadequacy of the companies' provision. This inadequacy was recognised by the institution when it granted annuities to clerks who already received reduced disability pensions from the companies' funds, and annuities to manual workers who already had a small pension from a company's friendly society. It may be inferred that the needs of the greater number who belonged to no fund or society were even greater.[2]

What was the general effect of security against injury, sickness death and old age? Nothing has so far been said about the proportion of men affected. This depended on the membership of the friendly and

---

1. London, Brighton & South Coast Provident Society Rules, 1868. Birkenhead Railway Friendly Society Rules, 1860.
2. Railway Benevolent Institution. Annual Reports, 1858-1871. W. F. Mills, *History of the Railway Benevolent Institution*, 1903.

insurance societies and superannuation schemes, and the extent of the companies' benevolence. The role of benevolence was to make good, to some extent, the deficiencies in the organised schemes of assistance.

Firstly, as regards manual workers the proportion which had, by 1870, some kind of security can be assessed because of the compulsory membership of companies' friendly societies. Out of approximately fifty societies in 1870 membership was compulsory in ten of the bigger ones, although this applied most often only to enginemen and traffic grades. In the other societies, in which membership was voluntary, there was often, in addition, a large membership. In most of the big companies, therefore, most men belonged to a company's society of some kind. On the other hand the kind of security obtained varied very considerably both in respect of the kind of benefit and its amount. The general effect was as follows: temporary disability, whether through accident or sickness - for many men about half pay; permanent disability - usually only a small sum and, when possible, alternative employment; death - small pensions for dependants for a few and a sum to pay for burial for the majority; old age - small pensions or gratuities for a comparatively few, and for the majority their savings, their children's support or the poor law.

For clerical workers, sickness was generally provided for by full or reduced pay. Old age meant, for the majority, dependence on their own efforts at life assurance; for a minority there were the superannuation schemes. But behind all this there was a great body of distress and insecurity in misfortune, indicated by the prevalence of 'contribution lists' to help the destitute families of railway servants, and by the rapid expansion of the work of the Railway Benevolent Institution.

The Price of Security

Security of employment and security against distress, so far as it went, were definite additions to the standard of living, but they were not net additions. Against that credit must be set certain considerable debits. The men paid for security in different ways, some simple and direct such as the finance of the companies' friendly societies, others more indirect and indefinable, such as the effect on wages and conditions of work.

The friendly societies were not unmixed blessings. They are open to criticism by reason of their two characteristic features: subsidisation and compulsory membership. Subsidisation involved in general a danger of laxity of management without strict attention to financial soundness. Actuarially these societies were unsound. It also meant that the companies were under no legal obligation to subsidise and could at any time disown a society, as in the case of the London &

North Western Euston Society. Compulsory membership involved a number of drawbacks of which perhaps the most serious was that full benefit depended on continuation of employment by the company. The men who left the companies, and there were many of them, lost some or all of their savings. The rules of the societies varied but those of the Midland Railway were fairly typical and they provided as follows. Members leaving the company after seven years with it and five years in the society might remain members but their sick benefit was reduced from 12s to 10s per week and their death benefit from £12 to £10. If such members left the society they received only 25 per cent of the excess of contributions over benefits received. Members leaving the company after less than seven years, and there were a good many, received only the same amount and of course had to leave the society. Such men might be too old to join another society.[1]

Another criticism is the deterioration in the financial position of members of societies. To some extent this was inevitable owing to heavy liability to injury and sickness which was then imperfectly appreciated. Reductions in benefits and conversely increases in contributions occurred in a good many societies, though they were most marked in the smaller ones, e.g. the Cambrian and Vale of Neath societies. Among the larger societies such changes occurred on the Eastern Counties, the London & South Western and the Great Western. In the last case, although the rules provided for pensions for old age and probably aroused such an expectation, in practice pensions were limited to men disabled by accident or disease.[2] Perhaps as a consequence the mortality of the societies was comparatively low and in fact occurred mostly after 1870. In most cases the companies maintained life by increasing their subsidies.

An interesting exception was what later became the London & North Western Friendly Society, established as early as 1840. The company's subsidy consisted of an initial £200 and one or two donations of the same size plus an allowance of fourteen days' sick pay to every sick member, which came to a total of £260 per annum. There were also various small sums of revenue from the sale of lost property, disciplinary fines and the rent of a newspaper stand which was subsequently withheld. This subsidy gave the society the impression that the company intended to guarantee its solvency and encouraged it to pay benefits considerably beyond those justified by the

---

1. Royal Commission on Friendly Societies. 4th Report, 1874. Midland Railway Friendly Society. Rules, 1870.
2. Railway Friendly Societies, Rules, 1856 - 1875. Great Western Railway Provident Society, Actuary's Report, 1871.

contributions. There is some doubt whether membership was compulsory but the directors wished that all men at Euston should join and most appear to have done so. The company's original circular promised not only sick and death benefits but also old age pensions. A little later contributions were reduced owing to 'the prosperous state of the funds', only once again to be increased as well as the benefits being reduced. There was continual criticism by the directors of the finances and an alternative proposal for a casualty fund specifically for accident injury began to make way, and with it a conflict developed between two groups of directors, one led by G. C. Glyn supporting the society, the other led by Richard Moon urging a new fund. By 1856, when the membership was 1015, an actuary's report referred to the society's 'irretrievable insolvency' and recommended its dissolution. Solvency would then have required a subsidy of £1,500 for five years and £1,000 thereafter, a not unreasonable sum in view of the advantages to the company. But this course was not followed and in 1863 the company divorced the society with a parting gift of £1,000. The society changed its name to the Railway Servants Friendly Society in 1871 at the company's request and by 1874 was reduced to six hundred and seventy members enjoying lower benefits and higher contributions. It was finally dissolved in 1878 with only one hundred and ninety-one members and assets nil. It had not been able to make any new members since the company began its own compulsory fund in 1871. After the divorce in 1863 there was nothing to take its place for eight years until the London & North Western Casualty Fund was established, and three years after that, the company's new provident society.[1]

This unedifying account is not typical of the companies' friendly societies but it serves to illustrate the dangers inherent in them. These were not encouraging for railwaymen who, in the words of the Commissioners of 1874, felt it 'a hard thing to be forced to join a society which must break in a few years'.

A further charge against the societies was that they gave the companies greater control over the men. Compulsory membership adversely affected not only the men who resigned from the service but also the many who were dismissed and who thereby lost all their contributions. The Commissioners of 1874 referred to 'many disputes between companies and servants in which the existence of a society enables a company by dismissing a servant to inflict a heavy fine as

---

1. London & Birmingham, Circulars, 1839, 1842. London & North Western Board, Coaching & Police Cte., Casualty Fund Cte., 1846 - 1870. R.C. on Friendly Societies, 4th Report, 1874.

well'. It was small comfort to know that disciplinary fines formed part of the companies' subsidies to the societies. The companies themselves were well aware of the increased power of punishment.[1] There was a strong financial inducement not to incur dismissal. Associated with this criticism is another, that attitudes of independence, self help and the formation of voluntary associations were discouraged by the existence of the companies' societies. A man could not afford to belong to two, the company's and an independent one. There was apparently much dissatisfaction with compulsory membership and the men suspected that they did not obtain the proper value for the stoppages from their wages. The Commissioners suggested that it was only when membership was optional that the societies were popular with the men.[2] It seems probable that a free choice by the men would, and in fact did, in many cases prefer an outside society. Where there was no compulsory society a considerable number of men belonged to ordinary benefit clubs or societies; it is evident that there was suspicion of the companies' interference and a desire for liberty of action.[3] It is not surprising therefore that in some cases it was difficult to persuade men to join companies' societies voluntarily and pressure was necessary to the extent of refusing help to men in distress unless they joined them, as on the London, Brighton & South Coast in the fifties.[4] It is not possible to say how far the formation of railwaymen's own associations was discouraged in this way but it may be significant that the only one of any size, strength or independence belonged to the enginemen, among whom compulsory societies were less common and whose wages may have been high enough to permit two memberships.

The inadequacy of the compensation for injury and death was another important item in the price of security from misfortune. There being no legal compulsion on the companies, it was entirely a question of how far the directors would feel obliged to pay something in lieu of compensation under the influence of public opinion and of their own consciences. In a conflict between the principles of political economy and humanitarianism the companies' position was expressed by the following characteristic statements made by the London & North Western in 1854 and by a contemporary chronicler in 1867. 'Engine drivers, guards, brakesmen, etc. enter voluntarily

---

1. Railway Clearing House. Report of Provisional Cte., 1850.
2. W. F. Mills, *The Railway Service*, 1867. Royal Commission on Friendly Societies. 4th Report, 1874.
3. London & North Western. Casualty Fund Cte. Report, 1854, Minutes, 1863, 1870.
4. London, Brighton & South Coast. Circulars, 1851, 1854; Board, 1852, 1854.

into the service of the company at wages mutually agreed upon, which must be considered (as in every other department of labour) equivalent to the nature and amount of the service required and to any unavoidable hardships or risks which belong to it. The directors accordingly have never held themselves liable to make compensation to their servants.'[1] 'The salaries and wages of the 219,970 persons employed by railway companies being ruled by contract, the welfare of the servants, unconnected with the due payment of the stipulated price of their labour, belongs to themselves and can only concern the companies in so far as they may consider to be practically expedient.'[2] Contrast with this the view represented by the secretary of the Railway Department of the Board of Trade when he expressed regret that the companies were not liable for injuries to servants, and by the opinion of the statistician to the Registrar General that railwaymen were 'justly entitled to compensation at a settled rate'.[3] On this side was the travelling public to whom petitions from distressed men were addressed. The public gave, but protested strongly that the 'companies ought to provide for their own servants'.[4]

It was a question therefore of how far the companies would have to go and, on the other hand, how far arrangements might be made for the men to pay for their own compensation. This problem was worked out through the companies' benevolence and their friendly societies. The more or less ready grant of a small sum in need lessened the likelihood of a man or his family thinking of their rights or any legal case they might have. There were very few cases like the guard's widow on the Eastern Counties who, refusing the proffered amount, gained a large sum through a summons in the County Court, or the guard on the Great Northern who had legal advice and was awarded £250 instead of the £100 offered.

But more important than this was the purpose of the subsidies made to the friendly societies. It was to provide the companies with relief from 'the burden of maintaining servants disqualified by age or accident, or contributing to the support of families of persons killed in their service'.[5] The London & North Western society, for example,

1. London & North Western. Special Cte., Report, 1854.
2. W. F. Mills, *The Railway Service*, 1867.
3. Report of H. of L. S.C. on Regulation of Railways (Prevention of Accidents) Bill, 1873. Evidence of T. H. Farrar. Registrar General. Annual Report for 1868, Appendix A.
4. W. F. Mills, *The Railway Service,* 1867.
5. Railway Clearing House. Provisional Cte. Report, 1850.

had been most useful in relieving the company from the chief part of the cost of maintaining their servants when sick or injured by accident, as the secretary of the Railway Clearing House pointed out in 1850. In fact a man who received benefit from a subsidised society was regarded as thereby having no claim on the company for compensation, as on the Great Western in 1865 and 1870.

The purpose of the subsidies was achieved because they were enough to serve two aims: to cover only a part of the extra risk from accident, and to persuade men to cover the other part with their own contributions. An example is the Midland Railway society membership of which was compulsory. During the five years 1862 - 1866 £6,240. was paid out for accident relief and death benefit whereas the company's subsidy was only £2,500. In 1873 accident pay was at the rate of £3,040 per annum whereas the Company's subsidy was only £1,000 per annum. 'Hence', as the Commissioners said in 1874, 'the company's donation is very far from making up to the society for the special risks and liabilities of so dangerous an occupation.' In this society part of the contributions which should have been used to cover the liability for ordinary sickness was being used for accident risk, in other words to pay compensation.[1] There was no question here of the accident risk being separated and covered by the company's subsidy; instead the men's contributions went in part to pay for compensation.

The same charge of 'self compensation' is made in the following criticism of the Railway Benevolent Institution.[2] It is somewhat exaggerated since members' contributions in fact supplied only part of the revenue of the Institution.

'The only awkward part is the circumstance that the railway servants themselves find the funds of this benevolent institution out of their own hardly-earned wages, and thus contribute to the support of the widows and children of those of their number who are killed through the mismanagement of economical directors. The arrangement is beautiful. The dividends of the shareholders are kept up, and the widows of mangled porters and stokers have a pension from a fund provided by the porters and stokers themselves. Can the most rigid justice require anything more?' A similar criticism of the Great Western Provident Society was made when the actuary's report

1. W.T.H., *History of the Midland Rly. Friendly Society*, 1928. R.C. on Friendly Societies, 4th Report, 1874.
2. *Pall Mall Gazette*, 10 May 1866.

pointed out that the annual subsidy had not increased with the growth of the society, it having been made when the membership was only half as large.[1] In fact the finance of compensation represented a compromise between the two extreme of companies' responsibility and men's responsibility.

Finally the possible effect of security on the level of wages must be considered. The connection between the two, though undoubted, is difficult to define. Provision for old age had some effect on the level of wages, though more for clerical than for manual workers and only for a minority of those. The practice in the Civil Service of remunerating partly by salary and partly by superannuation was discussed by a Parliamentary Committee in 1856 and the obvious advantage that it encouraged the retention of good employees was pointed out.[2] The railway companies also appreciated the possibilities in relation to wages. When in 1850 a general railway superannuation fund, widows' fund and friendly society was proposed one of the reasons put forward for the companies' support was that 'it would prove the means of permanently maintaining at moderate salaries the services of faithful and efficient servants'.[3] An illustration of the same point, in terms of cash, occurred in 1867. An agreement between enginemen and directors of the Great Western Railway, made to settle a dispute, included, as well as rates of wages and hours of work, a contribution by the company of £500 per annum to the Mutual Assurance Society. Since membership of this society had been made compulsory two years earlier it is likely that the subsidy was, if not requested, at least willingly accepted by the men as part of the general settlement. The link between security of employment and wages cannot be defined. But the fact that railwaymen were not generally liable to be thrown out of employment tended to increase the numbers of men anxious to work on the railways and improved the companies' ability to secure labour on favourable terms in a period when their demand for it was always increasing. Such a contribution to the supply of labour may well have had an important influence on wages at a time when, at least in this field, the original virtues of supply and demand were still unimpaired.

To conclude, security of employment was a marked addition to

---

1. Great Western Provident Society. Actuary's Report, 1871.
2. Report of S.C. on Civil Service Superannuation, 1856. Evidence of Dr. W. Farr.
3. Railway Clearing House, Provisional Cte., Report, 1850.

the standard of living although it may have had some adverse effect on the level of wages. Security against distress was more doubtful as an asset. The great liability to injury, sickness and death was only partly offset by the companies' provisions, and in so far as it was, serious though indefinable dangers of undue dependence on the companies and discouragement of independence were involved.

Chapter 10

THRIFT AND SELF HELP

The main significance of thrift and self help is as an indication of the standard of living, of respectability and social standing. A secondary consideration is the effect upon the attitude of labour to its employment, on the extent to which men were satisfied or dissatisfied; the possession of property gives a motive for a defensive attitude rather than an aggressive one. The questions raised here are these: What were the opportunities for thrift? What use was made of the opportunities? What were the limiting factors? The institutions to be examined are - savings banks, friendly societies, cooperatives, building societies, temperance associations, property, the family and its limitation.

In examining the opportunities for thrift and the institutions available, it is necessary to limit the field to the opportunities specifically connected with railway employment. This is the only possible course since no means of estimating the use made by railwaymen of the opportunities open to the working class in general are available.

By 1870 there were eight railway savings banks, the London, Brighton & South Coast Savings Bank established in 1852, the North Eastern in 1860, the Manchester, Sheffield & Lincolnshire in 1860, the South Devon in 1861, the Glasgow & South Western in 1865, the South Eastern in 1869, and the Wolverton (London & North Western) and the Crewe (London & North Western), both in 1859. The last two are distinct in that they provided mainly for artisans and labourers. The others were generally open to all grades. There had been only one casualty and even that unimportant. It was the case of the Provident Bank approved by the Bucks & Brackley Junction Railway in 1847, to be conducted by the chaplain. He however was discharged after five months and the bank, if it existed, disappeared with him.[1] In general the main advantage to the depositor was that the rate of interest was higher than in the Post Office or Trustee Savings Banks. Four of the banks gave 4 per cent interest, one gave 4½ per cent on amounts over £50, and one increased its rate from 3½ per cent to 5 per cent by 1870.[2] There

---
1. Bucks & Brackley Junction. Board, 1847.
2. London, Brighton & South Coast Board, 1860. North Eastern Rly. Savings Bank, Annual Reports, 1861 - 1870. London & North Western Crewe Savings Bank Cte., 1868, Special Cte., 1863. *Railway News*, 25 May 1870.

were also certain lesser advantages - such as members' control over management in most cases, the use of companies' premises, and the issue of free passes for representatives' meetings.

The establishment of these banks is not itself evidence of thrift. The initiative came from the management - 'the company being desirous of encouraging habits of Prudence and Economy amongst their servants in order to enable them to make Provision against accidents, sickness and old age, by investing and accumulating their savings'.[1] The exception was the North Eastern bank which originated from a Newcastle on Tyne Bible Society. The opportunity for saving through a bank therefore existed, though only for a considerable minority of railwaymen.

Next there were the friendly societies, that is, the societies of the railwaymen, quite distinct from the societies of the companies. They, being independent, are certainly evidence of self help, but there is less information about them than for the companies' societies. A list of all known societies is given in Appendix II p. 194 Apparently only sixteen existed in 1871, a much smaller number than the companies' societies. In addition there was probably a number of small local benefit clubs and societies on which no useful information is available.[2]

The benefits offered were all much the same (with two outstanding exceptions noted below). Sick pay ranged between 3s and 20s, being most usually 10s; death benefit between £6 and £30, being most usually about £10 and wives' death benefit between £4 and £10, being most usually £5. Most of these societies were small and local, the membership rarely going much above two hundred. The three main exceptions were the Railway Servants' Friendly, London, the Locomotive Steam Enginemen and Firemen's Society and the Railway Guards' Universal Friendly Society. The first, which may be briefly disposed of, had six hundred and seventy members in 1870 and was rapidly shrinking. This was the society, described earlier, which formerly belonged to the London & North Western Railway, was divorced by that company in 1863 and started on the downward path to its dissolution in 1878. The other two societies were both remarkable for the fact that, having been established in the early railway years, they lasted into the twentieth century, but they differed in important respects.

The Locomotive Steam Enginemen and Firemen's Society was

---

1. London & North Western Railway Act, 1858
2. London & North Western. Casualty Fund Cte., 1854, 1870. Rhymney Railway. Report, 1861. W. F. Mills, *History of the Railway Benevolent Institutions*, 1903.

established in 1839, by 1870 had over six thousand members and was not dissolved until 1936. It had an exceptionally favourable range of benefits. Sick pay was 10s per week for fifty-two weeks instead of the normal period of twenty-six weeks; death benefit was £18 (£10 if membership was for only twelve months); wives' death benefit was £5. The unusual feature was the disability pension of 5s per week. For unemployment it provided travelling cards and allowances. Moreover, the members' benefit position improved up to 1870. It developed early a strong organisation. By 1851 there were already twenty-five branches all over the country and by 1871 at least forty-two, controlled by annual delegate meetings. It was not confined to Britain but had members all over the world, for example in South America. It seem to have been completely independent of support from either companies or public. It is not surprising, therefore, that it was commended by the Royal Commissioners of 1874 for the favourable contrast it made with the companies' subsidised societies, and for its business-like accounts.[1] For one hundred years it was a bond of solidarity among the enginemen.

The Railway Guards' Universal Friendly Society was established in 1849, by 1870 had about nine hundred members, and was not finally dissolved until 1961. But its status was quite different. Its benefits was also unusually generous, the peculiar features being permanent sick pay in case of disability and a widow's pension. A disabled man who obtained less remunerative employment on the railway or elsewhere could earn up to £1 per week before losing all his pension. The society in this way paid some of the compensation due from the companies.

All this benefit could not come from the contributions which guards could afford to pay and the society depended greatly on help of various kinds from the companies and the public. According to one subscription list totalling £652, subscriptions came from Queen Victoria (£50), the London & North Western Railway (£105) and, inter alia, Sir Robert Peel (£10). A great deal of revenue was obtained from the public by concerts all over the country and by recurrent appeals. The donations from the companies, which continued into the twentieth century, implied approval if not control. Other lesser help was given by the issue of free passes to delegate meetings and free passage of parcels. More important, its funds were invested in railway debentures at a rate of interest one quarter per cent above the ordinary rate and it frequently received valuable

---

1. R.C. on Friendly Societies, 4th Report, 1874. Locomotive Steam Enginemen & Firemen's Society, Rules, 1851 - 1870. Registrar of Friendly Societies. Annual Reports, 1862 - 1871.

advice on investment from the Glyn family. Other bonds with the companies were close. The society's original rules were submitted to the London & North Western for approval and its reports and accounts were sent to every railway board. Directors and chief officers were honorary officers and trustees. It was, in fact, an independent society indirectly controlled by patronage. Within these limits its organisation flourished, and grew from twenty-two districts all over the country in 1854, only five years after establishment, to twenty-eight districts by 1873. It was businesslike and democratic with its continual reference of policy to districts' decision. The respectability of the society was always prominent, as indicated by the following extract from the rules of its widows' and orphans' fund in 1851, and it was severe on the immorality of members or widows. Its secretary had been a nobleman's servant and in fact its benefits depended greatly on the beneficence of the nobility, gentry and middle class.[1]

'In conclusion it may be stated, that the object in adopting this plan was, because it was felt to be in *proportion to the means of the members*, although not to the *extent* of their *wishes*. The sum granted weekly is admitted to be small, but it is hoped that the *certainty* of receiving a certain sum weekly will prove a stimulus to exertion on the part of the widow, to make up the deficiency of such sum as may be found necessary to support her self and family. On the contrary, the knowledge that *no support* would be rendered except by the *uncertain* hand of CHARITY would doubtless frequently cause the poor widow to despair of ever maintaining her position in the world, or of providing food for her children and being overpowered by the gloomy prospect before her, sink under her troubles, and leave her children living monuments of a system of *thoughtlessness* and *improvidence* too often indulged in by the working classes, but which evil, this Society (being a humble portion of a vast and well directed system of provident and frugal principles, happily rapidly extending) is intended to remedy in a large class of men, daily increasing in numbers and importance.'

To sum up railwaymen's friendly societies as a means of thrift existed only for a minority, and that minority was the better paid. There were no other institutions of any importance. Cooperative

---

1. Railway Guards' Universal Friendly Society. Minutes, 1849 - 1873; Rules, 1849 - 1863. London & North Western Rly., Board, 1849, 1850. Eastern Counties, Traffic Cte., 1850. Great Western, Board, 1869. Great Northern, Executive Cte., 1858, 1868.

societies were infrequent and insignificant. Only four can be found: a Great Western society at Paddington established in 1866, a Railway Clearing House society established in 1868, a Great Eastern society in 1867 and a Bristol & Exeter society in 1868. They were small and do not seem to have lived long. Although the potentialities among railwaymen were appreciated by some interested observers the movement did not take root in this period, and it may be that the companies' prohibition of men engaging in trade may have had something to do with it.[1] Railway building societies did not appear either. There was only one small one, the Railway Permanent Benefit Building Society established at the Clearing House in 1850. Its membership in 1867 was only six hundred and fifty-one, nor was it to expand, and it included many persons outside railway employment. House-owning ambitions found expression elsewhere.[2]

It now remains to see how much the institutions were used and the extent of self help; secondly to attempt an estimate of family limitation. Table XLIV below gives the number of depositors and the average amount deposited per annum in Railway Savings Banks and, for comparison, the average amount deposited per annum in the Post Office Savings Bank, the Trustee Savings Banks and Military and Seamen's Banks.[3] It shows that the number of railway depositors was very small compared with the total employed on railways, i.e. about 2 per cent. But the average amount deposited per annum was higher than in other banks except the Trustee Banks, and very much higher than in the Post Office Bank.

The question is, what grades of men were able to save at this rate? In view of the general level of wages most of the savers must have been in the more highly paid grades. The available evidence supports this. Of all the depositors in the Manchester, Sheffield & Lincolnshire bank in 1862 numbering three hundred and seventeen, 58 per cent were officers, clerks or supervisors, 11 per cent were workshop artisans, 2 per cent were enginemen, and only 29 per cent were in the rank and file traffic grades.[4] In the case of the London, Brighton & South Coast Bank 59 per cent of all station masters and station

---

1. Returns of Industrial & Provident Societies, 1867, 1870. W. F. Mills, *The Railway Service*, 1867. South Devon Railway Board, 1868.
2. Railway Permanent Benefit Building Society Rules, 1850; Annual Report, 1913. M. Riebenack, *Railway Provident Institutions in English Speaking Countries*, 1905.
3. Return of Deposits in Savings Banks, 1876.
4. Manchester, Sheffield & Lincolnshire Savings Bank, Annual Report, 1863

Table XLIV

Railway Savings Banks.

Year	Number of Banks	Number of Depositors	Average Amount Deposited during year £ s d
1867	7	1,933	16 4 6
1868	7	1,969	18 19 2
1869	7	2,056	19 0 9
1870	8	2,614	20 14 10
1871	8	3,221	17 17 4
1872	8	3,968	18 11 2
1873	8	4,576	18 6 0
1874	8	5,309	20 16 1
1875	10	6,626	20 18 11
1876	10	7,898	19 8 9
Average for 10 years			19 7 5

Average Amount deposited each year in:-

Year	Post Office Savings Bank £ s d	Trustee S. Banks £ s d	Military S. Banks £ s d	Seamen S. Banks £ s d
1866	6 2 6	25 18 2	9 15 11	17 1 0
1867	5 13 6	26 7 3	8 12 11	21 0 8
1868	5 15 9	26 17 6	10 13 1	18 2 5
1869	5 12 1	27 4 10	10 16 7	21 1 6
1870	5 7 1	27 8 3	10 18 8	18 5 2
1871	5 8 0	27 12 11	11 8 4	20 5 3
1872	5 12 9	27 16 10	9 9 3	17 7 5
1873	5 8 4	28 0 9	9 2 8	18 6 9
1874	5 6 3	28 6 4	9 7 4	20 17 6
1875	5 5 3	28 13 1	11 2 0	19 0 1
Average	5 10 1	27 8 11	10 2 8	19 3 1

clerks in 1856 admitted to being depositors. Since the membership of the bank was probably not more than three hundred, it is improbable that many of the depositors were manual workers.[1] An analysis of all single deposits in two banks in the year 1870, as shown in the table XLV, supports this argument. The fact that one third of all deposits were made in sums of 10s and upward, and over a half in sums of 5s and upward confirms the view that most of the depositors belonged to the higher paid and smaller grades and that few of the others saved in this way, if at all.[2]

Table XLV

Amount of Single Deposits	Number of Single Deposits	Percent of all Single Deposits
Under 5s	3 771	48
5s & under 10s	1,478	19
10s & under £1	1,170	15
£1 and under £2	741	9
£2 & under £5	338	4
£5 & upward	380	5

Comparison with the trustee banks suggests that the depositors in the railway banks were in the ranks of the lower middle class associated with the trustee banks, and the conclusion must be that very few of the mass of low paid men saved in these banks.

Accumulation of savings by railwaymen is shown in Table XLVI below. It shows the average total of savings held by depositors in two banks, the Manchester, Sheffield & Lincolnshire and the North Eastern from their first financial year, compared with the Post Office Savings Bank. This indicates a steady and solid accumulation, but it was by a membership which was a very small proportion of all men employed.[3]

An analysis of the savings of depositors in the North Eastern Railway bank in 1870, ten years after its establishment, confirms this view.[4] Table XLVII shows that 16 per cent of depositors had saved £100 or more and 60 per cent had saved £5 or more.

---

1. London, Brighton & South Coast, Census, 1856.
2. Manchester, Sheffield & Lincolnshire Savings Bank and South Eastern Savings Bank, Annual Report, 1870. 1874. *Railway News*, 2 July 1870.
3. Manchester, Sheffield & Lincolnshire Savings Bank and North Eastern Savings Bank, Annual Reports, 1870.
4. North Eastern Railway Savings Bank, Annual Report, 1870.

Table XLVI
Manchester, Sheffield & Lincolnshire and North Eastern Savings Banks

Year	Number of Depositors	Average Total Savings per Depositor £ s d
1861	558	5 1 0
1862	636	8 1 8
1863	660	10 15 3
1864	671	14 8 2
1865	713	15 16 7
1866	656	24 6 3
1867	723	27 8 1
1868	751	36 16 0
1869	773	47 16 2
1870	859	51 6 1

Post Office Savings Bank

Year	Average Total Savings per depositor £ s d
1866	10 17 8
1867	11 8 1
1868	12 1 9
1869	12 9 1
1870	12 15 3
1871	13 1 1
1872	13 7 10
1873	13 12 0
1874	13 17 1
1875	14 3 6

After the savings banks there are the independent friendly societies as an indication of the extent of saving. Some indication has already been given in this chapter. With three exceptions the societies were small. Of all known societies the membership of most in 1870 or thereabouts is known. The total was not more than eight to nine thousand, a very small proportion of those employed, and of that number about 70 per cent was accounted for by the Locomotive Steam Enginemen and Firemen's Society. The two exceptionally strong societies built up by the enginemen and the guards did accumulate considerable funds. By 1871 the enginemen's society had

Table XLVII
North Eastern Railway Savings Bank
1870

Total Savings	Percent of Depositors %
Under 1s	7
1s - 5s	10
5s 1d - 10s	3
10s 1d - £1	4
£1 0s 1d - £2	7
£2 0s 1d - £4	7
£4 0s 1d - £5	2
Over £5	60

funds of £42,304, or about £7 per member, while the Railway Guards' Universal Friendly Society had more than £13,000 invested in railway debentures or perhaps £1 10s 0d per member.[1] But the reserves of the guards' society were the result partly of charity. Moreover, neither society included anything like all the men employed in the grades for which they catered. At its highest level the enginemen's society had certainly not more than 50 per cent of all enginemen in its ranks and the guards' society had not more than 25 per cent. Further, even of those funds which were accumulated only that part which was earmarked for pensions and death benefits could be described as savings. The rest allocated to sick pay was merely a provision for day to day contingency. This applies also to the unknown number of small benefit and sick clubs in which the surplus was often divided for an annual spree. So far as railway cooperatives or building societies are concerned the saving effected was insignificant.

There remain the commercial and state institutions used by the population in general. Into these probably went a considerable proportion of whatever savings were made but very little information is available. Certain companies' friendly societies gave help towards the taking out of life assurance but the effect is not known. Members of the Railway Benevolent Institution enjoyed from 1860 specially favourable terms for commercial life assurance. By 1866 it was

---

1. Registrar of Friendly Societies. Report for 1871. Railway Guards' Universal Friendly Society. Minutes 1864 - 1873.

claimed that assurance for £50,000 had been effected.[1] But even on the assumption that the average policy was for £100 that amount would represent only five hundred men from among the better paid.

Little can be said about the property owned by railwaymen although some evidence is provided by the cases of the widows assisted by the Railway Benevolent Institution. In most of these cases the amount of property left to the widow, if any, was given. In no case of a manual worker is there mention of any property being left. But in about 50 per cent of the cases of station masters' and clerks' widows there were life assurances and occasionally other property-shares, houses, savings bank deposits. This, however, could hardly be taken as representative since only the more thrifty men would probably be members of the Institution. And even among those a considerable proportion of their families were reported as destitute.[2]

The question of family limitation is related to self help and thrift and is certainly important in consideration of the standard of living. Were railway men thrifty in reproduction? Two sources indicate a possible answer, the annual reports of the Railway Benevolent Institution, and of the Great Western Railway Provident Society. In the first, in each case of relief the number of children is given. In the period 1861 to 1880 one hundred and forty-four station masters and clerks or their widows who received relief and who also had children had an average of 4.3 children each. Sixty-seven manual workers who had children had an average of 3.9 children each. These figures are not however representative in view of the probability that the most distressed cases were relieved at the expense of others and the true average of all applicants would be lower.[3] From the Great Western Provident Society annual reports the approximate number of children to each widow having children may be calculated, given the amount of benefit to each family per annum and the standard rates of benefit per widow and per orphan up to eleven years of age. In 1867 there were 218 widows and 216 orphans receiving pensions; of the 218 widows 115 also received orphans' pensions and had an average of 1.9 orphans. In 1870 there were 250 widows and 185 orphans receiving pensions; of the 250 widows 92 also received orphans' pensions and had an average of 2.0 orphans under the age of eleven.[4] This is a lower figure than in the first case but some of the difference

---

1. Railway Benevolent Institution. Report of Half Yearly Meeting, 1868.
2. Railway Benevolent Institution. Annual Report, 1871.
3. Railway Benevolent Institution. Annual Reports, 1861-1880
4. Great Western Railway Provident Society. Annual Reports, 1867 & 1870.

would be explained by the limitation to age eleven in the second case. In comparison the national figures from the 1861 census show an average of 2.2 children, living with the family, per family of which the head was a widow or widower, and 2.94 for families with both husband and wife. Similar figures for 1871 and 1881 are not available but it may be inferred from the numbers of persons to a family at all three dates that they were slightly higher.[1] It should be emphasized however, that these averages are based on all families whereas the railway figures are based on those families which had children. No definite conclusion can be drawn but the railway families may well have been somewhat smaller than the average for that period and some kind of limitation may be indicated.

The limiting factors on thrift in the railway institutions were three — compulsory saving, suspicion of the institutions, and the level of wages. By the first is meant compulsory membership of friendly societies. It is only briefly mentioned here since it has already been shown that most of the big companies had societies, compulsory membership of which made it more difficult for men to save voluntarily through other organisations.

The suspicion of the railway savings banks felt by the men was an equally important though less definite factor. A good deal of persuasion, moral and otherwise, was exercised by the companies on behalf of their banks. In an age when thrift was the panacea for distress railwaymen were also issued with that prescription. 'The savings of the children too, can be deposited and so they may be trained to habits of frugality and providence - the surest foundation for the attainment of honourable independence and social prosperity.[2] Perhaps the activity of Samuel Smiles as a chief railway officer for twenty-one years had something to do with advocacy of the banks. One of the greatest enthusiasts for railway savings banks, Sir Edward Watkin, became chairman of the South Eastern Railway in the same year (1866) in which Smiles vacated the secretaryship. The managements' reasons why the men should save were various. The rate of interest was relatively high. Saving was both the path of independence and a means of raising the price of labour. 'A man who put money in a savings bank rendered himself independent and was in a position to ask such terms as he considered adequate remuneration for his labour.' It was the way to advancement since it could be known who were depositors and preference in promotion and appointment to positions of trust would be given to the provident.

---

1. Census Reports. 1861, Appendix Table 38, 1871, Appendix Table 11; 1881, Appendix Table 3.
2. London, Brighton & South Coast Traffic Manager's Circular, 1864.

Political rights might be won through the county vote which the purchase of a house with his savings would confer on a man. If forty men at the Manchester, Sheffield & Lincolnshire works at Gorton had bought their houses so could their fellows at the South Eastern works at Ashford.[1]

The force of all these excellent arguments was considerably reduced for some years by suspicion of banks which belonged to employers: this was a major obstacle to their use. The workingmen's fear that knowledge of his savings would be used to reduce his wages was not a new thing. It was prevalent before the establishment of the Post Office Bank. In 1850 it was said that the working man concealed from his employer his ability to save by going to a distant bank to make his deposits.[2] Railway men were no exception. Twenty years later the railway labourers at Bristol refused to have their annual benefit club converted into a society with accumulating funds, even with the offer of a subsidy. They asked; 'Why should we accumulate to bring down wages?[3] This attitude was a considerable deterrent from the beginning of railway banks. At the first meeting of the Manchester, Sheffield & Lincolnshire bank the chairman referred to an impression (erroneous in his view) that the bank might act unfavourably towards advances in wages. Although the suggestion was repeatedly repudiated and the rules of secrecy were adduced, the impression remained until well after 1870. The belief that the ability to save must, in the absence of trade unions, weaken any demand for increased wages which was advanced on the grounds of the cost of living, and that the companies could use their knowledge of the men's savings was still held in 1875. This belief was considered a stumbling block to the savings banks by both station master and manual worker.[4]

About the third limiting factor, the level of wages, little need be said here since it has already been shown that wages in general were such as to make saving difficult. A man's reply to the admonition to save might well have been: 'I would if I could and will if you will only show me how it is possible to provide for a wife and children on such small wages.[5]

---

1. *Railway News*. 25 June 1870. South Eastern Railway Savings Bank. Annual Reports, 1871, 1872.
2. Report of S.C. on Savings of the Middle & Working Classes, 1850. Evidence of J. Millbank.
3. R.C. on Friendly Societies. 4th Report, 1874.
4. Manchester, Sheffield & Lincolnshire Savings Bank. Minutes of General Meeting, 1860. *Railway News*, 25 June 1870. South Eastern Rly. Savings Bank. Annual Report, 1873.
5. W. F. Mills, *History of the Railway Benevolent Institution*, 1903.

In conclusion, the available information is hardly conclusive since the institutions for thrift were not available to the majority and the suspicion of even those that existed prevents their being regarded as an accurate indication of saving. But, due allowance having been made, it may be said that the proportion of savers either in banks or friendly societies, to the number employed, was very small, even after the institutions had been in existence for some years. That proportion was very largely composed of the skilled men, enginemen and guards and the better paid station masters and clerks. They were sometimes able to accumulate considerable sums but of those amounts only a part, especially in friendly societies, could be regarded as long term saving, the rest being provision for everyday contingencies. If by 1870 the enginemen's and guards' societies were widely supported the banks were not widely used. It was in the period after 1870 that the bank depositors grew more rapidly in numbers and much faster than the numbers employed. Between 1870 and 1890 on the North Eastern they multiplied eight times, and on the Manchester, Sheffield & Lincolnshire, ten times. In 1870 savings were in the future, except for the small minority who, by hard work, strict discipline and good fortune, had been able to rise in the railway world.

BIBLIOGRAPHY.

I. MANUSCRIPT SOURCES.

Railway Companies' Minute Books.
Birmingham & Derby Railway
  Board, 1842
Birmingham & Gloucester Railway
  Board, 1840
Brighton Croydon & Dover Railway
  Board, 1843
  Locomotive Committee, 1842 - 1846
Eastern Counties Railway
  Board, 1845 - 1851
  Traffic Committee, 1844 - 1851
  Locomotive & Engineering Cte., 1849 - 1851
Grand Junction Railway
  Board, 1839 - 1844
  Church Cte., 1843
Great Eastern Railway
  Board, 1862 - 1864

    Traffic Cte., 1865, 1866
    Locomotive Cte., 1862 - 1867
    Way & Works Cte., 1866, 1867
Great Grimsby & Sheffield Railway
    Board, 1845 - 1848
Great Northern Railway
    Board, 1846 - 1851
    Occasional Cte., 1846 - 1874
    Salaries Cte., 1851 - 1853, 1874
    Traffic Cte., 1850, 1851
    Locomotive Cte., 1863 - 1869
    Executive Cte., 1849 - 1868
    Appointments Cte., 1848
    Station Cte., 1850, 1851
    Expenditure Cte., 1863.
Great Western Railway
    Board, 1833 - 1871
    London Cte., 1833 - 1841
    Bristol Cte., 1833 - 1841
    General Cte., 1840, 1841
    Appointments Sub Cte., 1837 - 1840
    Traffic Cte., 1840 - 1867
    Expenditure Cte., 1849 - 1863
    Locomotive & Permanent Way Cte., 1863 - 1867
    Swindon Church & School Cte., 1843 - 1878
Lancashire & Yorkshire Railway
    Board, 1847 - 1873
Leicester & Swannington Jcn. Railway
    Board, 1830
Liverpool & Manchester Railway
    Board, 1830 - 1844
London & Birmingham Railway
    Board, 1838 - 1846
    Administrative Cte., 1838
London & Brighton Railway
    Board, 1837 - 1846
    Police Cte., 1839 - 1841
    Establishment Cte , 1839 - 1843
London & Greenwich Railway
    Board, 1831 - 1838
London & North Western Railway
    Board, 1846 - 1875
    Special Cte., 1850 - 1861
    Salaries & Wages Cte., 1848 - 1861

Locomotive Cte., 1848 - 1855
　　Coaching Cte., 1845, 1846
　　Grand Junction Cte., 1848
　　Road & Traffic Cte., 1849 - 1853
　　Traffic Cte., 1865 - 1870
　　Northern Sub Cte., 1858
　　Law Cte., 1861
　　Medical Cte., 1870 - 1875
　　Casualty Fund Cte., 1854 - 1870
　　Church & Schools Cte., 1849 - 1870
　　Crewe Savings Bank Cte., 1868.
London & Southampton Railway
　　Traffic Cte., 1836 - 1845
London & South Western Railway
　　Board, 1845 - 1875
　　Traffic Cte., 1846 - 1866
　　Special Cte., 1849 - 1858
　　Locomotive Cte., 1849 - 1872
London, Brighton & South Coast Railway
　　Board, 1846 - 1875
　　Traffic Cte., 1849 - 1875
　　Locomotive & Construction Cte., 1848, 1849
Manchester, Sheffield & Lincolnshire Railway
　　Board, 1847 - 1869
　　Officers' Cte., 1848
　　Executive Cte., 1848 - 1858
　　Traffic Cte., 1847, 1848
　　Conference on Working Expenses, 1855 - 1858
　　Management Cte., 1845
Midland Railway
　　Board, 1844 - 1870
　　Management Cte., 1845 - 1849
　　Locomotive Cte., 1853 - 1860
　　Wages Cte , 1871
Newcastle & Carlisle Railway
　　Management Cte., 1833 - 1842
Sheffield & Manchester Railway
　　Board, 1836 - 1842
　　Management Cte., 1840, 1841
　　Sheffield Cte., 1842 - 1845
South Devon Railway
　　Board, 1859 - 1861
South Durham & Lancs. Union Railway
　　Traffic Cte., 1856 1857

South Eastern Railway
  Board, 1836 - 1860
South Yorkshire Railway
  Board, 1846 - 1852
Stockton & Darlington Railway
  Board, 1821 - 1863
  Sub Cte., 1821 - 1834
  Coach & Carrying Cte., 1846 - 1847
  Dues Cte., 1847 - 1849
  Finance Cte., 1847 -1849
  Shildon Works Cte.,1847 - 1849
  Locomotive Cte., 1851 - 1854
Vale of Neath Railway
  Board, 1859 - 1863
York & North Midland Railway
  Board, 1835 - 1840

Railway Companies' Record Books, Reports & Correspondence
Newcastle & Carlisle Railway
  Establishment Book, 1841
London & North Western Railway
  Reports to Board, 1852 - 1872
London Brighton & South Coast Railway
  Census of Station masters and clerks, 1856
  Staff Books, 1861 - 1893
  Black Book, 1863 - 1863
  Salary Book, 1864
  Registers of Appointments, 1860 - 1870
  List of Staff in All Departments, 1871

Miscellaneous Reports and Correspondence including the following:-
Great Western Railway
  General Manager's Reports, 1865, 1870, 1879
  Secretary's Reports, 1863, 1871, 1878
  Report on Working Expenses, 1863
  Return of Station masters' Houses 1890
  Application for Employment, 1842
London & Birmingham Railway
  Memorials to the Directors, 1838
  Applications for Employment, 1837
  Return of Gratuities, 1842
London & North Western Railway
  Applications for Employment, 1857
  Locomotive Supt.'s Report 1848

London Brighton & South Coast Railway
  Applications for Employment, 1860 - 1890
Railway Guards' Universal Friendly Society
  Minute Book, 1849 - 1873

II. PRINTED REPORTS, RULE BOOKS ETC.

Registrar of Friendly Societies.
  Rules of Railway Friendly Societies, 1830 on
  Railway Companies' Rule Books, 1830 on
Great Western Railway Provident Society
  Annual Reports, 1865 - 1870
Great Western Railway Enginemen & Firemen's Mutual Assurance Society
  Annual Reports, 1865 - 1870
Railway Benevolent Institution
  Annual Reports, 1858 - 1880
Manchester, Sheffield & Lincolnshire Railway Savings Bank
  Annual Reports, 1860 - 1880
North Eastern Railway Savings Bank
  Annual Reports, 1860 - 1880
South Eastern Railway Savings Bank
  Annual Reports, 1870 - 1875
Railway Permanent Benefit Building Society
  Annual Report, 1905
  Rules, 1850
Liverpool & Manchester Railway
  Answer of the Directors, 1832
Railway Companies' Association
  Minutes, 1867 - 1876
London Trades Council
  Trades Union Directory, 1861

III. PARLIAMENTARY PAPERS

Reports
S.C. on State of Communication by Railways, 1839, 1840
S.C. on Railway Labourers, 1846
S.C. on Accidents on Railways, 1857, 1858
R.C. on Railways, 1867
S.C. on Railways (Law of Compensation), 1870
S.C. on Regulation of Railways
  (Prevention of Accidents) Bill, 1873

R.C. on Friendly Societies, 4th Report, 1874
Papers & Returns
Friendly Societies: Returns relative to, 1837 - 1870
Rules & Regulations proposed to be observed by Enginemen, Guards, Policemen and others on Railways, 1841
Registrar of Friendly Societies
                              Annual Reports, 1842 - 1875
Number & Description of Persons Employed on Railways, 1847 - 1860
Railways - Return of Persons Employed, 1874
Railway Employees: Returns of Accidents, 1893-4
Railway Companies' Savings Banks, 1876
Statistical Abstracts for U.K., 1847 - 1884

IV. NEWSPAPERS AND PERIODICALS

Beehive, 1862 - 1870
Household Words, 1851
Illustrated London News, 1867
On the Line, 1883
Pall Mall Gazette, 1867
Patent Journal, 1848
Railway Magazine, 1898
Railway Review, 1898 - 1899
Railway Times, 1836 on
The Times, 1845 - 1867
The Train, 1884 - 1886

V. BOOKS

(Except where stated otherwise the place of publication is London)
G. W. Alcock, *Fifty Years of Railway Trade Unionism*, 1922
J. M. Baernreither, *English Associations of Working Men*, 1889
P. S. Bagwell, *The Railwaymen*, 1963
Vincent C. Bassett, *An Authentic History of Railway Trade Unionism*, 1902
W. H. Chaloner, *The Social and Economic Development of Crewe*, Manchester, 1950
G. D. H. Cole and R. P. Arnot, *Trade Unionism on the Railways*, 1917
C. H. Ellis, *British Railway History, 1830 - 76*, 1954
J. W. Fletcher, *Railways in their Medical Aspects*, 1867
C. P. Gasquoine, *Story of the Cambrian*, 1922
L. V. Grinsell, *Studies in the History of Swindon*, Swindon, 1953

Sir F. B. Head, *Stokers and Pokers*, 1849
J. R. T. Hughes, *Fluctuations in Trade, Industry and Finance*, Oxford, 1960
R. Kenney, *Men and Rails*, 1913
R. Langdon, *Life of Roger Langdon*, 1908
Leone Levi, *Wages and Earnings of the Working Classes*, 1867
J. M. Ludlow and L. Jones, *Progress of the Working Classes*, 1867
S. Maccoby, *English Radicalism 1853-1886*, 1938
E. T. MacDermott, *History of the Great Western Railway*, 1927
W. F. Mills, *The Railway Service*, 1867 *History of the Railway Benevolent Institution*, 1903
B. P. Mitchell and P. Deane, *Abstract of British Historical Statistics*, 1962
G. P. Neele, *Railway Reminiscences*, 1904
H. Parris, *The Government and the Railways*, 1965
J. Parsloe, *Our Railways*, 1878
M. Riebenack, *Railway Provident Institutions in English Speaking Countries*, 1905
R. M. Robbins, *The Railway Age*, 1962 *Points and Signals*, 1967
R. Young, *Timothy Hackworth and the locomotive*, 1923

VI. ARTICLES AND PAMPHLETS

Amalgamated Society of Railway Servants, *Souvenir History*, 1910
A. G. Kenwood, 'Railway Investment in Britain, 1825-75', in *Economica*, Vol XXXII, 1965
J. Fitzgerald, *The Duty of procuring for the labouring classes the earlier closing of shops and the Saturday half holiday*, 1856
F. C. Mather, 'The Railway, the Electric Telegraph and Public Order during the Chartist Period, 1837 - 48' in *History*, Vol 38, new series February 1953, No 132, and correction June 1953, No 133.
W. T. H., *Outline of History of the Midland Railway Friendly Society*, 1928

VII UNPUBLISHED THESES

P. S. Gupta, *The History of the Amalgamated Society of Railway Servants, 1871-1913*, D.Phil. thesis, Oxford, 1960
G. C. Halverson, *The Development of Labour Relations in the British Railways since 1860*, Ph. D. thesis, London, 1952

INDEX

A

Accident benefit, 157
Acts of Parliament:
    Act for Regulating Railways, 1840, 14, 15
    Act for Better Regulation in Railways, 1842, 14
    Great Western Railway, 1835, 17
    Liverpool and Manchester, 1826, 29
    Railway Clauses Act, 1845, 30
Advancement, 128–147
Age distribution, 36
Agricultural labourers, 2
Amalgamated Society of Railway Servants, 47, 84, 119
Applications for employment, 7
Apprentices, clerks, 61, 134
Artisans, 81, 86
Assurance, life, 178

B

Board of Trade, 70, 115
Bonuses, 105
Boy clerks, 60–61
Boy porters, 60
Building societies, railway, 174

C

Capital, 62
Cautions, 25
Chartism, 85–86, 122
Churches, railway, 75
Classes, 132–133
Clergy, 74, 75, 76
Clerks, 56, 96–97, 107, 132–133, 140, 142, 160
Clothing, 111–113
Compensation, 152, 165–167
Combination, 80, 84
Cooperative societies, railway, 173
Cottages, railway, 94, 126
Crewe, 75, 86

D

Death by accident, 47, 155, 158
Dickens, Charles, 80
Disability payments, 153, 157
Discipline, 13–34, 145
Dismissal, 19–22, 37, 44
Disputes, 64–71
Document, the, 79
Drunkenness, 17, 20, 21, 22, 25

E

Early Closing Association, 75, 119
Education, 72–74
Educational standards, 9
Election, 1868, 86
Employment, terms of, 149
Engine drivers, 19, 20, 97–98, 132
Engineman, 4, 14, 22, 28, 45, 52, 58, 64, 65, 66, 67, 70, 77, 78, 79, 80, 81, 82–84, 97–99 108, 117, 131, 138, 171

F

Families of railwaymen, 179–180
Fines, 22–25
Firemen, 98, 132
Foremen, 95

Free travel, 113–114
Friendly societies, companies', 35, 45, 48, 156–160, 162–167
Friendly societies, railwaymens', 83, 171–173, 177–178
Fuel, domestic, 111
Funeral expenses, 155

G

Gangers, 99
Gatekeepers, 94, 142
Gooch, Daniel, 82
Grades, 2, 57, 77, 134
Gratuities, 28–29, 104
Great Exhibition, 1851, 103, 113
Guarantee funds, railway, 33
Guarantee societies, 32
Guarantees for honesty, 29–34
Guards, 65, 67, 78, 92, 107, 117, 130, 137, 172–173

H

Hospitals, 156
Hours of work, 71, 115–120
Housing, 110–111, 121–127
Hudson, George, 70

I

Industrial relations, 64–85
Injury at work, 47, 153
Inspectors, 94, 143
Intimidation, 80
Investment, 62

J

Juvenile labour, 60–61, 151

L

Lad clerks, 60
Lad porters, 61
Lampmen, 91
Langdon, Roger, 57
Levi, Leone, 100
Limbs, loss of, 154

Locomotive Steam Enginemen and Firemens' Friendly Society, 83
Lodging allowances, 108

M

Master and servant legislation, 14
Medical fees, 155
Metropolitan police, 4
Missions, city, 81
Mobility, 55–58, 144
Mortality, 49

N

Nine Elms, 78

O

Overtime payment, 103–104

P

Patronage, 5–7
Permanent Way Men, 99–100, 108, 138
Petitions, 67–70
Physical standards, 9
Platelayers, 24, 100, 138
Pointsmen, 91, 130, 136
Policemen, 4, 23, 89, 129, 134, 142
Porters, 23, 65, 67, 78, 89–91, 95, 117, 129, 135, 141
Promotion, 128–147
Property of railwaymen, 179
Prosecutions, 14, 15, 18
Punishment, 13–15

R

Railway Benevolent Institution, 158, 161, 167, 178
Railway bye-laws, 19
Railway Clearing House, 114, 174
Railway Clerks' Association, 84
Railway Companies:
  Birkenhead, 161
  Birmingham and Gloucester, 30
  Bristol and Exeter, 144–174

INDEX

Railway Companies (cont.):
  Bucks. and Brackley Junction, 170
  Cambrian, 163
  Canterbury and Whitstable, 19
  Chester and Holyhead, 74
  Eastern Counties, 17, 60, 65, 78, 80, 85, 99, 103, 116, 121, 124, 131, 154, 156, 163, 166
  East Lincolnshire, 6
  Edinburgh and Glasgow, 149
  Glasgow and South Western, 170
  Grand Junction, 74, 75, 80
  Great Eastern, 99, 154, 155, 174
  Great Northern, 6, 8, 11, 21, 32, 40, 55, 74, 80, 103, 105, 107, 113, 120, 121, 122, 123, 125, 126, 130, 131, 133, 139, 143, 144, 146, 147, 150, 153, 154, 155, 166
  Great Western, 7, 8, 9, 11, 17, 21, 23, 24, 28, 43, 45, 47, 52, 53, 55, 59, 60, 67, 74, 75, 103, 104, 107, 108, 109, 111, 112, 113, 115, 117, 120, 123, 125, 129, 130, 131, 132, 136, 140, 144, 146, 149, 150, 153, 154, 155, 160, 163, 167, 168, 174, 179
  Grimsby and Sheffield, 126
  Lancashire and Yorkshire, 33, 74
  Leicester and Swannington, 30
  Liverpool and Manchester, 3, 5, 14, 29, 119, 149
  London and Birmingham, 15, 17, 30, 37, 75, 81, 115, 119, 125, 131, 145, 149, 153
  London and Brighton, 20, 23, 30, 59, 109
  London and Greenwich, 80
  London and North Western, 5, 7, 8, 9, 10, 11, 17, 20, 32, 33, 37, 47, 53, 59, 65, 67, 71, 72, 74, 75, 76, 77, 78, 79, 80, 82, 84, 98, 107, 108, 109, 113, 116, 117, 122, 124, 129, 130, 131, 132, 133, 134, 136, 145, 150, 151, 153, 154, 155, 156, 159, 160, 165, 170, 173
  London and South Western, 7, 8, 10, 23, 55, 56, 59, 61, 67, 78, 103, 108, 115, 121, 123, 124, 130, 133, 134, 140, 144, 145, 146, 154, 160, 163,
  London, Brighton and the South Coast, 5, 9, 21, 24, 25, 29, 32, 35, 37, 38, 41, 42, 43, 45, 55, 56, 57, 65, 66, 70, 71, 78, 83, 84, 85, 86, 100, 103, 105, 109, 111, 113, 115, 117, 122, 123, 124, 125, 126, 130, 138, 139, 140, 143, 144, 147, 150, 151, 153, 154, 156, 160, 161, 165, 170, 174
  Manchester, Sheffield and Lincolnshire, 17, 56, 60, 61, 86, 99, 103, 116, 119, 121, 125, 133, 140, 144, 145, 170, 174, 176, 181
  Midland, 65, 76, 104, 112, 120, 130, 131, 133, 145, 156, 160, 163
  Midland Counties, 80
  Newcastle and Carlisle, 59, 103, 109, 111, 120, 121, 122, 123, 124, 150
  North British, 78
  North Eastern, 66, 67, 78, 80, 81, 87, 117, 136, 138, 170, 176, 178
  North Staffs., 10, 74, 113
  Sheffield and Manchester, 8, 55, 80, 121, 144, 149
  South Eastern, 33, 74, 114, 123, 124, 126, 145, 170, 180
  Stockton and Darlington, 19, 20, 22, 30, 64, 67, 80, 98, 108, 111, 114, 121, 123, 125, 154, 155
  Taff Vale, 20, 76
  Vale of Neath, 163
  York and North Midland, 6
Railway Companies' Association, 80
Railway Department, Board of Trade, 70, 115
Railway Guards' Universal Friendly Society, 172, 178
Rationalisation, 58–63
Recruitment, 1–12
Reform League, 86
Religion, 74–76
Rents, 123–125, 127
Resignations, 37, 44, 146
Retirement pensions, 159
Rewards, 28–29
Risks of work, 46–53, 152, 167

Savings banks, railway, 170, 174–178, 180–181
Savings of railwaymen, 177
Schools, railway companies', 73
Security, 148–169
Shunters, 93, 131
Sick benefit, 157
Sick pay, 159–160
Sickness, 48–53
Signalmen, 24, 28, 58, 77, 91, 107, 117, 130, 136
Special constables, 29, 85–86
Station masters, 56, 95–96, 106, 109, 122, 132, 141, 160
Stephenson, George, 6
Strikes, 64–67
Sunday observance, 75, 76, 119
Sunday pay, 83, 120
Sunday travel, 73, 76
Superannuation, 160, 168
Supernumaries, 150
Swindon, 74, 75
Switchmen, 24, 28, 91, 107, 130, 136, 142

T

Ten hour day, 117–118
Thrift, 170–182
Ticket collectors, 93, 137, 142
Trade unions, 82–84
Turnover of labour, 35–44, 53

U

Uniform, 111–113

V

Volunteer corps, railway, 76

W

Wages, 88–108, 181
Wastage, 33–54
Widows, payments to, 155
Wolverton, 81
Working expenses, 60

APPENDICES

Appendix I

RAILWAY COMPANIES' FRIENDLY SOCIETIES IN 1871

Name and Date of Origin		Sick Allowance (Full) per week s d	Ordinary Death Allowance £	Accident Sick Allowance per week	Accident Death Allowance £	Wives' Death Allowance £	Superannuation per week s d	Widow's Pension per week s d	Children per week s d	Members' Contributions per week	Railway Company's subsidy £	Grades Covered	Membership
Birkenhead Rly. Friendly	1860	10 0 to 20 0	—	as for sickness	—	—	—	—	—	2½ to 1 0	—	All	—
Bristol & Exeter Labourers Annual Benefit		4 0 to 12 0	—	as for sickness	—	—	—	—	—	1½ to 5	Miscellaneous concessions	Compulsory	300
Caledonian Sick	1856	8 0 to 16 0	4–8	as for sickness	—	2–4	—	—	—	—	—	All	640
Cambrian Friendly	1865	12 0	12	15	25	5	—	—	—	1 0 to 4 0	—	All	503
Great Eastern Friendly	1860	8 0 to 16 0	10–20	as for sickness	as for sickness	3–6	—	—	—	4 to 8	500 p.a.	Traffic	392 (1863)
Great Eastern Loco. and Per. Way Friendly	1851	10 0 to 20 0	5–10	as for sickness	as for sickness	5	—	—	—	4 to 1 1	—	Enginemen Artisans	—
Great Northern Loco. Sick	1850	5 0 to 10 0	6–10	by levy	by levy	4–6	—	—	—	3 to 5	—	Enginemen	3946
Great Northern Provident	1853	3 6 to 20 0	2–10	as for sickness	as for sickness	4–7	—	—	—	2 to 11	—	Compulsory below clerk	—
Great Western Enginemen and Firemen's Mutual Assurance	1864	12 6 to 15 0	60–100	as for sickness	as for sickness	5	7 6 to 12 6	4 0 to 6 6	1 6 to 2 0	10½ to 1 3	500 p.a.	Compulsory Enginemen	1220
Great Western Loco. & Carriage Fund	1843	4 0 to 12 0	4–12	as for sickness	as for sickness	2–6	2 0 to 6 0	—	—	2 to 9	?	Compulsory Artisans	8824 (1890)
Great Western Medical Fund	1847	Free medical attendance	—							1½ to 4	—	Swindon Works Employees	—

Fund	Year									Membership	Members (Year)
Great Western Provident	1838	12 0 to 20 0	7–12	as for sickness	5.10.0 to 6	4 0 to 10 0 (Disablement)	4 0	1 0 to 6 0	1 0 to 8 4	1000 p.a.	Compulsory Traffic	4202
Highland Loco.		9 0	4–5	as for sickness	3	–	–	–	1 0	–	Enginemen	288
Highland Per. Way Sick		9 0	4–5	as for sickness	3	–	–	–	1 0	–	Way Men	306
Highland Loco. Brotherly		9 0	4–5	as for sickness	3	–	–	–	1 0	–	Enginemen	281
London & North Western Insurance Fund	1871	–	12 0	35 to 40	–	–	–	–	–	1500 p.a.	Compulsory Traffic	–
London & North Western Crewe Sick & Burial	1843	4 0 to 8 0	2–4	as for sickness	1–2	–	–	–	1½ to 3	–	Artisans Enginemen	160 (1860)
London & North Western Earlestown Sick & Burial	1855	10 0	10	as for sickness	–	–	–	–	3	–	Artisans	436 (1860)
London & North Western Longsight Sick & Burial	1847	10 0	4	as for sickness	–	–	–	–	2 to 3	–	Artisans Enginemen	160 (1860)
London & North Western Wolverton Provident Sick	1855	half wages	4 weeks wages	as for sickness	–	–	–	–	1 hour's work	–	Artisans	1500 (1860)
London & South Western's Friendly	1844	10 0 to 20 0	10	as for sickness	5	One half sick pay	–	–	5 1 4	600 p.a.	Compulsory Traffic	1186 (1862)
London & South Western Sick Fund	1856	?	?	–	–	–	–	–	½ to ½	300 p.a.	All	London only
London & South Western Widows & Orphans Friendly	1861	–	–	–	–	–	2 0 to 10 0	–	1½ to 8	?	All	85 (1862)
London, Brighton & South Coast Insurance Fund	1852	–	–	10 0 to 20 0 50 to 1000	–	–	–	–	Half premiums	Half premiums	All	–
London Brighton & South Coast Provident	1842	9 0 to 30 0	6–20	as for sickness	3–10	–	9 to 12 6	–	5 to 1 5	Unspecified	All	2774

Name and Date of Origin	Sick Allowance (Full) per week s d	Ordinary Death Allowance £	Accident Sick Allowance per week s d	Accident Death Allowance £	Wives' Death Allowance £	Superannuation per week s d	Widow's Pension per week s d	Children per week s d	Members' Contributions per week s d	Railway Company's subsidy	Grades Covered	Membership
Lancashire & Yorkshire Insurance 1854	—	10	5 0 to 20 0	12 to 62	—	—	—	—	1 to 4	780 p.a.	Compulsory All	—
Manchester, Sheffield & Lincolnshire Plate-Layers Provident Sick 1867	10 0	10	as for sickness	as for sickness	5	—	—	—	3	?	Way men	—
Manchester, Sheffield & Lincolnshire Sick & Burial 1866	4 0 to 15 0	5–10	as for sickness	as for sickness	5–7	—	—	—	?	?	All	—
Midland Friendly 1841	12 0	12	15 0	25	5	—	—	—	8	1000 p.a.	Compulsory traffic & loco	8295
Lancaster & Carlisle Sick & Burial 1856	9 0	8	as for sickness	as for sickness	3	—	—	—	3	50 p.a.	All	210 (1860)
North British Insurance 1853	—	—	80 0 to 12 0	10 to 45	—	—	—	—	1 to 3	84 p.a.	All	—
North Eastern Provident 1857	2 0 to 16 0	1.10.0 — 12	as for sickness	as for sickness	15–6	—	—	—	1 to 8	?	All	878
North Eastern York Per Way & Provident 1855	10 0	10	as for sickness	as for sickness	5	—	—	—	3	?	Way men	—
North Eastern Darlington Superannuation 1865	Percentage of wages according to membership at 65	4.10.0 to 9							—	2½% of wages	Equal member contributions	—
North London Provident 1865	6 6 to 15 0								5 to 8	?	All	503
North Staffs. Friendly 1848	10 0	5–10	as for sickness	as for sickness	5	—	—	—	3	Fines	Traffic & Loco	900
Rhymney Accident Fund 1861	—	—	half wages	10	—	—	—	—	—	1/80th wages	deficiencies	—

Society	Year	Contribution	Sickness Benefit	Accident Benefit	Funeral Benefit	Other	Annuity/Pension	Other Benefits	Membership Conditions	Members
South Devon Incapacitation Fund	1868	3 0 to 4 8	as for sickness		8 0		2	100 p.a.		All	548
South Devon Provident	1847	10 0 to 25 0	6–10	as for sickness		5		1 4 to 5 0	Unspecified	Compulsory All	540
South Eastern Sick Fund	1843	10 0		as for sickness				1 0	?	All	—
Vale of Neath Provident	1856	4 0 to 11 0	3.4.0 to 10	as for sickness		2–6		2 to 1 3	50 Irregularly £1 per member	Compulsory traffic & loco	385 (1862)
West Midland Provident	1853	10 0	10	as for sickness		5		6	?	Traffic & loco	900
Great Western Superannuation	1865	Percentage of average salary according to years of contribution at age 60						2½% of salary	Equal to Member's contribution	Compulsory Salaried Staff	—
London and North Western Superannuation	1883										
London and South Western Superannuation	1864	Deferred Annuity at age 60									
Midland Superannuation	1870	As for Great Western									

NOTES:

1. Disablement Benefits also given as follows:- London and North Western Insurance Fund £25 — £35; Lancashire and Yorkshire Insurance Fund £18.10s. — £50; North British Insurance £15 — £27; North Eastern Provident £5.4s. — £41.12s.; North Eastern York P.W. and Provident £10.

2. The following societies are also known to have existed although no further information is available:-

    Caledonian Life Assurance Enginemen and Firemen's Friendly (1865); Glasgow and South Western Locomotive Friendly (1852); Great Central Mutual Provident (1867); Furness Employees Sick Club and Benefit (1855); Great Northern Locomotive Sick Fund Peterborough (1866); London and North Western Insurance Fund Running Department (1867); London Chatham and Dover Sick and Benefit (1870); Manchester and Milford Friendly (1867); Midland Enginemen and Firemen's Life Assurance (1865); Taff Vale Friendly.

Appendix II

RAILWAYMEN'S FRIENDLY SOCIETIES 1871

Name and Date of Origin		Full Sick Benefit Per Week s d	Death Benefit £	Wives' Death Benefit £	Member's Contributions s d	Grades Covered	Membership	Remarks
Engine Drivers Benevolent Friendly	1854	6 0 to 12 0	10–20	5–10	7 to 8	Enginemen		
General Railway Benefit	1860	10 0 to 20 0	10–30	–	5 to 1 9½	All	150 (Manchester only. 1862)	
Great Northern Carmens Friendly	1867	12 0	5	5	As necessary	Carmen	33	
Great Western Chester Sick and Funeral	1866	4 0 to 14 0	6–10	4–6	2 to 7	Artisans	103 (1866)	
Locomotive Provident	1868	12 0	10–16	5	9	Enginemen	25	Travelling Relief 1s 2d per day
Locomotive Steam Enginemen and Firemen's	1839	10 0	10–18	5	6½ to 8	Enginemen	6221	Disability Pension 5s 0d
London and North Western Servants	1864	10 0	5	Unspecified	3 to 4	Traffic	205 (1866)	
London and South Western Guards' Mutual Benefit	1869	5 0	–	–	1½	Guards	112	
North of England Railway Servants Benefit	1868	12 0 to 20 0	10–16	5–8	4½ to 1 1½	All	22	
Railway Guards Universal Friendly	1849	10 0 to 20 0	5–20	–	7½ to 1 5	Guards	903 (1866)	Disability Pension 10s 0d – 20s 0d Widows Pension 5s 0d
Railway Servants Sick Benefit	1871	8 0	–	–	3½ to 5½	Traffic	24	Dissolved 1873
Railway Servants Friendly	1864	12 0	10	5	7 to 8	All	670	Dissolved 1878
U.K. Railway Officers and Servants Association	1861	–	–	–	5s 0d p.a.	All	–	Disability – £15 – £25 p.m.
Waterloo Tontine Friendly Sick and Burial	1859	10 0	8	5	6	All	66	

NOTES:

The following societies are also known to have existed although no further information is available:-
Chester and Holyhead Platelayers Sick Fund (1854); membership 217 in 1867. Hull Benefit (1866); Railway Signalmen's United Aid (1869).